WILD HORSES

WHITE STAR PUBLISHERS

Lucia Lauffs

TEXT
PAOLO MANILI

PROJECT EDITOR
VALERIA MANFERTO DE FABIANIS

EDITORIAL COORDINATION
GIADA FRANCIA

GRAPHIC DESIGN
MARINELLA DEBERNARDI

CONTENTS

INTRODUCTION
PAGE 8

THE LITTLE KING OF THE ICE
PAGE 10

THE WATER HORSE
PAGE 54

THE LORD OF THE BUSH
PAGE 108

BORN OF THE WIND
PAGE 124

THE KING OF THE PAMPAS
PAGE 186

THE ELEGANT SON OF THE HIGH PLANES
PAGE 206

INTRODUCTION

In some corners of the planet there are still breeds of untamed wild horses living far from man, often in large numbers. In reality nearly all of these horses were once domesticated and, having escaped or been abandoned by their owners, have run wild again to create new breeds.

The only truly wild horse remaining on the planet that has never been tamed by man, is the so-called Przewalski's Horse (taken from the name of the Russian officer and naturalist who discovered it in 1879 near Askania Nova). It is a direct descendent of the ancient Tarpan that was once widespread in Europe and western Asia.

The Tarpan (in origin there were two types: the forest one, which was larger and slower, and the steppe variety) had been hunted to extinction and the last one died in Poland in 1879, however, the breed was revived via 'genetic reconstruction' thanks to the presence of a few survivors in European zoos. Today the descendents of the ancient Przewalski's Horse roam in semi-free herds in the Polish forestry reserves of Popielno.

Having clarified the difference between truly wild horses and horses that have returned to the wild, it would also be true to say that they resemble each other given that the latter, returning to live in nature, have reacquired the atavistic instincts and characteristics of wild animals.

What are these characteristics according to the experts? Besides living and reproducing freely far from man, they have resumed living in a way typical to their species. They gather together in herds, each one led by a dominant stallion who protects the herd from dangers such as predators and who fights any other adult stallions that come too close to his 'harem.' The wild horse does not know man and generally runs away from him, however it has never been tamed by human hand, so does not fear him, but if cornered they will attack human beings.

Horses that have escaped man and returned to their wild state forming herds within a given territory were at first just 'extended families.' However, with repeated free cross-breeding and hybridizations they truly became 'new' breeds.

This was also due to the fact that, over the course of time, certain characteristics of a particular equine population have gained the upper hand over other characteristics and thereby became typical to the group. They became so 'fixed' as to make that group homogenous in terms of features, temperament and behavior. The environment to which a given population has had to adapt determines these transformations: the climate, the type of food available, the presence or absence of other animals with whom to live or at times from whom to defend themselves, have all directly influenced them and led to their current 'status.'

This is what happened to the Spanish horses abandoned by the 'Conquistadors' of the sixteenth century, whose descendents became the wild horses of North America (Mustang) and of South America (Argentine Criollos). The same thing took place much later for a number of animals abandoned by colonists in nineteenth-century Australia (Brumbies). It also occurred in an earlier epoch, at the time of the Moors, in the marshes of southern France (Camargue ponies), while in AD 871 the Norwegians colonized Iceland along with their horses (Icelandic ponies). It was the same with the Arab raids and trade in the arid highlands of central-northern Africa, in particular in Sudan and Eritrea (Dongola), in an era from which no records remain.

Finally, the descendents of the horses of South African and German troops that survived the clashes in that region at the start of the First World War now scrape a meager existence in the arid lands of Namibia, bordering the Kalahari Desert.

There are also breeds of wild horses in Italy, and Sardinia has its Giara ponies, whose origin is obscure, but who may have arrived on the island with the Greeks in the Nuragic era, and are certainly not indigenous. Or as in Sicily on the Nebrodi mountain range, the Sanfratellani horses, half oriental and half Norman in origin, but are today bred and tamed. Italy's most famous wild horse is still the Maremmano (Tuscan horse), which lives in the region between Tuscany and Lazio, from which it takes its name. The Butteri, the maremma cowherds of the big Tuscany-Lazio landed estates, rode Maremmano horses. They even became famous in the early 1900s when they beat Buffalo Bill's touring 'Wild West Show' cowboys. The artist, Fattori, also immortalized them in his paintings. The first horses in Maremma date back to the pre-Roman period, however, in the centuries that followed continual crossbreeding, due both to man and nature, made the current Maremmano quite different to the small, coarse and rough original horse: it was bigger in Tuscany than in the Tolfa Mountains of Lazio. They can still sometimes be found living in the wild.

5 Two young Camargue horses clash; part fight, and part play. • 7 Sure of foot and graceful, an Icelandic pony moves confidently over the icy ground.

THE LITTLE KING OF THE ICE

Icelandic ponies are famous the world over mainly for two reasons. Firstly, they live freely, out in the open day and night even in the 'arctic' temperatures of winter. And secondly, they have a characteristic gait, the 'tölt,' a sort of quickstep, which is very comfortable for the rider.

Many believe the 'tölt' to be similar to the amble, for which the horse performs a lateral gait, however, the amble is a rather tiring gait, requiring a lot of training. It is good on flat terrain, but conversely, Iceland is very rough; the land is often icy and, until a few years ago, it did not have many roads.

The 'tölt' however, is a 'quick' step, performed on a four-beat, which also allows the horse to keep one foot on the ground. The Icelandic pony must have developed this particular stride spontaneously in order to give it greater 'hold' on snow and ice when it had to flee from predators. While it would have been easy to fall when trotting or galloping, the tölt made it possible for a horse to keep its balance and run over long distances, until its pursuers were too tired to keep up the chase. Naturally the Icelandic pony also knows how to perform the other natural gaits: the step, trot, and gallop.

When one of these very hardy ponies is trained to take a saddle, the tölt is so comfortable that it is said that while the pony is running at top speed, '…you could hold a glass full of water in your hand without spilling a drop.'

A rider is able to travel across very great distances in terrible weather conditions on this robust, safe and speedy means of transport, especially given that the Icelandic pony is also very hardy. You could say that it is a sort of tireless 'mini-tractor.'

There were no horses in Iceland in ancient times – the Arctic fox was the largest animal on the island, however in AD 871 the Vikings landed, in dispute with Harald Haarfagre who had been proclaimed king of Norway despite great opposition. The new arrivals brought domestic animals with them including a number of ponies, most likely Fjord ponies. Subsequently ponies were also introduced from Scotland and its islands, from Ireland and from the Isle of Man. Crossbreeding between these ponies, all of a rather homogenous 'Nordic' type, led to the current Icelandic pony, which since then has developed without 'contamination' from other breeds for a thousand years. In fact, the first 'modern' selective breeding was performed in 1879.

The Icelandic pony is 1.20 to 1.35 meters high at the withers and is generally chestnut or burned chestnut in color, but can sometimes be dun, palomino and grey, but rarely black or dappled. In reality there are about fifteen color variants. It has a strong body with a thick neck and a large but not heavy head, a thick tail and mane, smooth limbs and very hard hooves. To someone seeing them for the first time in their natural habitat of volcanic, icy moors and flocks of sheep, they appear to be European horses at the dawn of the medieval period. Having lived far from external influences and in difficult environmental conditions for centuries, they have grown up healthy and free of illness. However behind this very hardy exterior and individualistic character there hides a sharp intelligence and, once accustomed to man, also great docility. This seems extraordinary in animals that have known complete freedom until adulthood and who often continue to live in the wild afterwards.

They have very acute vision together with a very well-developed sense of direction, meaning that the tame ones always know how to find their way home alone. It was once quite common practice for people who didn't own a horse, to 'hire' someone else's pony, using it for a single stage of their journey (the Icelandic pony besides being used for riding was also used for loads and light pulling), after which, they would remove the saddle or load and let the horse return home alone. To continue on, they simply had to 'hire' another horse.

Even today one of the most enjoyable ways of visiting Iceland is to do so in the saddle on a strong pony walking at a 'tölt.'

11 A stallion walks confidently over the ice, demonstrating the sense of balance, refined over the centuries, that enables it to survive in Iceland's hostile environment. • 14-15 Two ponies ford a lagoon during the ice melting season. The small size of this breed is emphasized by the grandeur of the surrounding countryside. • 16 and 17 The two pictures show Iceland's typical wild and harsh countryside, which is well reflected by these small, fierce-looking quadrupeds.

18 and 18-19 • Icelandic ponies have various coat colorings, which recall the many breeds from which they derive: principally the Fjord ponies introduced by the Norwegians who landed in AD 871, as well as the horses imported from Scotland and its islands, and those from the Isle of Man.

20 and 21 • Ponies galloping in the Skagafjordur and surrounding zones, in the north of Iceland, which in the brief summer are covered by rich green pastures.

22-23 • Some Icelandic ponies also have sky-blue eyes, however most have dark eyes, which cope better with the dazzling reflections from the ice.

24 and 25 • A wild horse prances near the herd's mares, displaying features typical to all breeds of horses: the trot or 'passage,' left – that in this photo looks a lot like the 'tolt,' the Icelandic's typical gait – and the caracole, right.

26 and 26-27 • The pleasures of the Icelandic summer: the long grass of the fields and the flowers bursting forth transform the island into a great big pony 'health center,' where, after the ice and difficulties of the arctic winter, they can finally rest.

28 • Icelandic ponies, which lived in 'splendid isolation' for centuries, are disease free, incredibly hardy and able to survive in extreme conditions.

29 • A male and female sniff each other, the prelude to the very brief courtship and mating ritual, which eleven months later will lead to the birth of a very tough little foal.

30-31 • A herd of ponies slaking their thirst near one of the Icelandic countryside's countless cascades.

32-33 and 33 • Fun and games between month-old ponies in the Skagafjordur, one of the most evocative parts of the North of Iceland.

34-35 • A mother suckles her darkly coated and maned foal, however its fetlocks are already lightening: as an adult it will be a fierce gray stallion.

36 • This foal, born with honey-colored hair on dark skin, will be chestnut as an adult.

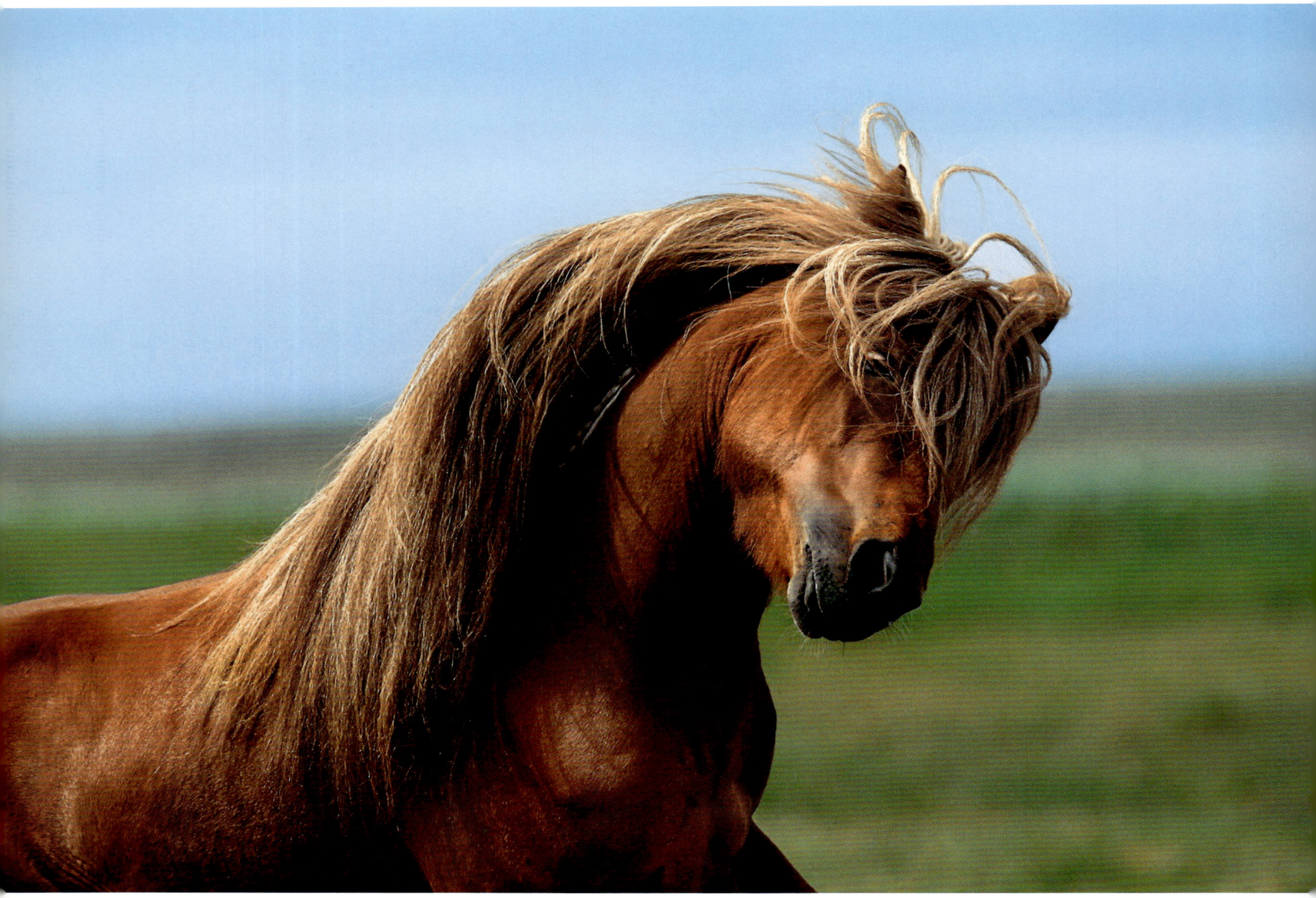

38 • A wild Icelandic pony tosses its neck and head, a typical sign of excitement, joy, and also aggression.

39 • The 'flehmen' is typically equine behavior, which involves raising the upper lip to 'smell' the infinity of olfactory messages carried on the air, such as for example whether a female is in heat, or the presence of a predator nearby, and many other things besides.

40 the little king of the ice

40 A very long mane and forelocks are characteristic of adult stallions, here they are golden chestnut. • **40-41** A life of freedom: the stallion courts and sniffs the female who, being in heat, doesn't reject him.

42 and 43 • The yawn of this Icelandic Pony shows his gums, the lower ones of which have oval teeth with the cups very evident inside, which indicates youthfulness. The lack of lateral 'bands' means that it is a female. The youth of this mare is also confirmed by the side view, showing its vertical incisors, rather than the decidedly more protuberant ones of old horses.

the little king of the ice

44-45 • Water is always cold in Iceland, even in summer, but this is no problem for the hardy local ponies used to living free among the ice.

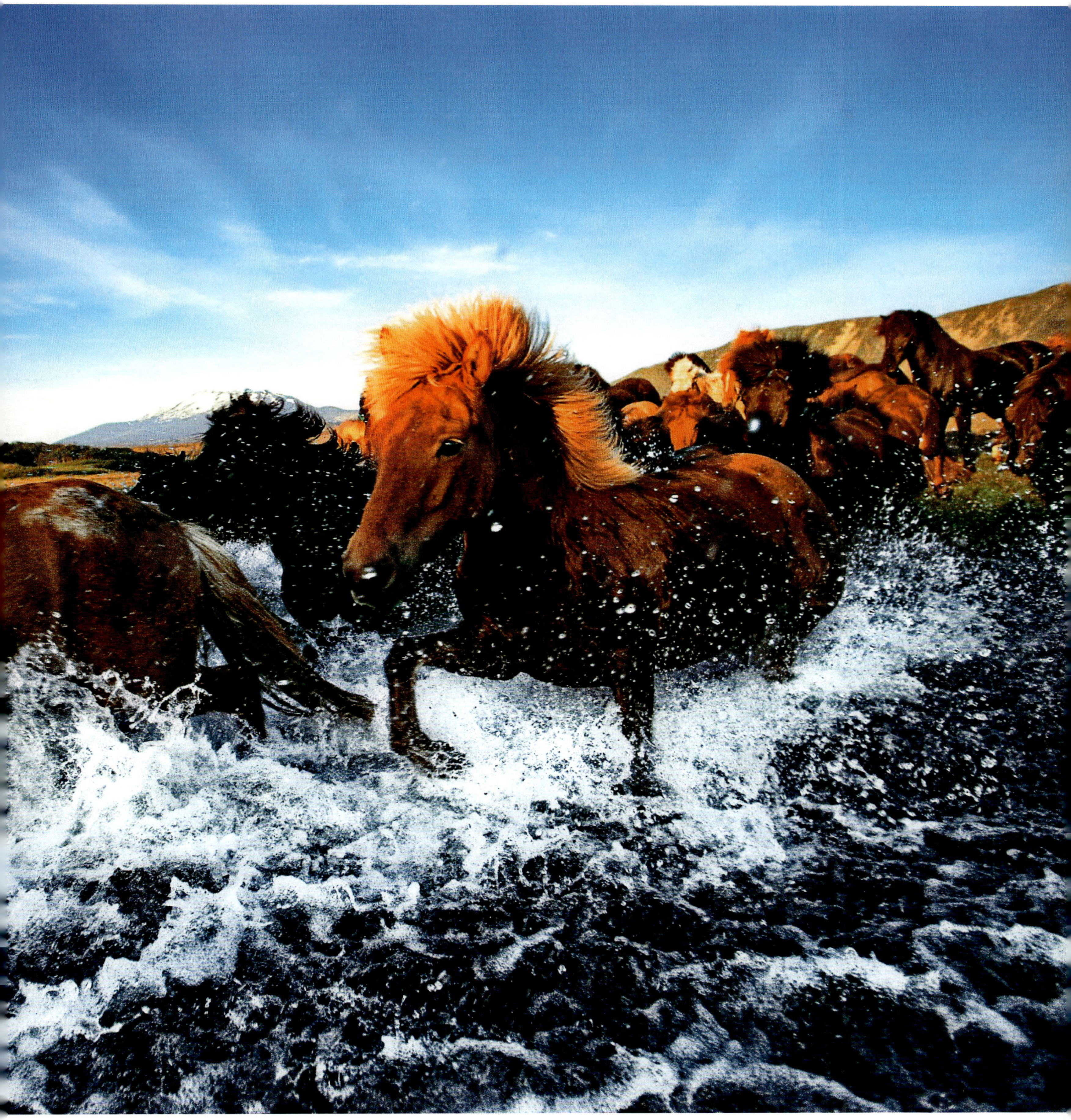

the little king of the ice

46-47 • The picture of this herd of galloping Icelandic ponies conveys a sense of energy and strength.

the little king of the ice

48-49 • A splendid chestnut horse in the middle of a moss-covered volcanic rocky moraine.

50-51 A herd standing in the snow 'warming' in the timid rays of the arctic sun. • 51 This gray is quietly drinking the icy water, which would cause serious harm to other breeds of horses.

the little king of the ice

52-53 and 53 • Two very beautiful pictures of wild ponies in a typical Icelandic environment, which in winter is completely covered in snow and ice, despite the numerous volcanoes dotted around.

the little king of the ice

THE WATER HORSE

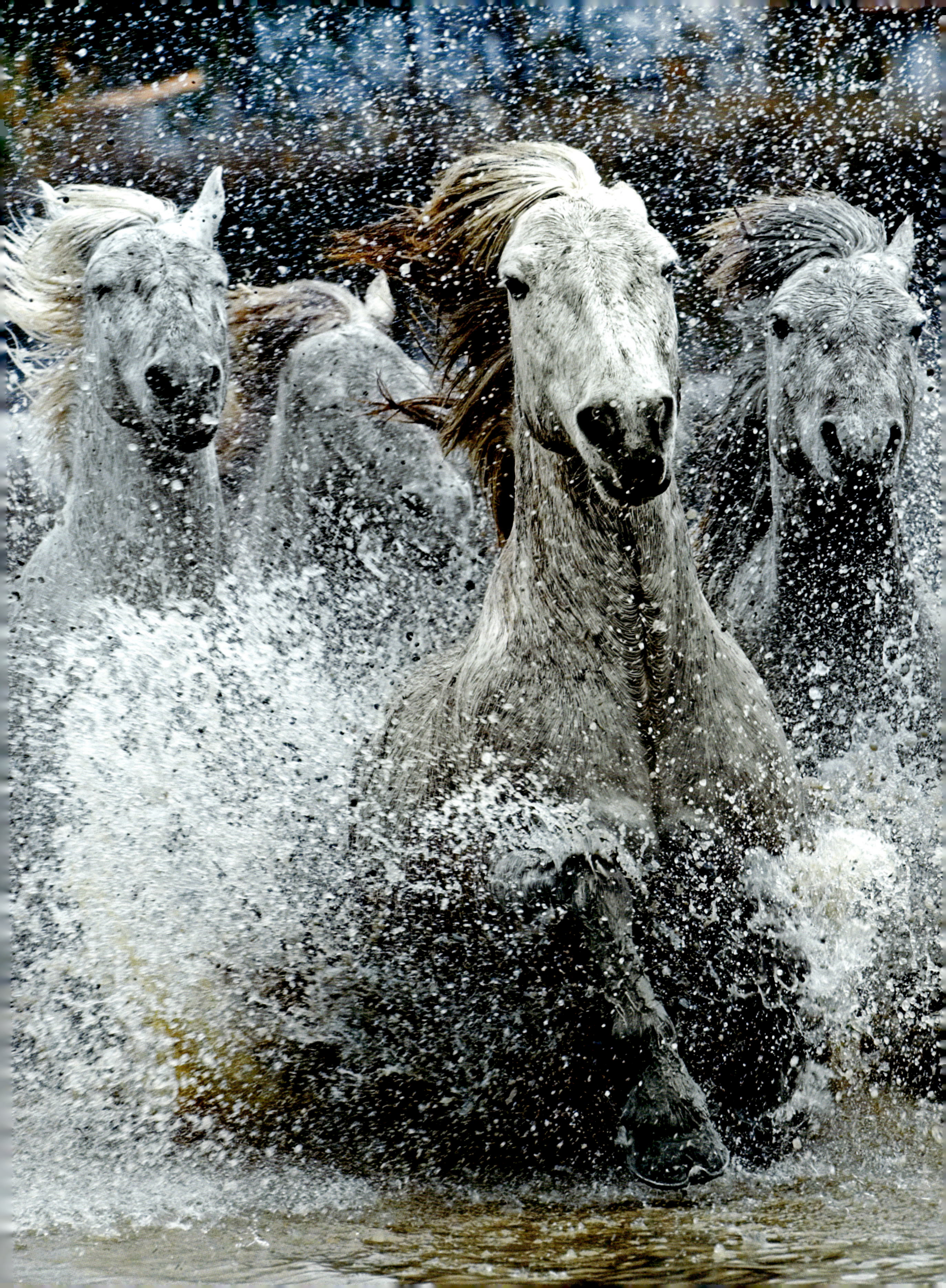

When Julius Caesar arrived in a small region of southern Gaul between the Rhône and the Mediterranean, he found an inhospitable and swampy land, constantly flooded by river, and an indigenous breed of wild white horses. These animals miraculously lived and prospered in that uninhabited sodden land, which was generally bad, if not fatal, for other breeds of horses.

Even though they were short, these wild horses were nevertheless very robust and hardy and above all very brave, accustomed as they were to living in close contact with the other large animals that prospered in the region — the wild black bull with its lyre-shaped horns. It is likely that when the ancient Romans crossed the ponies of the Carmargue with oriental horses, they intended to strengthen the breed in order to produce four-legged warriors worthy of their legions.

In reality the Camargue ponies had survived from prehistory, but of course Julius Caesar could not have known this. Today in fact, most experts believe that the Camargue pony descends from the prehistoric Solutré horse, named after a cliff in Burgundy, from which it seems that prehistoric hunters stampeded entire herds to their deaths. The many equine remains found on that site by nineteenth-century archeologists provide solid evidence for this theory. Primitive drawings of horses (dated 1500 BC) found in the Lescaux caves also resemble the Camargues.

It is certain that the Camargue pony was infused with Berber blood at the time of the Moorish invasions, after which it again prospered in isolation. In short, the Camargues that we see today have experienced very little genetic 'interference' and continue to live untamed, if not truly wild, in the marshes of the Rhône Delta.

More recently the region's herdsmen, the famous Gardians, have learned how to tame these horses and breed them in the wild. They make excellent cattle horses and are used for bullfighting in a similar way to the south of Spain and Portugal (but in Camargue they are only games of skill and there is no cruelty to the bull). Today the Camargue ponies, together with their Gardians and the black bulls with the lyre-shaped horns, are a major part of religious festivals and tourists attractions. They contribute on the one hand to the preservation of traditional local costume and on the other to the maintenance of the region's unique ecosystem.

The Camargue pony is 1.37 to 1.47 meters high. Its head has a 'gracious' and sometimes convex profile, which is similar to oriental horse types. This sits atop a robust body, with a broad chest and a short trunk, with a normally sloping rump. The tail and mane are long and thick and its limbs are thin but strong-boned, while its hooves are wide and suited for soft and watery ground. They don't even need shoes when they are tamed and used as workhorses. The breed was officially recognized in 1978.

The Camargues live and die in complete freedom: the foals are born very dark, but their coats lighten as they grow, finally becoming gray (white is not the correct term) in adulthood, which is around four years of age. When weaned the Camargue pony feeds itself on whatever it finds in the marshes during the summer and on the scrub of the salt steppes in winter.

At one time the horses that were captured and tamed were not just used by the Gardians to drive herds in the marshes, because of their 'safe feet' even in the most difficult swamplands, but were also employed to 'tread' the harvest, after which they were set free again. Today Camargues are often used to conduct tourists around the Rhone Delta and its marvelous countryside, trees and fauna.

A horse trip in the Camargue, riding a solid and reliable pony, is an incredible experience: you can admire flocks of pink flamingoes and myriads of other birds sheltering in the oxbows of the wind-battered swamps, or cross inlets during low tide, so that you look as if you are 'walking on water' as the sunset turns the horizon red.

Then of course there are also the equestrian games, bullfighting and the folklore associated with them. At Les Saintes Maries de la Mer the 'course à la cocarde' is when the 'razateur' (bullfighter) attempts, while on foot, to grab hold of a rosette placed between the bull's horns. On horseback however the Gardians capture calves and bulls in the rodeos and in picturesque gymkhanas. The whole scene, coupled with the encouragement and applause of the crowd, takes place amidst a kaleidoscope of colors and sounds.

Once a year, the Camargue and Les Saintes Maries de La Mer also becomes the religious center of all of Europe's gypsies. On 24 and 25 May the Gitani, Roma and Sinti converge from all over Europe to celebrate their saint, Sarah. The origin of the pilgrimage is unclear, but it has been performed for 500 years. Today it is the main tourist attraction in Provence and the Camargue. After the horses, naturally...

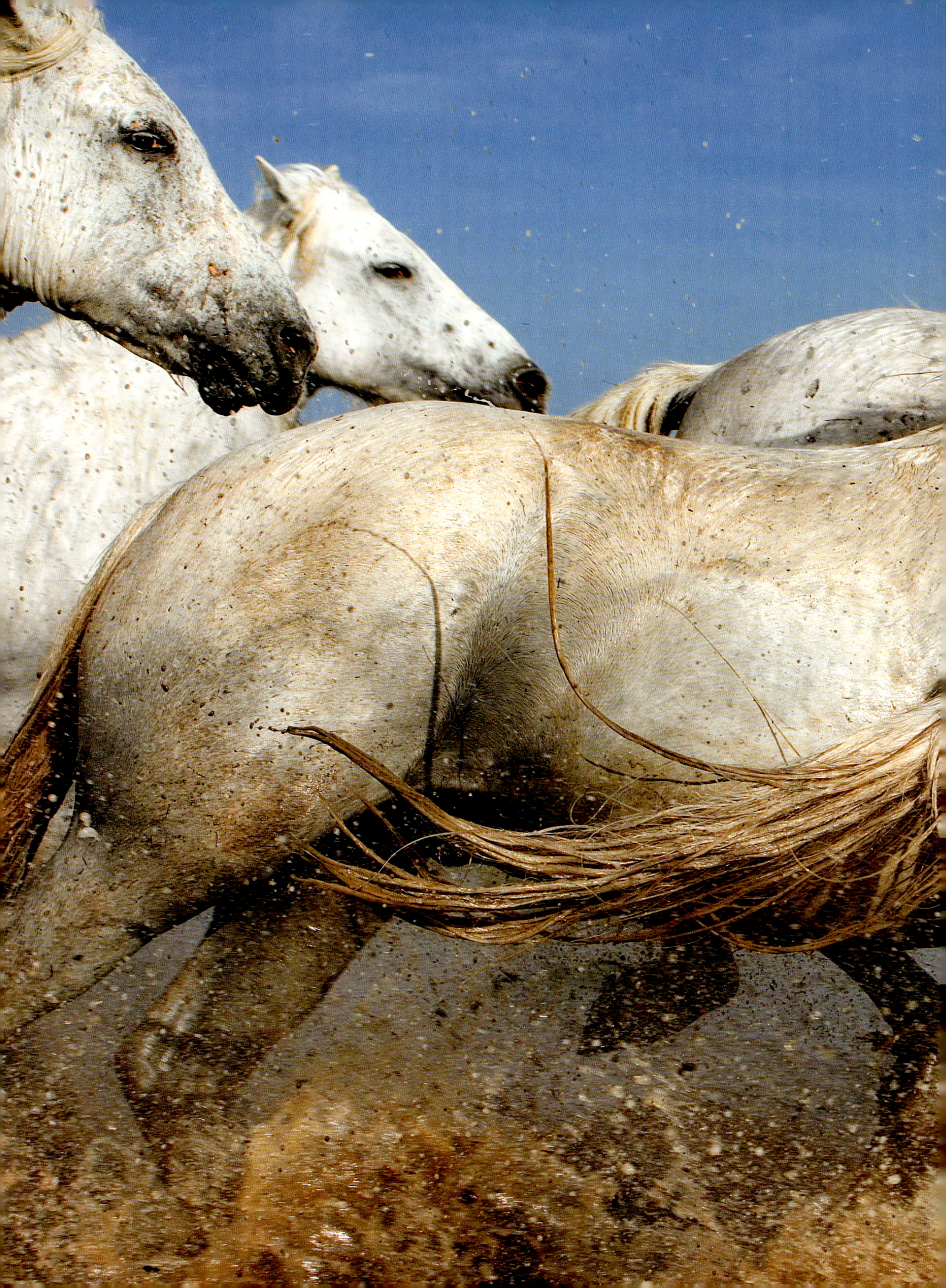

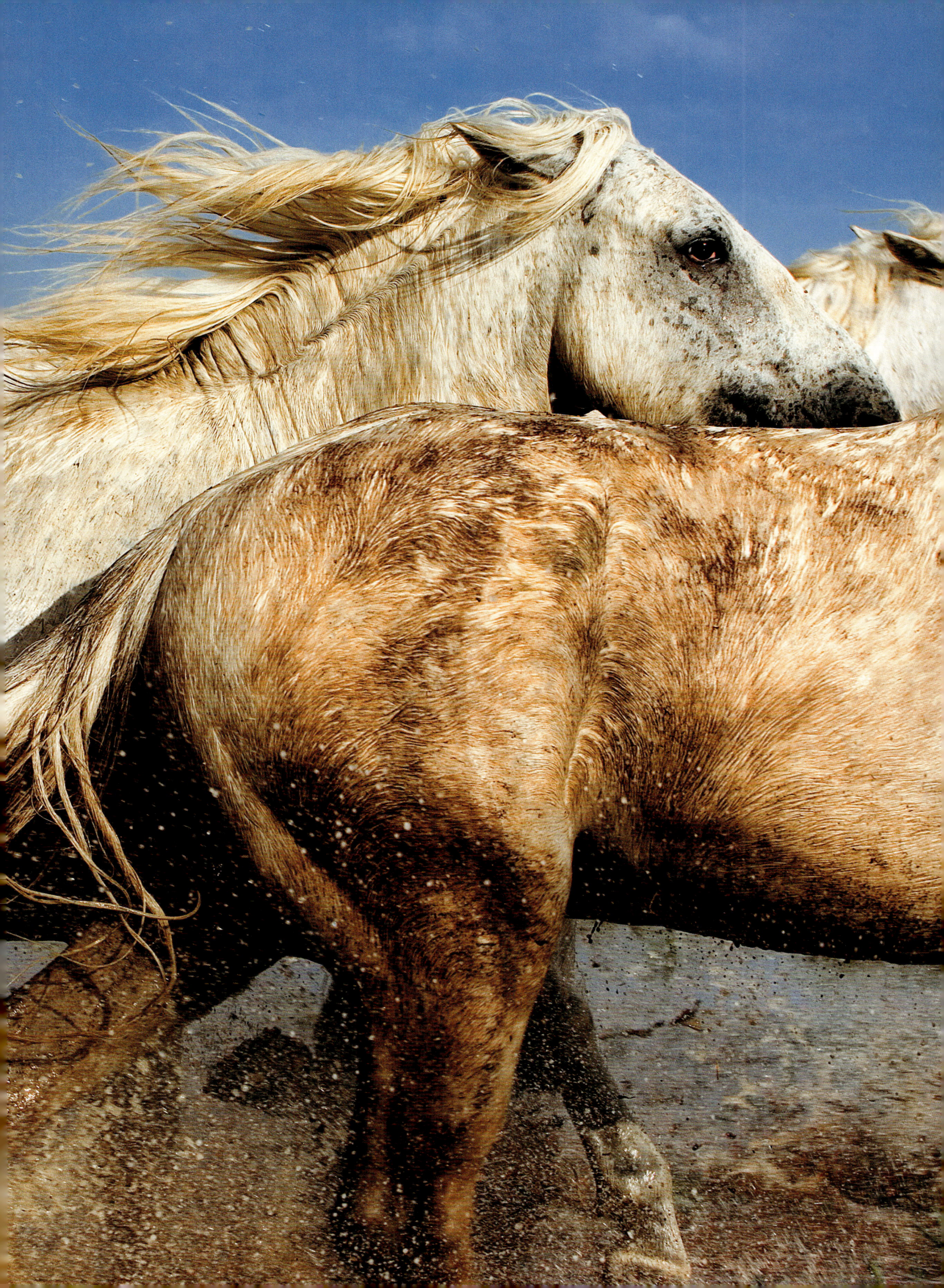

55 Camargue ponies are universally known for their capacity to survive and prosper in swampy, brackish environments that are usually harmful, if not fatal like all damp zones, for other breeds. • **58-59** A herd of Camargues gallop across marshland: these horses feed on what they can find in the marshes during the summer and on the scrub of the salt steppes in winter. • **60-61** This intense foreground shot of a Camargue stallion emphasizes another basic characteristic of the breed: the plain gray coat.

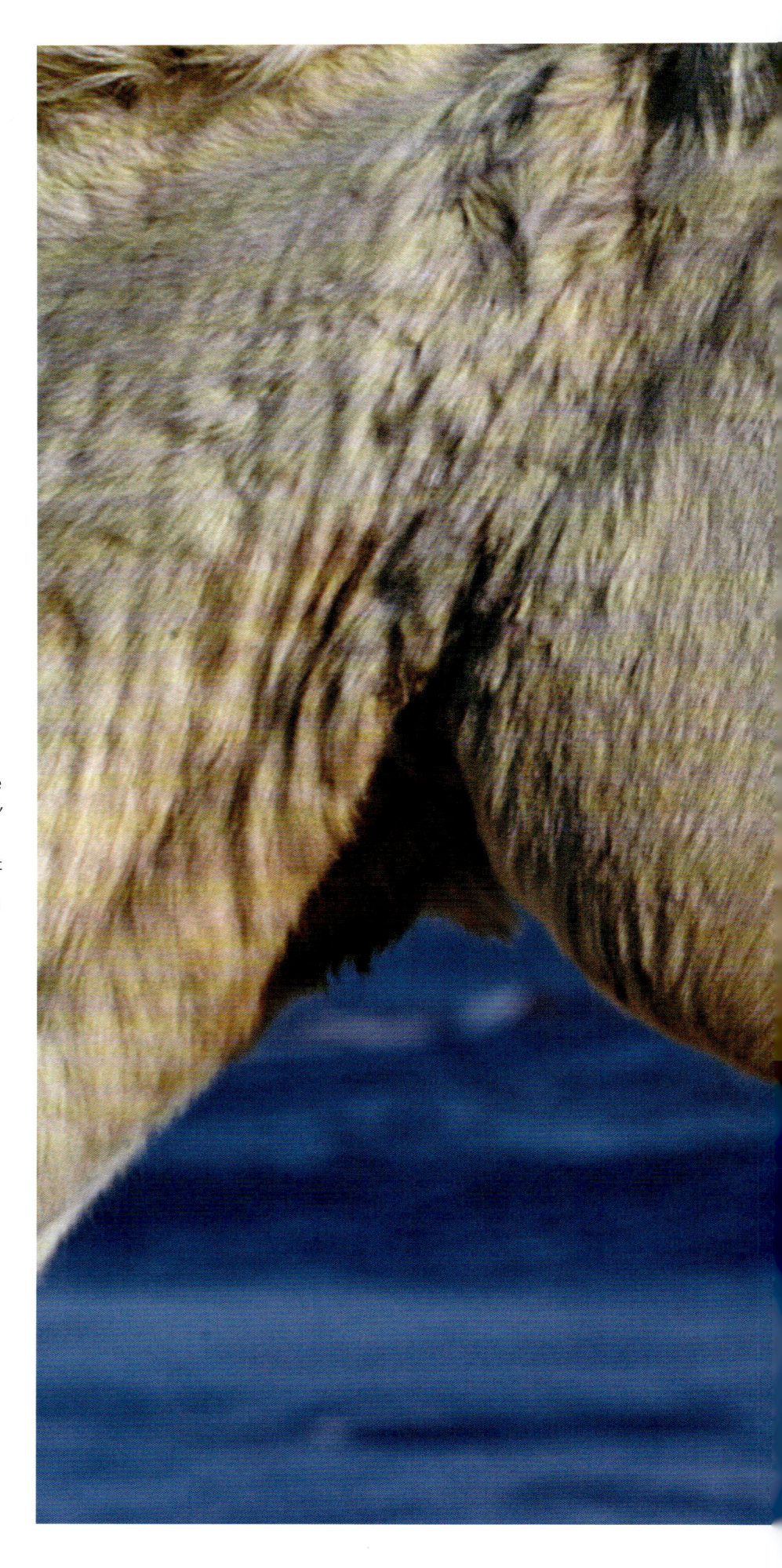

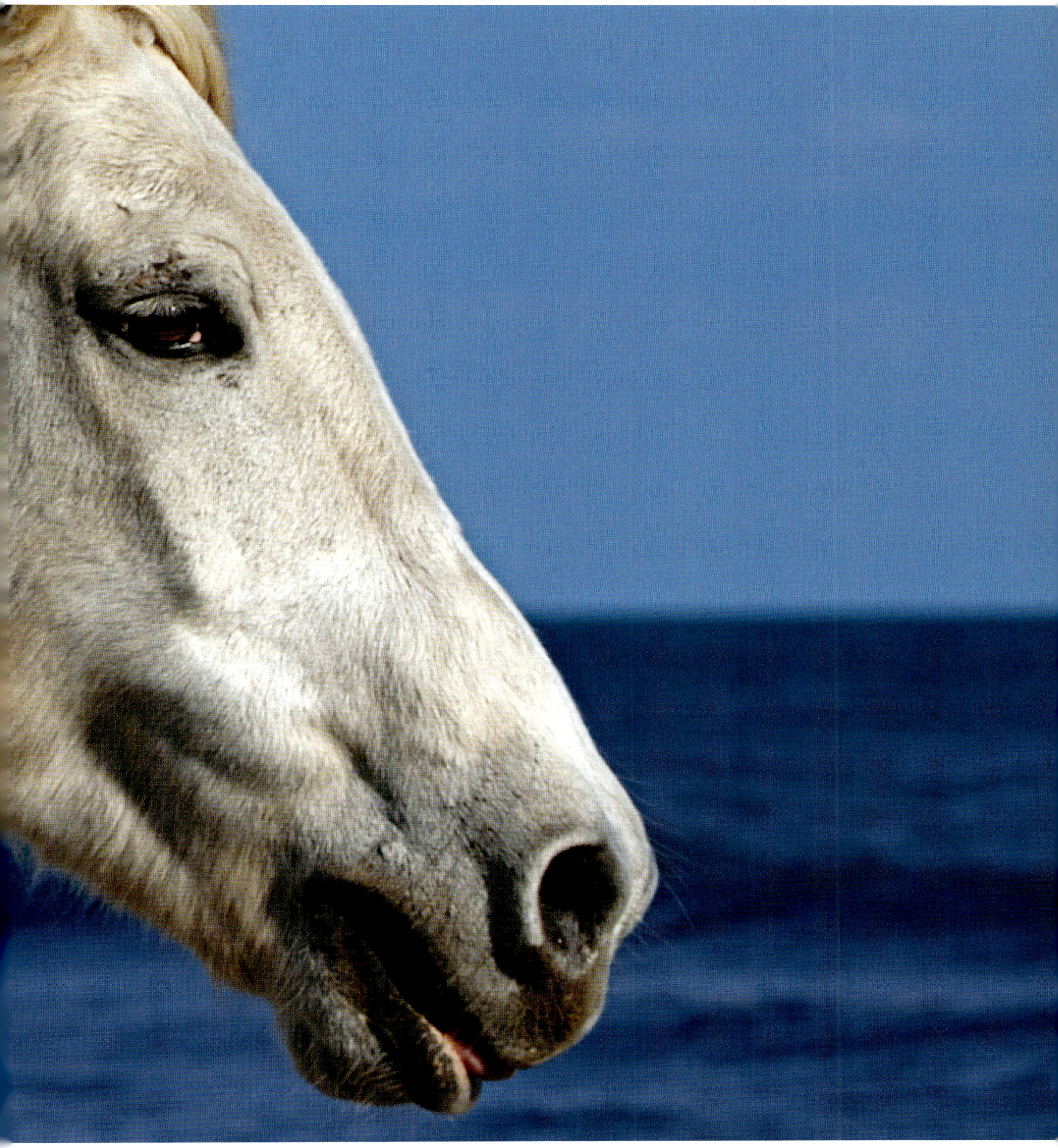

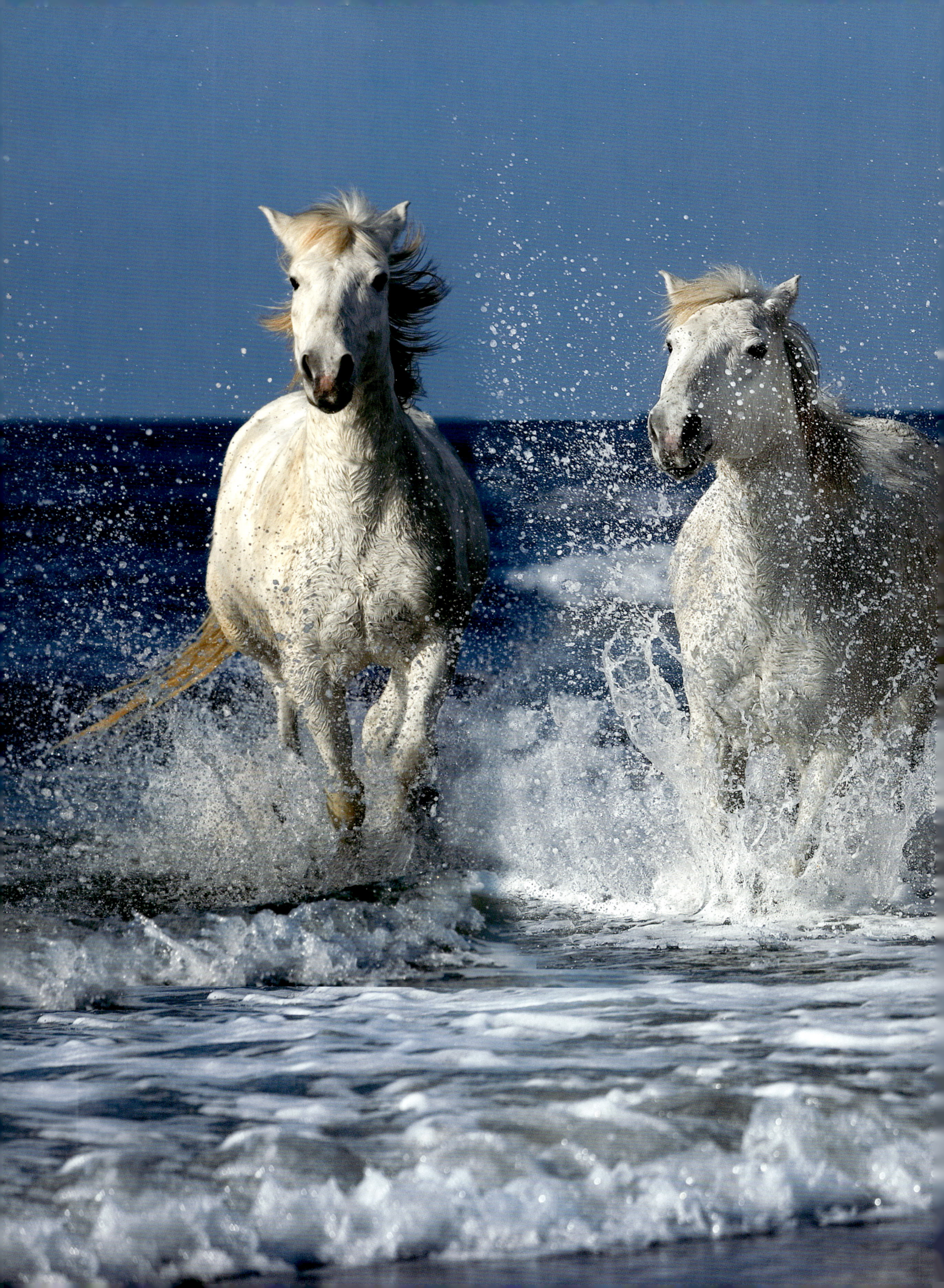

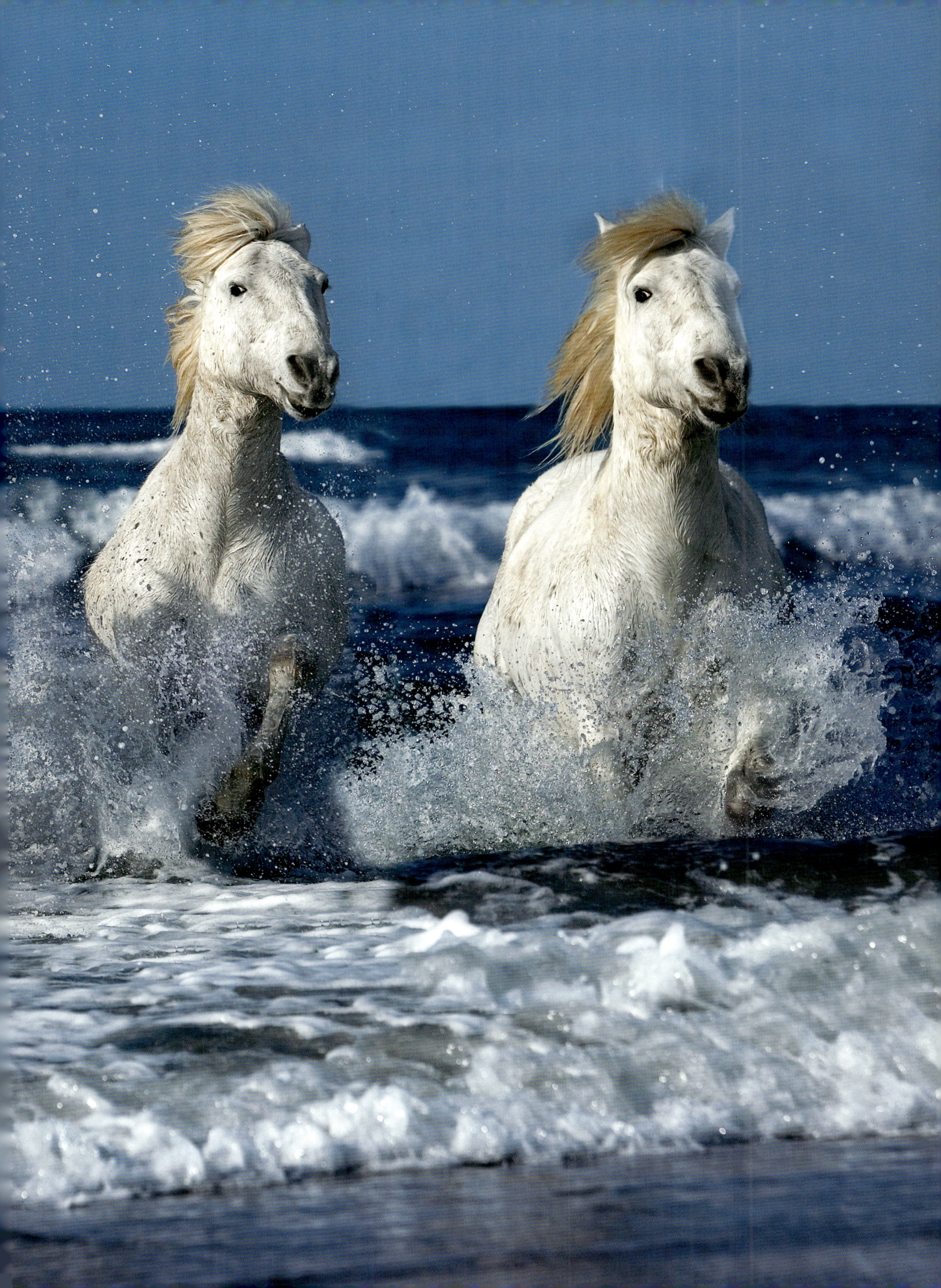

62-63, 64-65 and 65 • Camargue ponies live between the sea and marshland. They are excellent swimmers and sometimes look as if they are walking on water: when the low tide permits, it is not unusual to see a herd crossing vast but shallow lagoons and pools.

the water horse

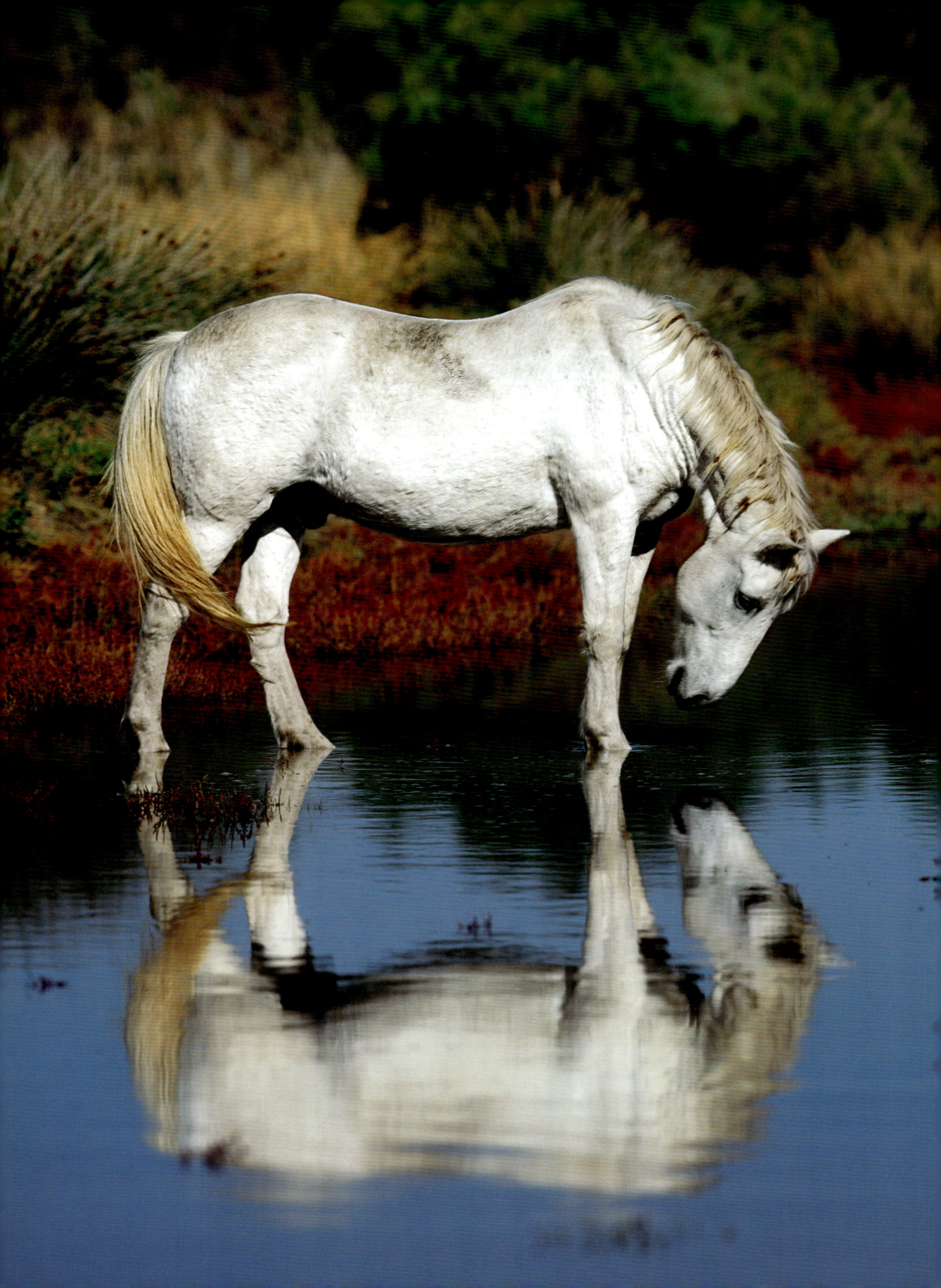

66 • These horses also play in the water, like this one looking at its own reflection on the surface of a pool — a real equine Narcissus.

67 • A herd of Camargues run alongside a marsh bordered and dotted with marsh grass, an excellent natural food for horses and wild bulls.

68 and 69 • The strips of land between the lagoons of the Camargue are often covered in sand, which is ideal for powdering the horse's coat and then removing the excess with a nice little shake. This type of 'ritual' rolling over on the ground, is common to horses in every part of the world.

70 • A detail of the dark eye of a Camargue, an ancient breed that certainly received an infusion of oriental blood, probably Berber, at the time of the Moorish invasions.

71 • We can clearly see how the gray coat of the Camargue Pony is made up of both fair and dark hairs on dark skin and how its limbs are sturdy, which is known as 'short-jointed' in the fetlock-fetter-hoof portion.

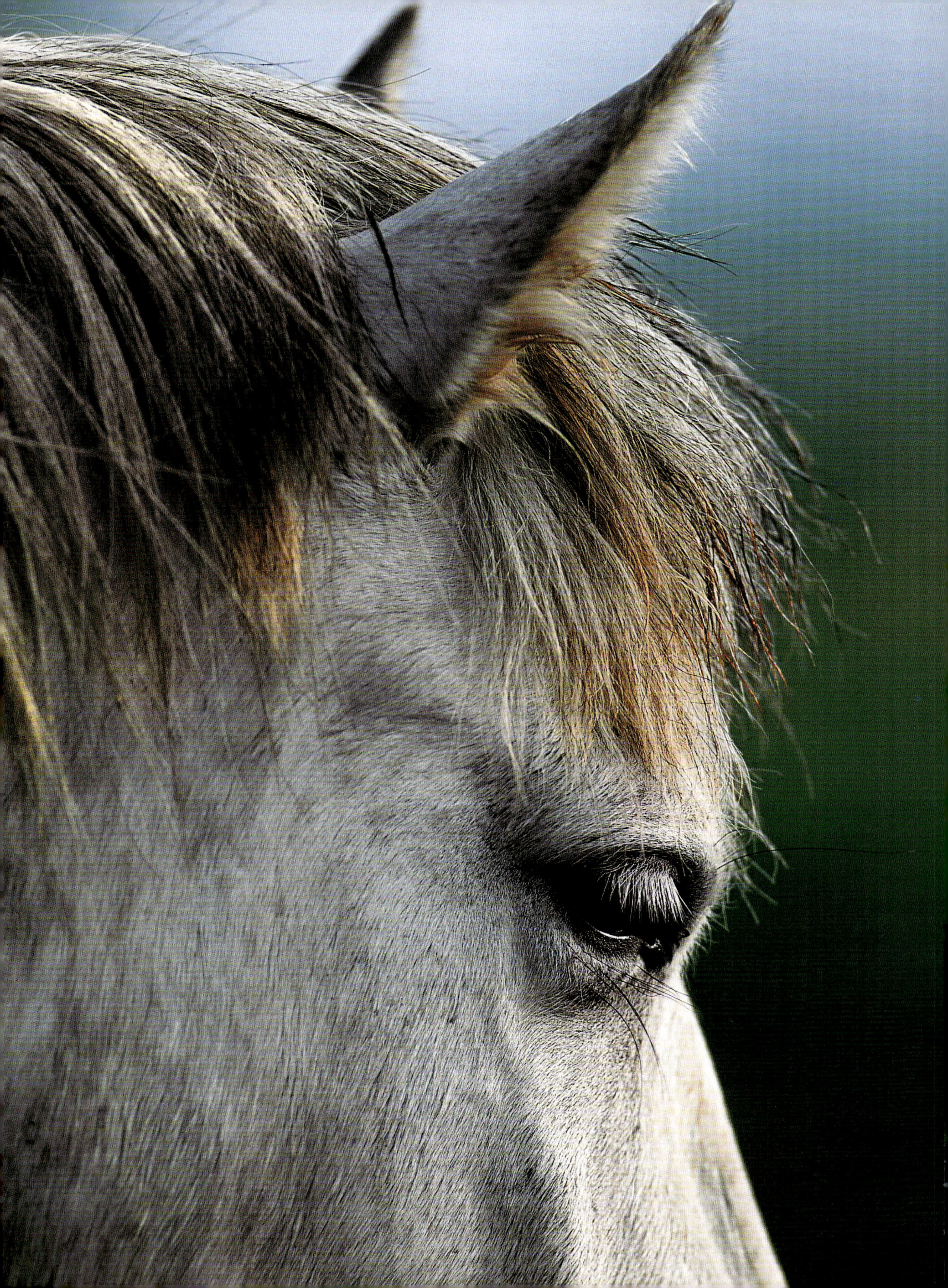

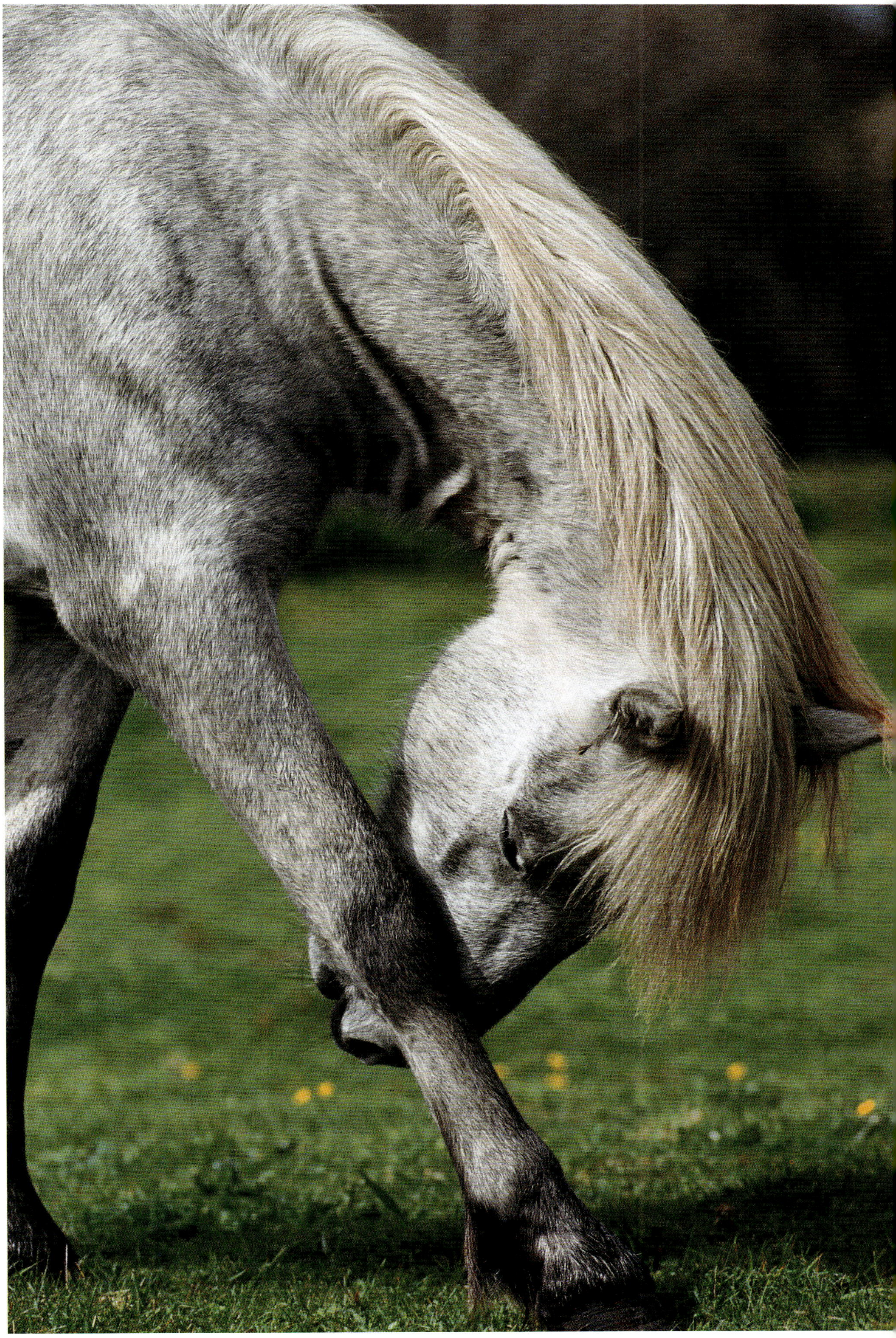

72 • Two Camargue ponies sniff and rub against each other, a behavior that emphasis the spirit of mutual aid that has developed in the life of the herd.

73 • From this adult stallion's head shape and its very long mane it is very clear that oriental blood flows through the veins of Camargue ponies.

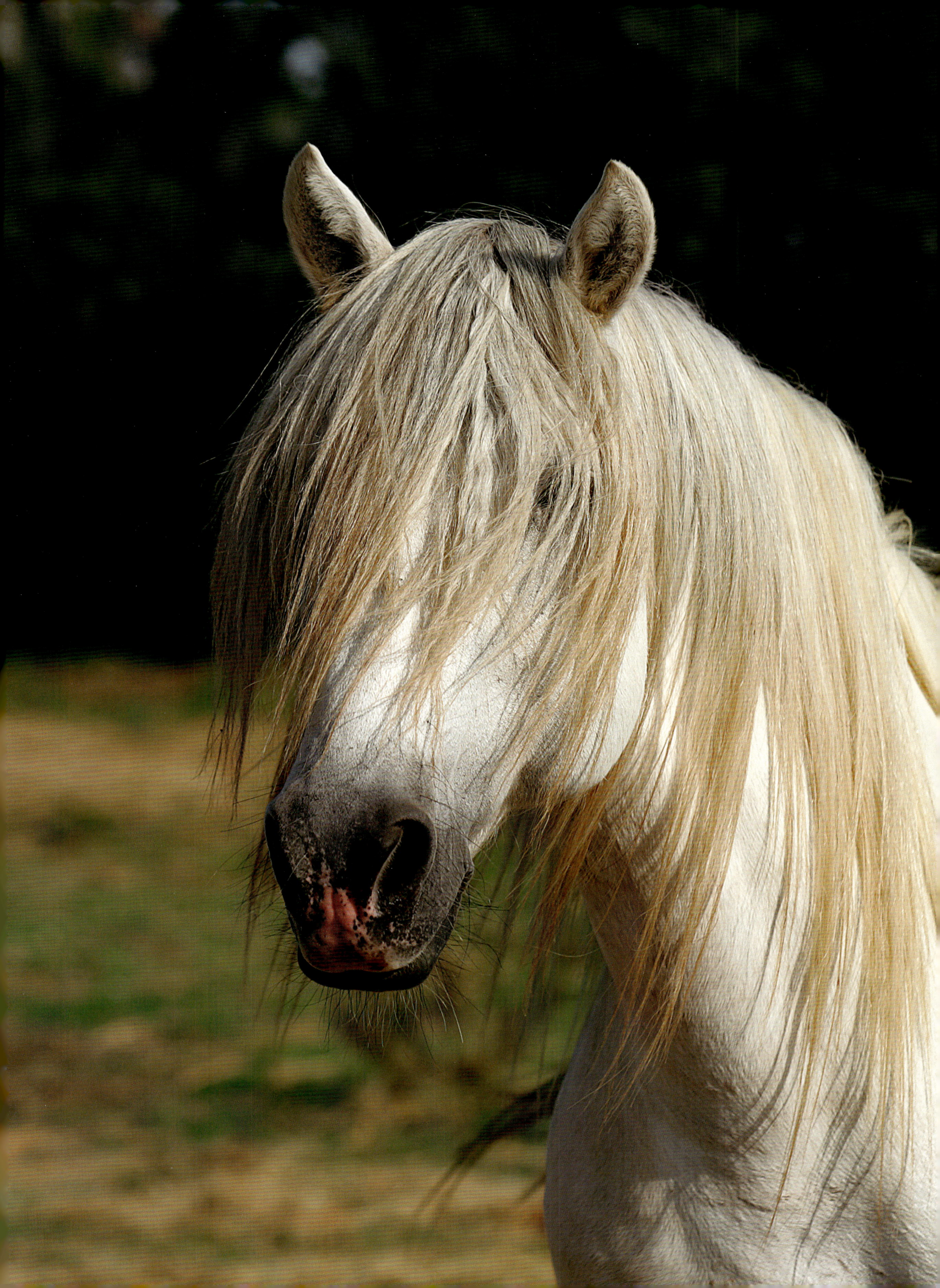

74-75 • According to the most recent studies, the Camargue Pony descends from the prehistoric Solutré horse, named after a cliff in Burgundy. It appears that prehistoric hunters slaughtered entire herds to provide them with food. The archaic origins of the breed are confirmed by findings, in the caves of Lescaux, of many equine remains and also drawings (dated 1500 BC), which show horses markedly similar to today's Camargue Ponies.

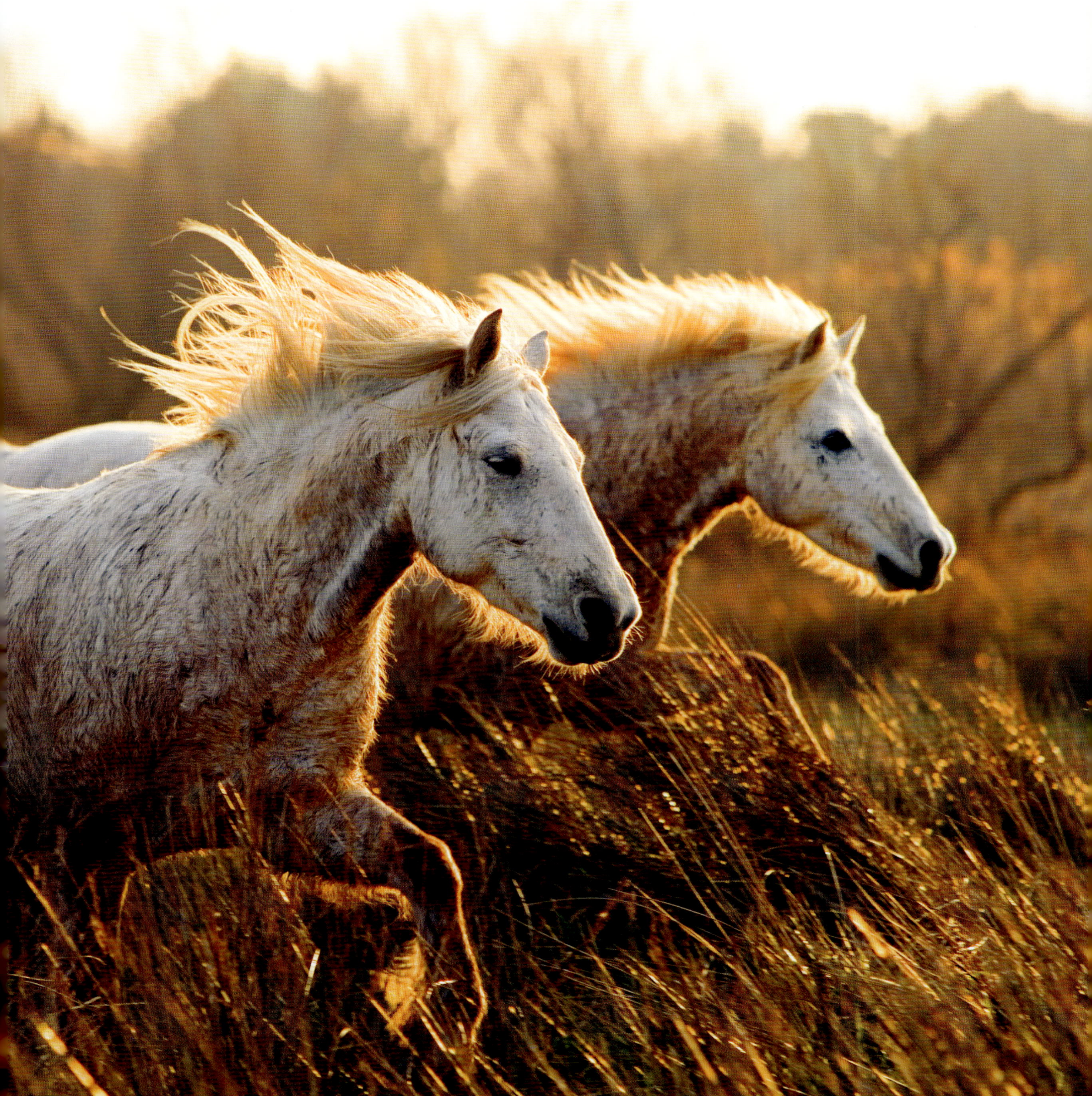

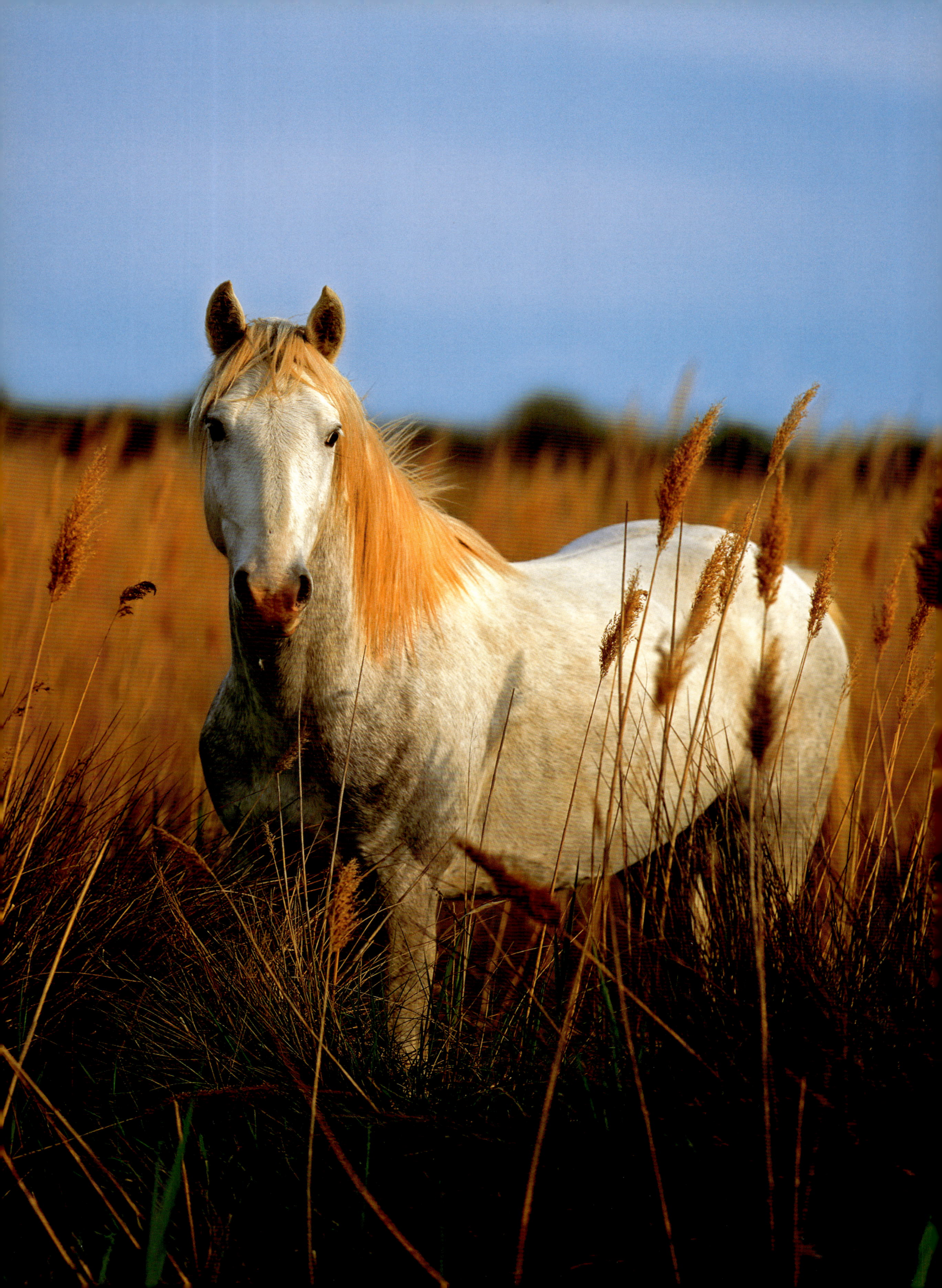

76 • In the Camargue sunset, the horses' coats occasionally give out blondish reflections, as do the hairs of the mane and the tail, above all in winter when the hair thickens.

77 • In the winter, Camargue Ponies push deeper into the ground in search of food, which they also find in the farmlands alongside the marshy zones, rich with grasses and shrubs.

78 • The stallion pictured is cleaning its mane by rubbing it against the branches of a tree; it is also sheltering from the sun and the wind.

79 • A pair of ponies graze the brackish but highly nutritious grass, which is their basic food.

80-81 • The picture shows complete harmony with birdlife: the horse in the foreground has probably been through a few scrapes, judging by the scars on its back.

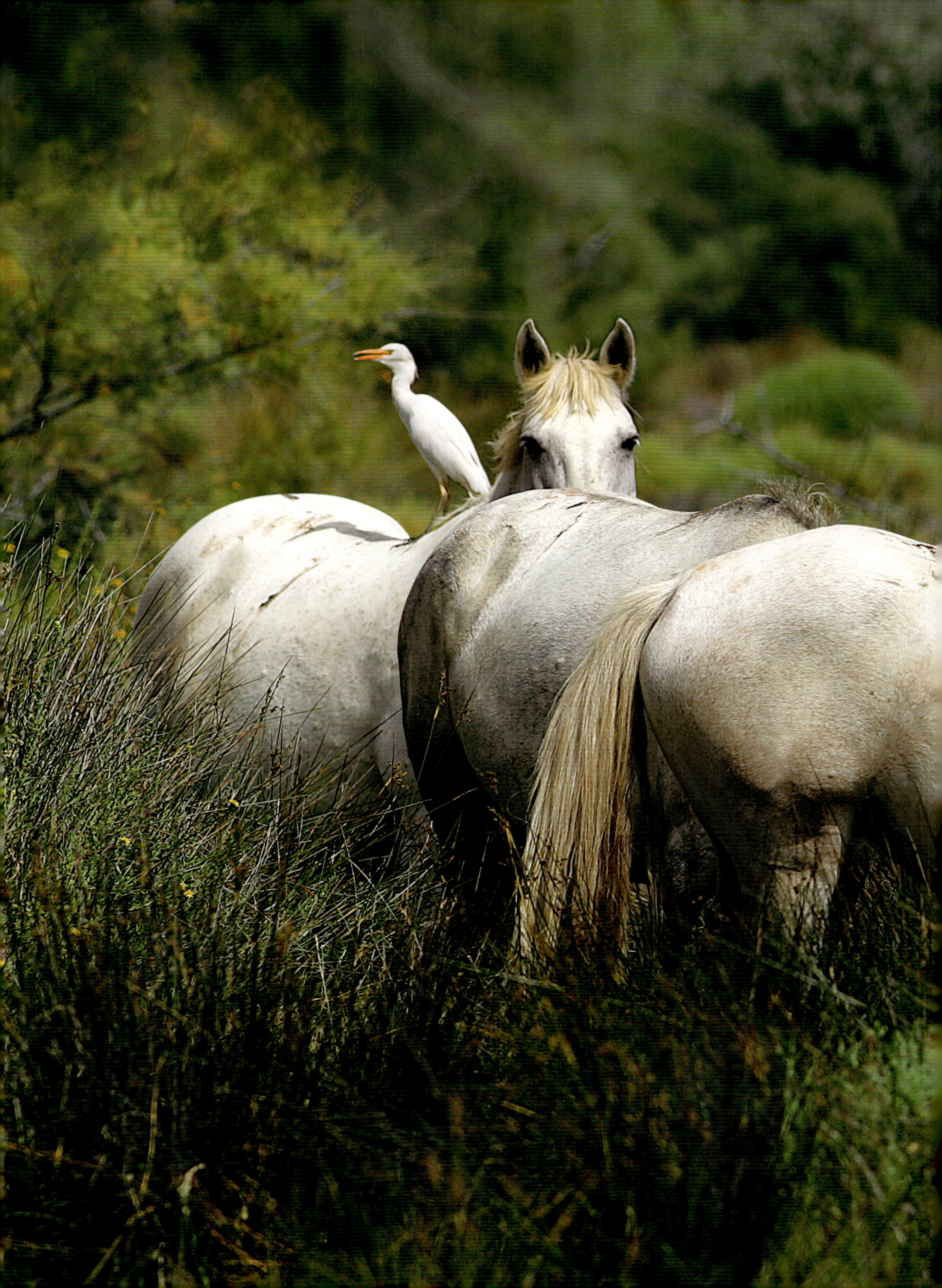

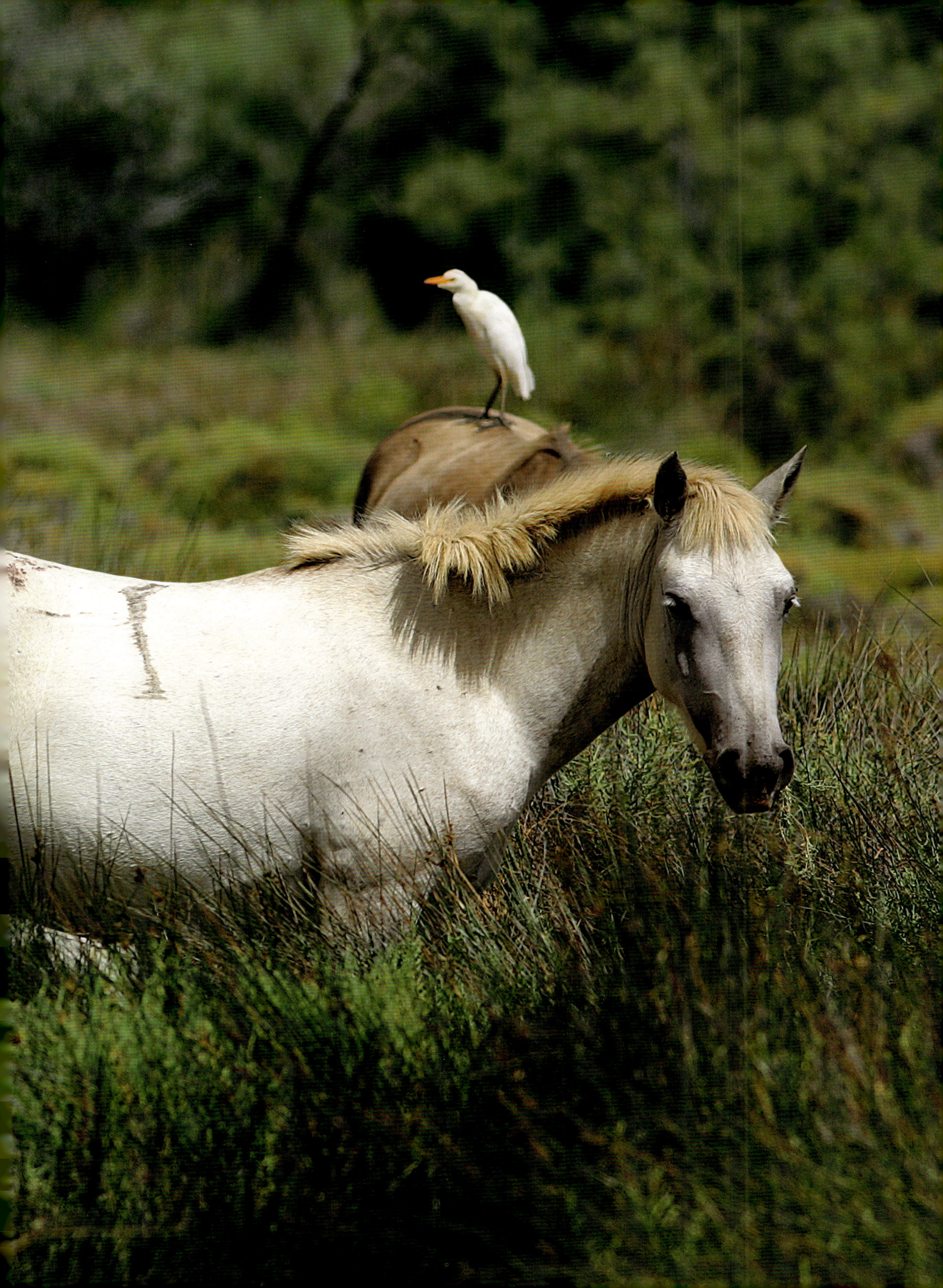

the water horse

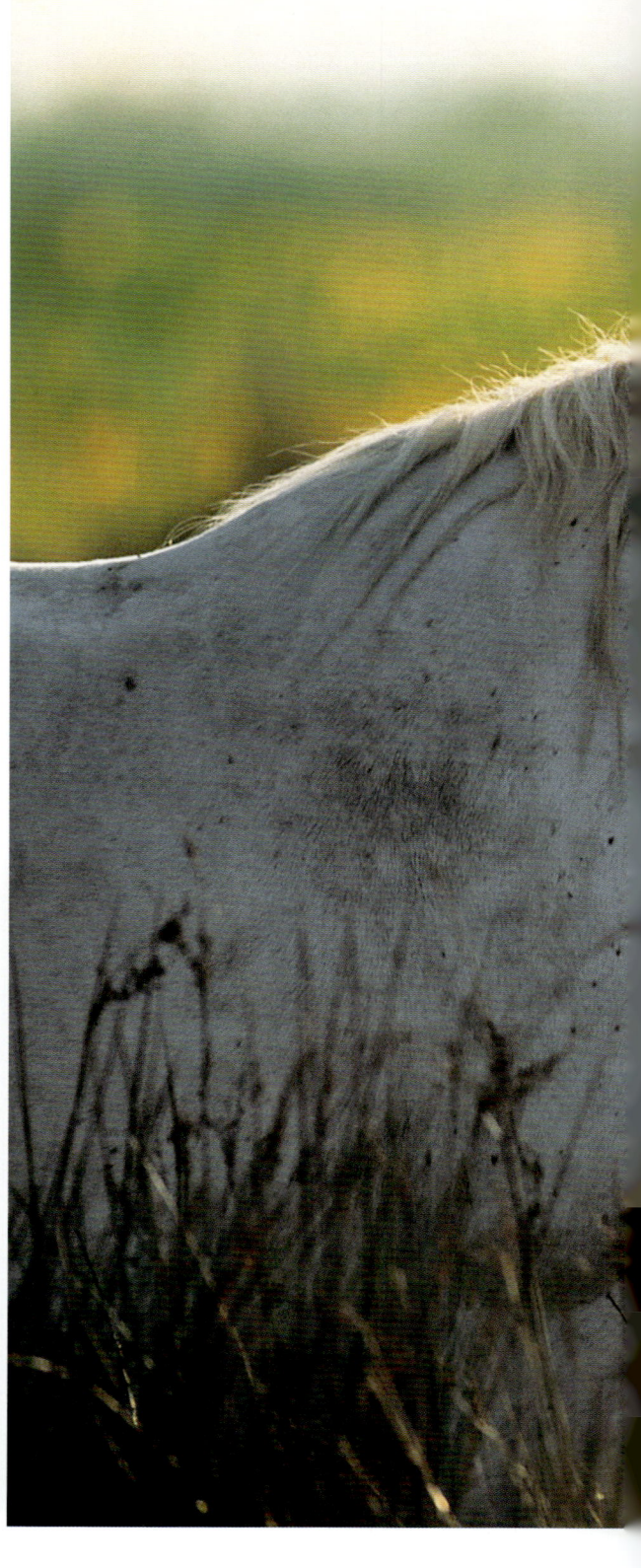

82 Two foals play enthusiastically: their dark coat lightens as they grow. • 82-83 The picture shows a mother with her foal that is just a few weeks old: the two are inseparable.

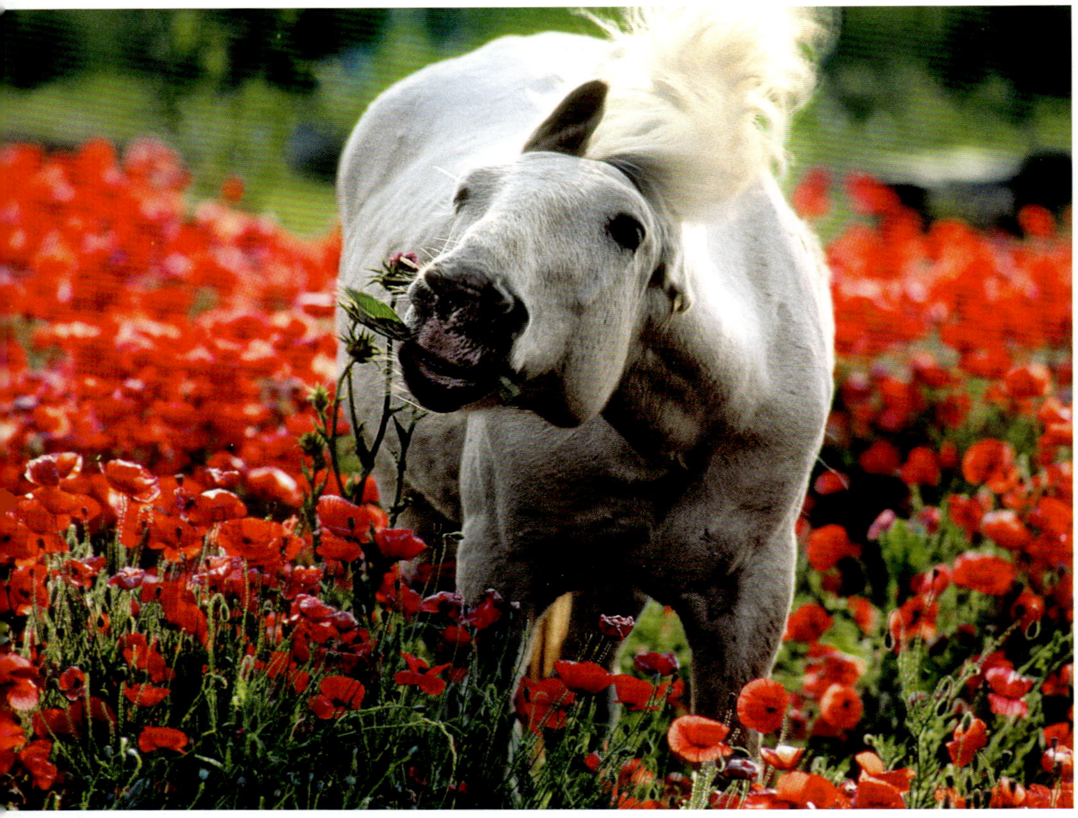

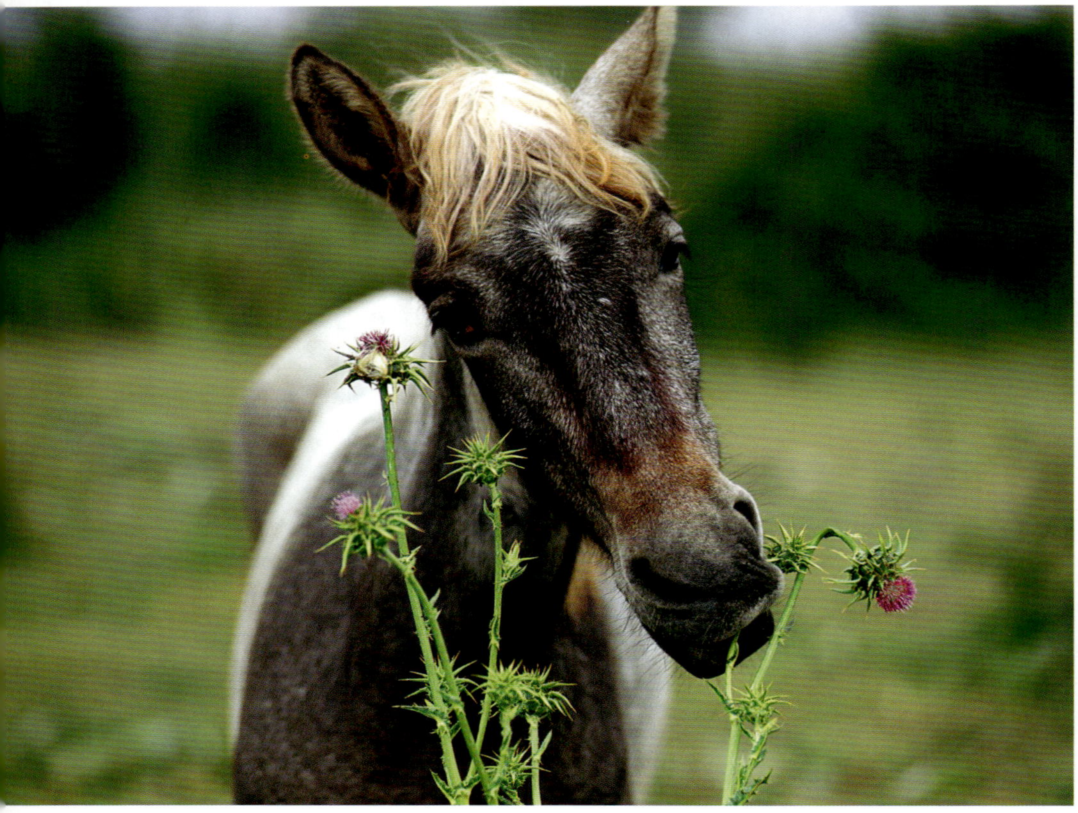

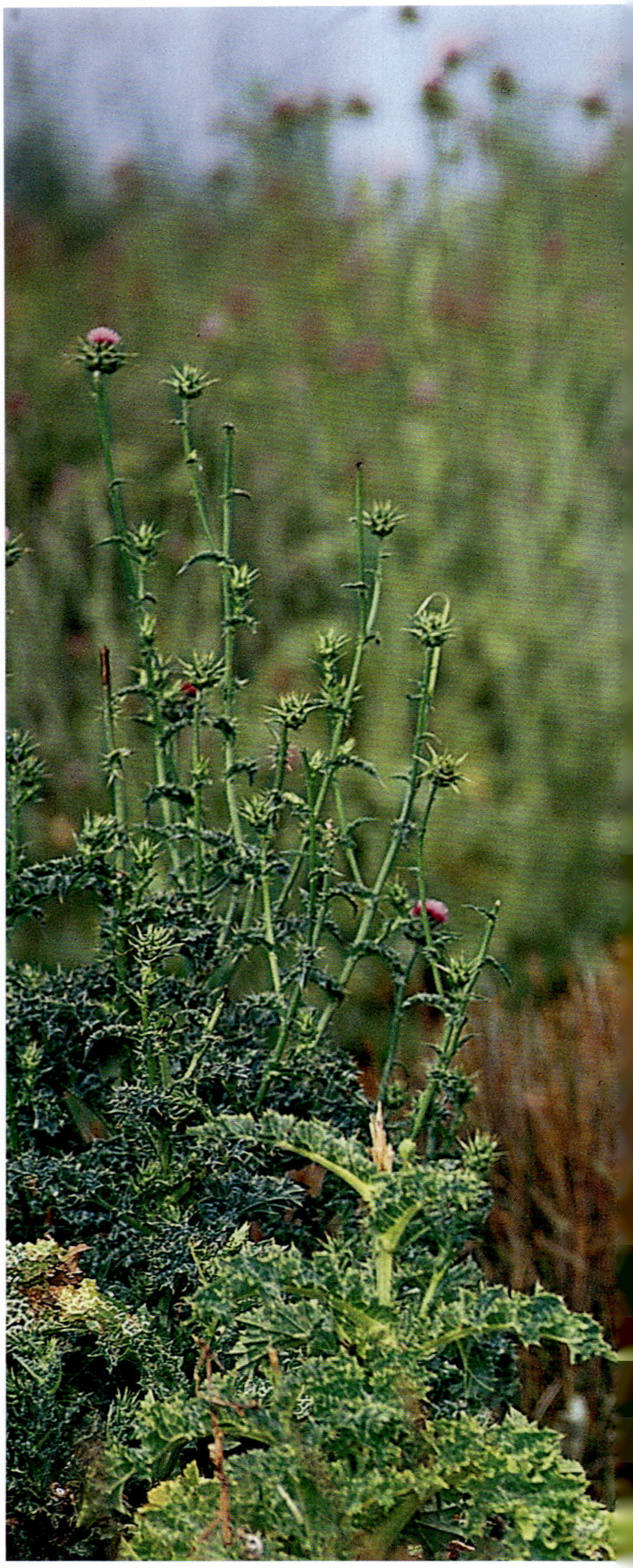

84 and 84-85 • Besides the color of the coat, which differentiates adults and foals, the latter's ages are shown by the shades: a few months for the horse in the bottom left, ten months for the dark one above and over a year for the two beside him that are already gray.

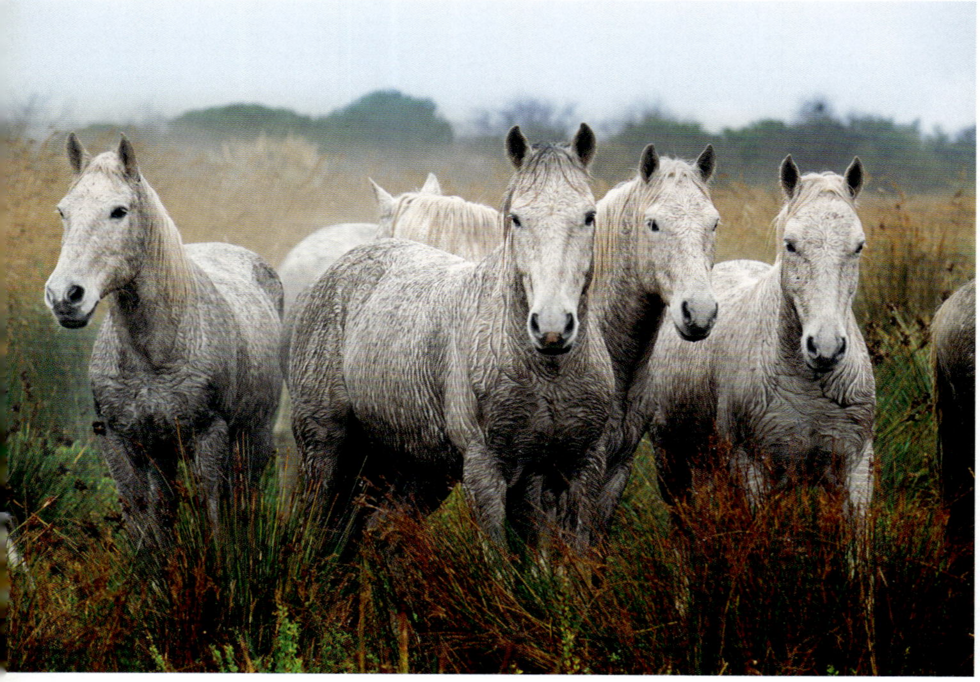

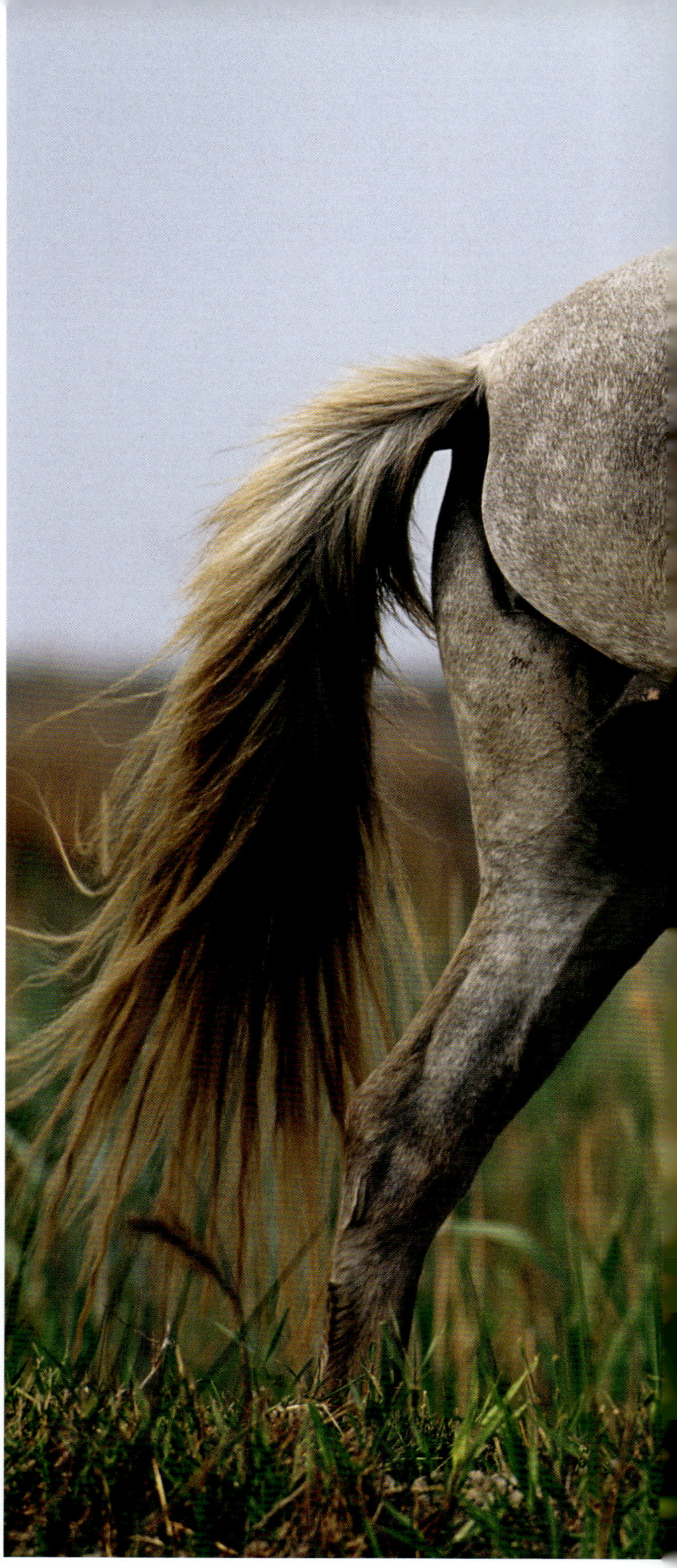

86 and 86-87 • A wild female horse scrapes a rear fetlock with the typical flexibility of a horse. Her foot has the perfect shape of a wild horse, even though it is not protected by a shoe.

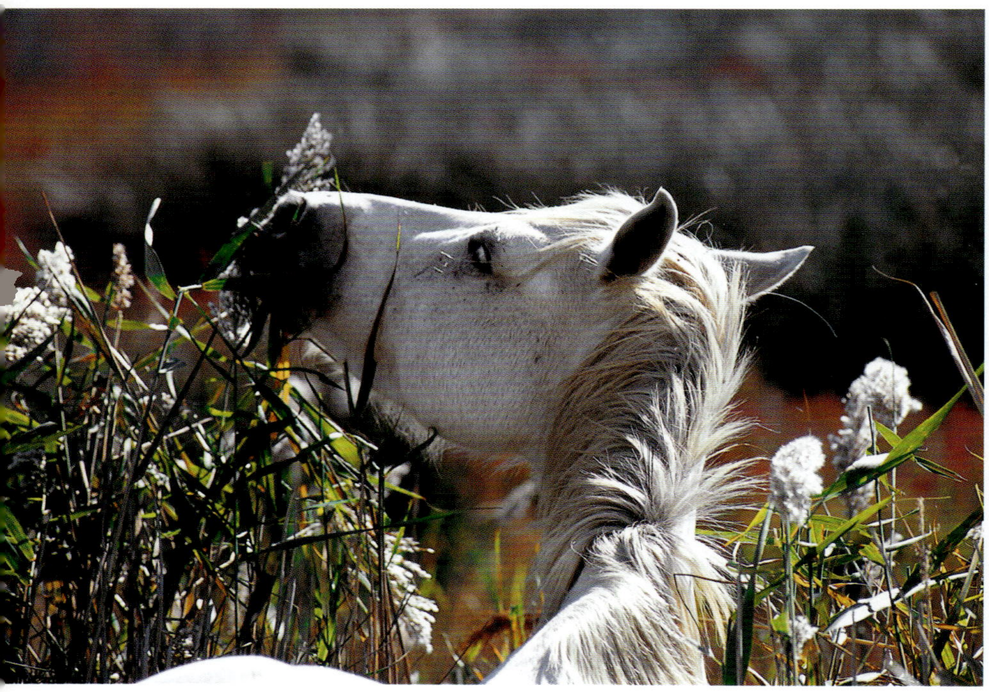

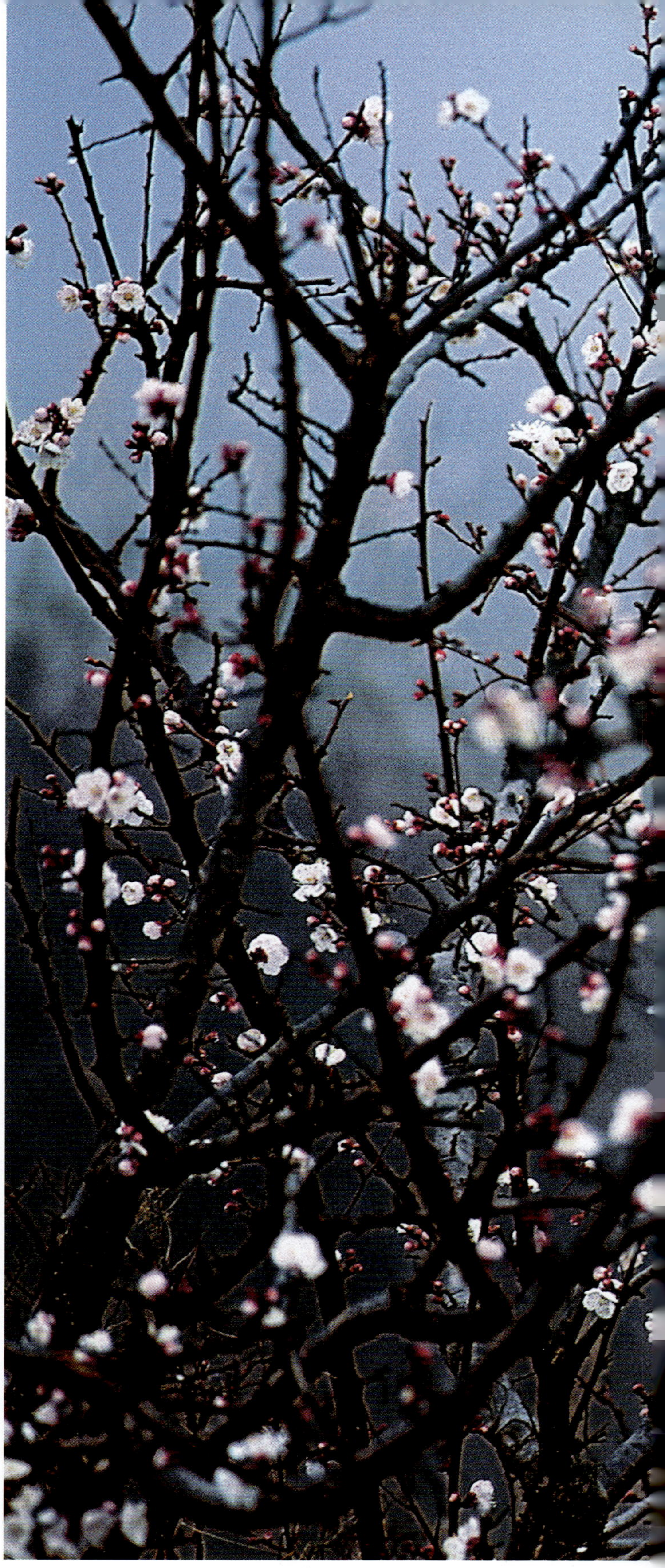

88 and 88-89 • In spring peach-blossoms and other of the Camargue region's innumerable arboreal species, are tasty tidbits full of nutrition, a good addition to the daily diet of the wild horses.

90 and 91 • In winter it sometimes snows even in the Camargue, but the horses' coats are already thicker by the autumn and protect them both from the colder temperatures and from the abundant snowflakes.

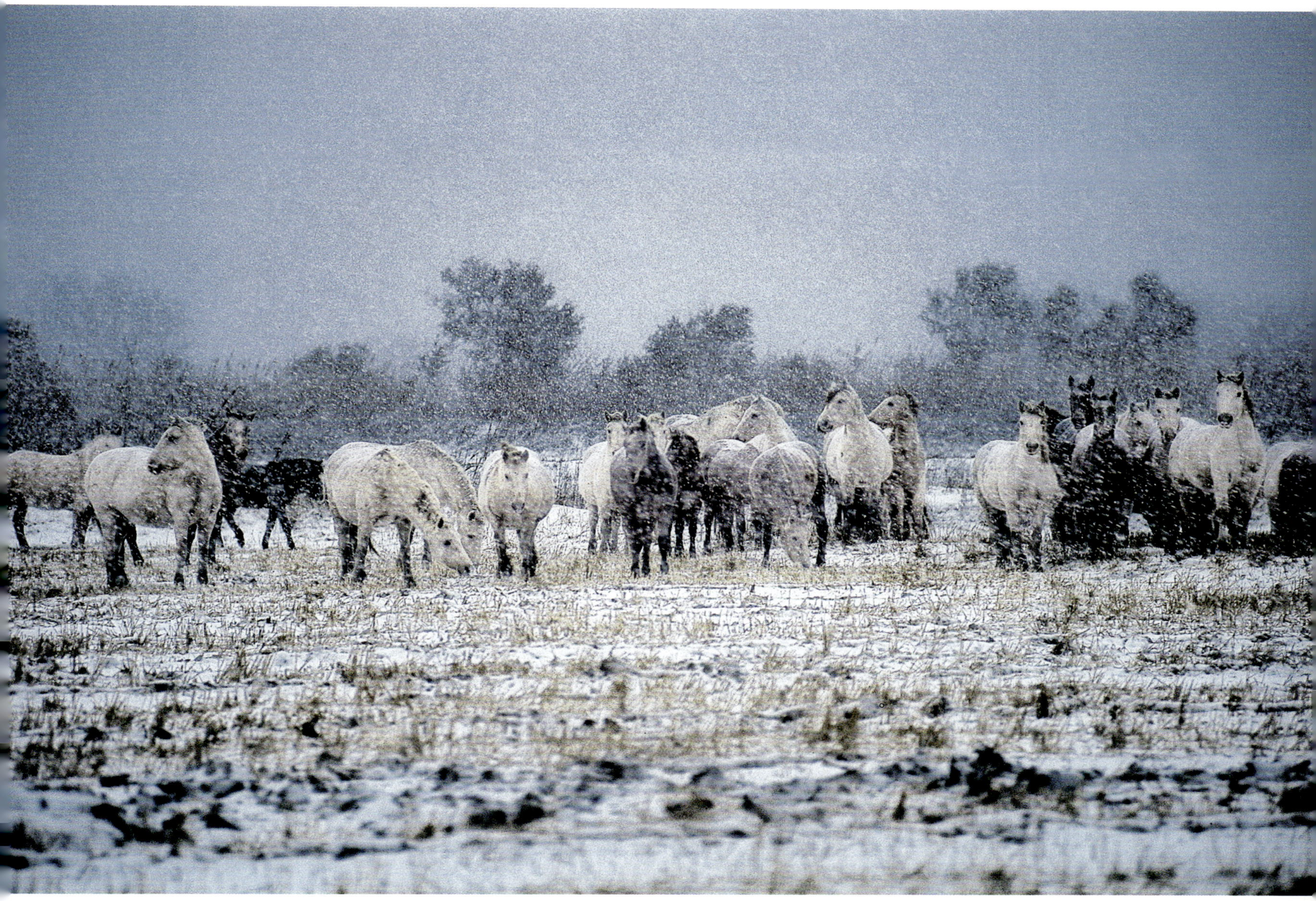

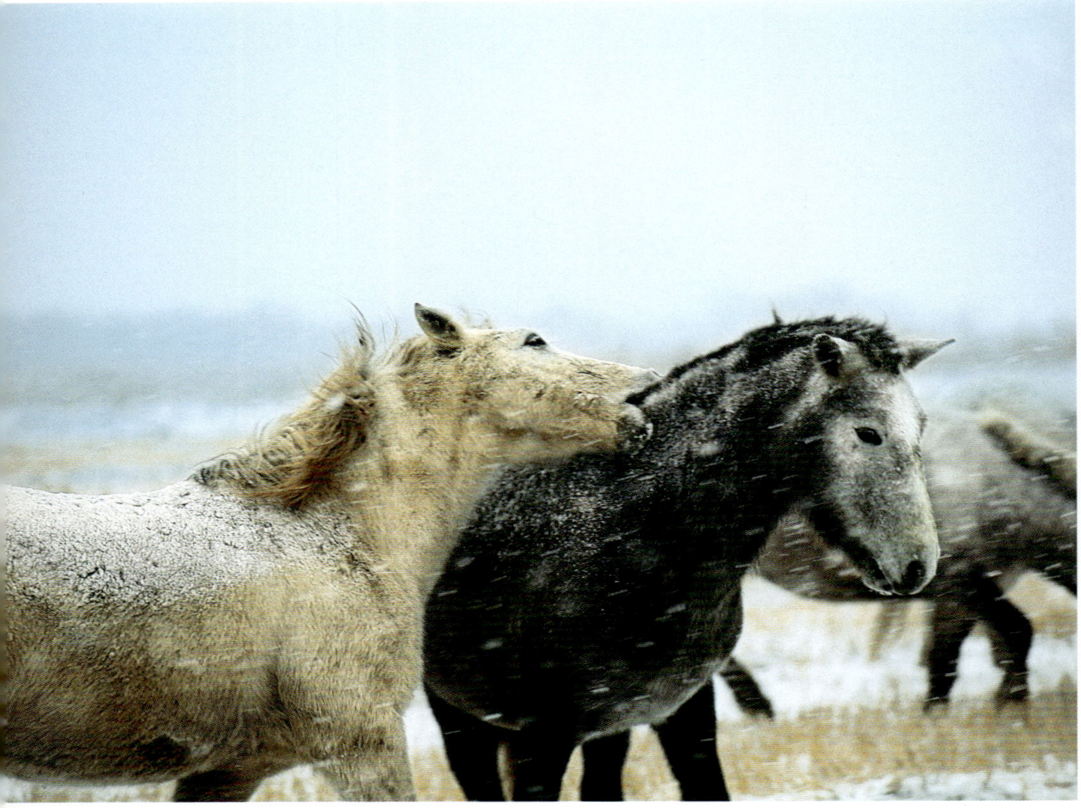

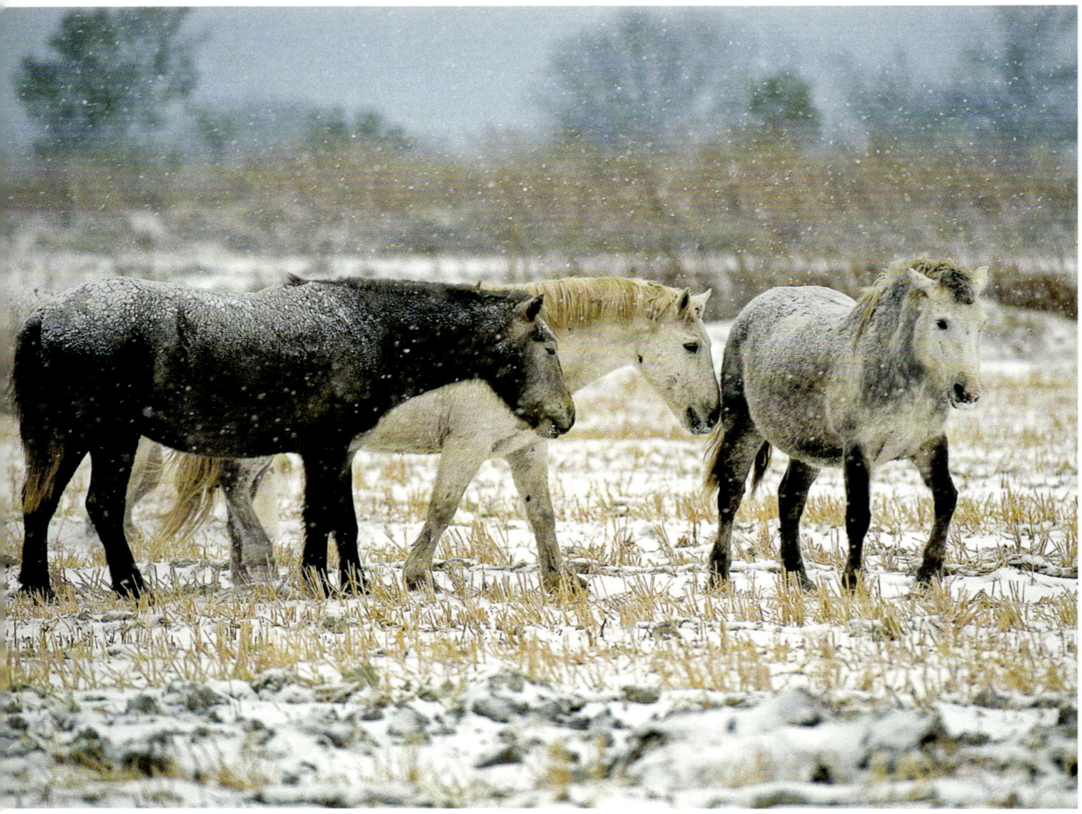

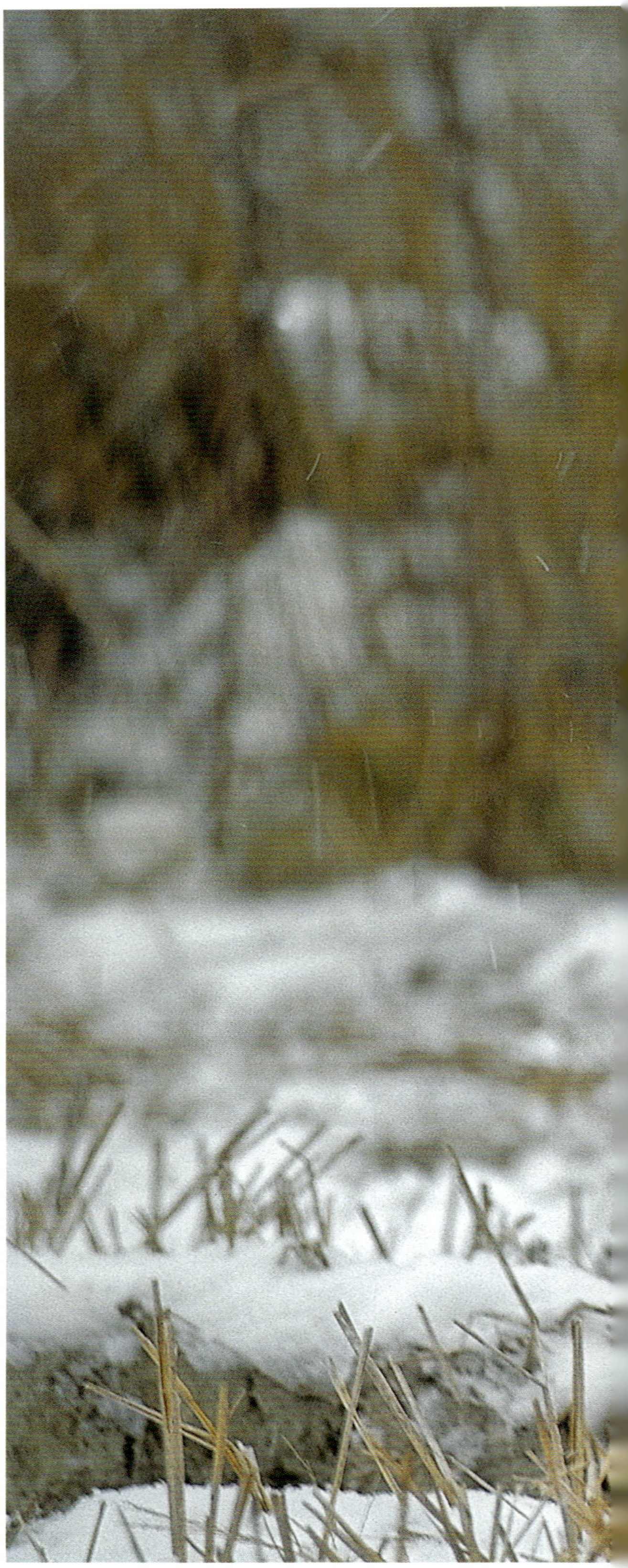

92 and 92-93 • Despite the snow, these youngish pregnant brood-mares — as the color of their coat shows — continue their daily lives undisturbed, cleaning themselves. Meanwhile the foals forage for food before it is buried by the white blanket.

94 the water horse

94 and 94-95 In the photographs on the left a horse is performing the 'flehmen,' an olfactory analysis of the air from which the horse extracts a great deal of information, while on the right two Camargues are photographed 'swapping ideas.' • **96-97** A stallion in the foreground is performing the 'flehmen.'

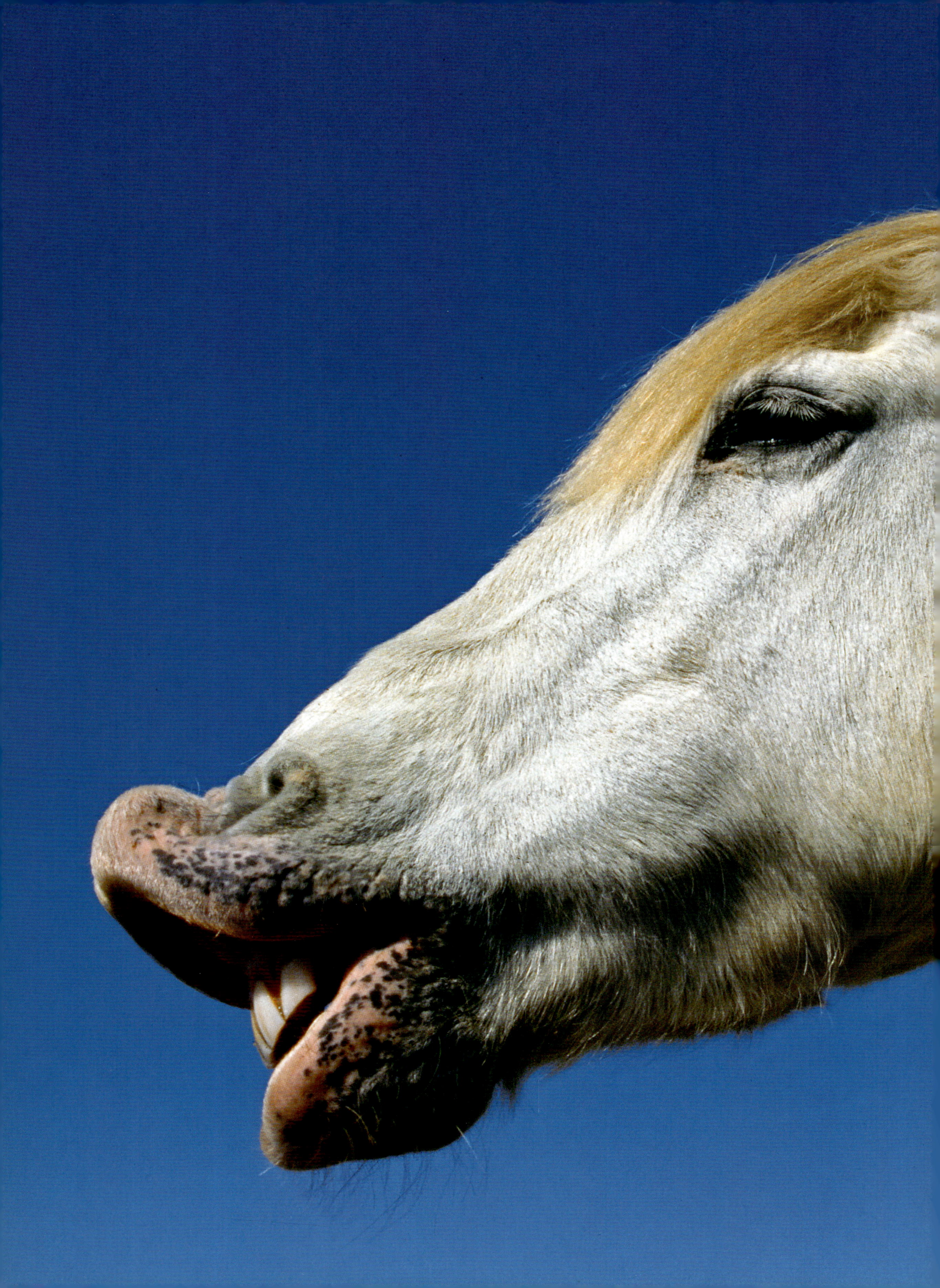

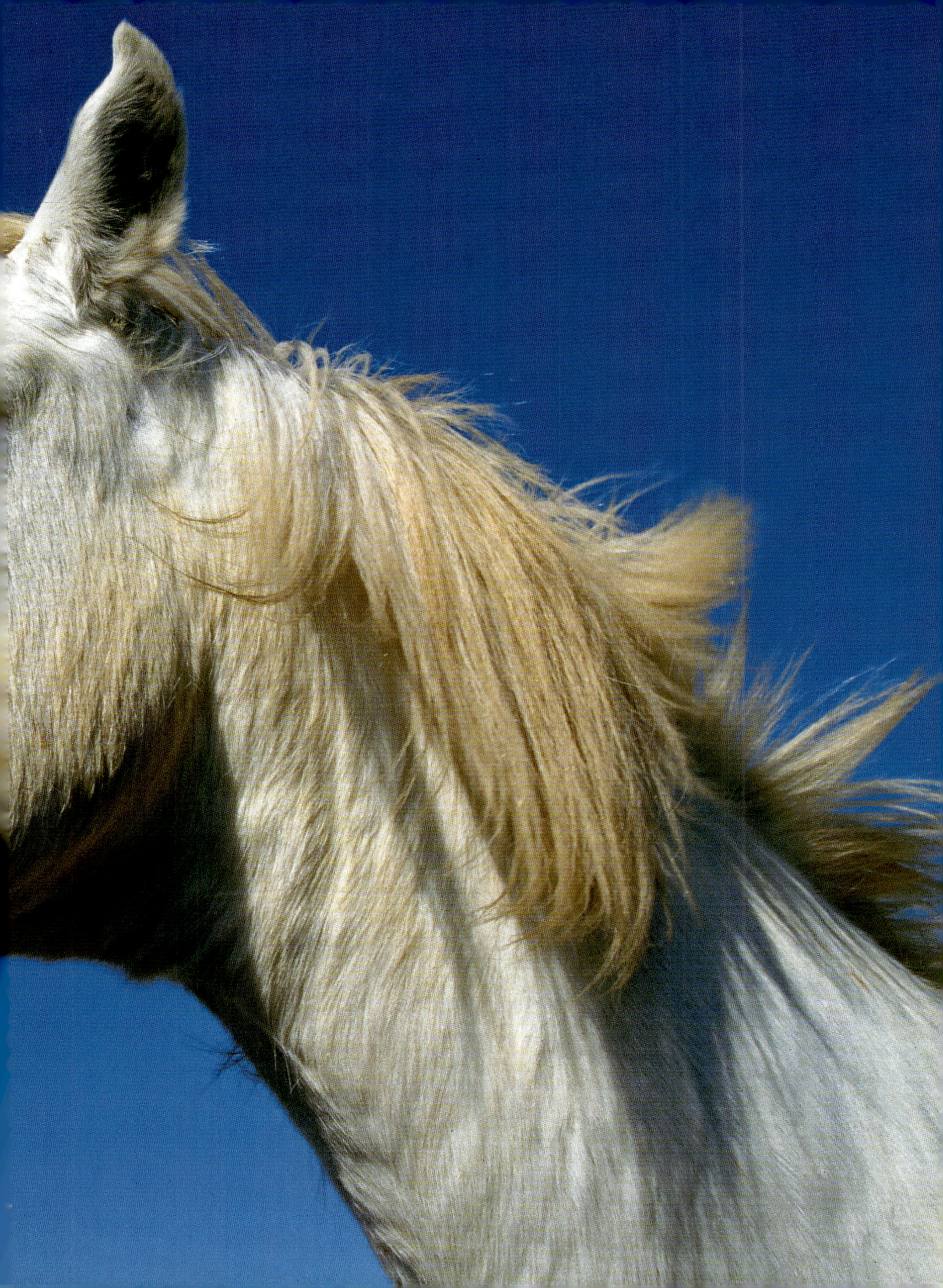

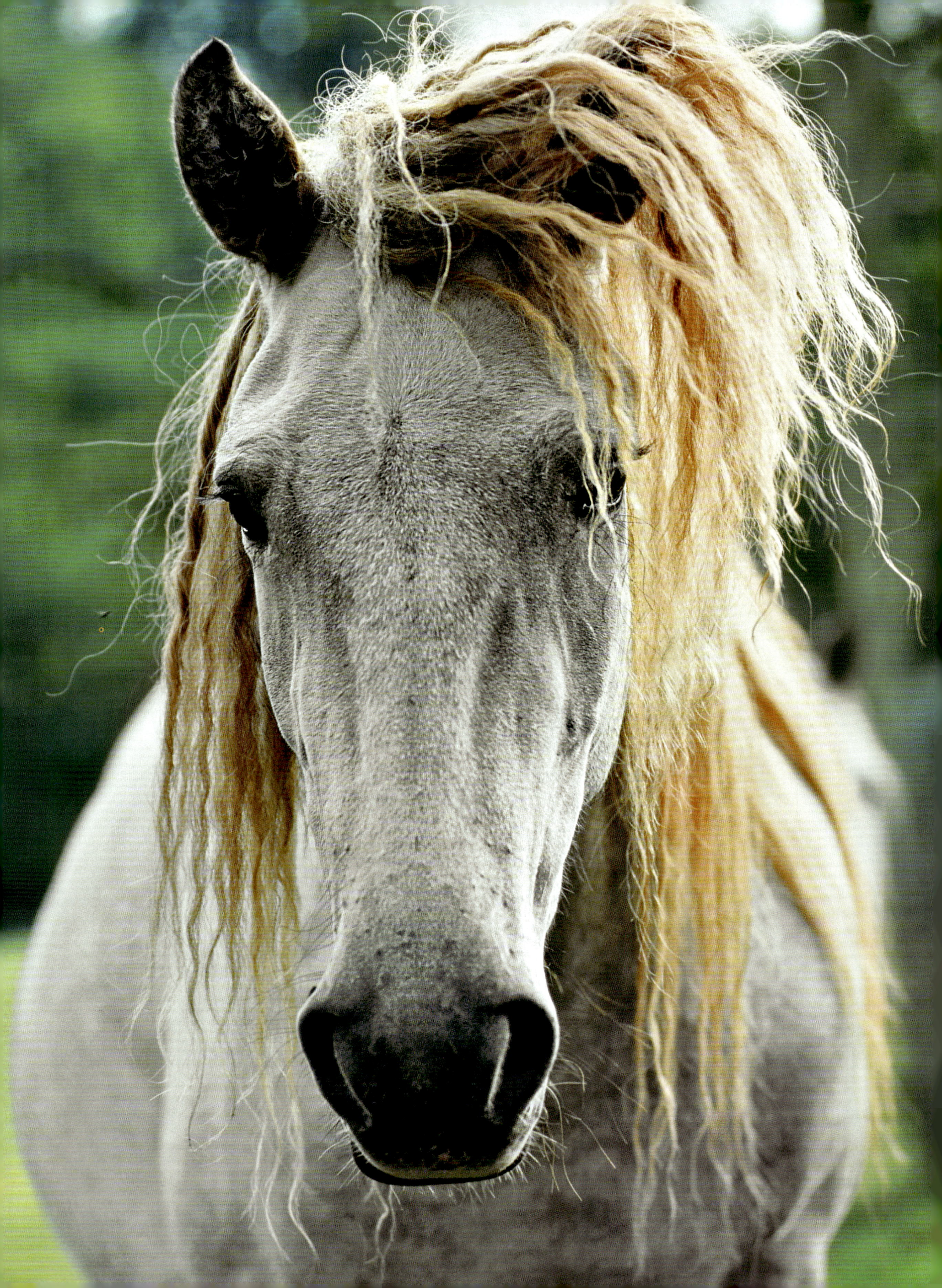

98 • Spring is back and blood flows faster and hotter in the veins; thus the males resume their struggle for supremacy in the herd and to win the youngest and most fertile females.

99 • Expression and physical power are combined in this thick-haired dominant male, who will father many foals.

100 and 101 • With the onset of summer the wild Camargue Ponies resume their wanderings in the lakes and marshes that form the immense nature reserve of the Rhône Delta. The Gardians capture some of them for riding, working with cattle, or tourist rambles, but they will never entirely lose their freedom because they will be left out in the open after every job.

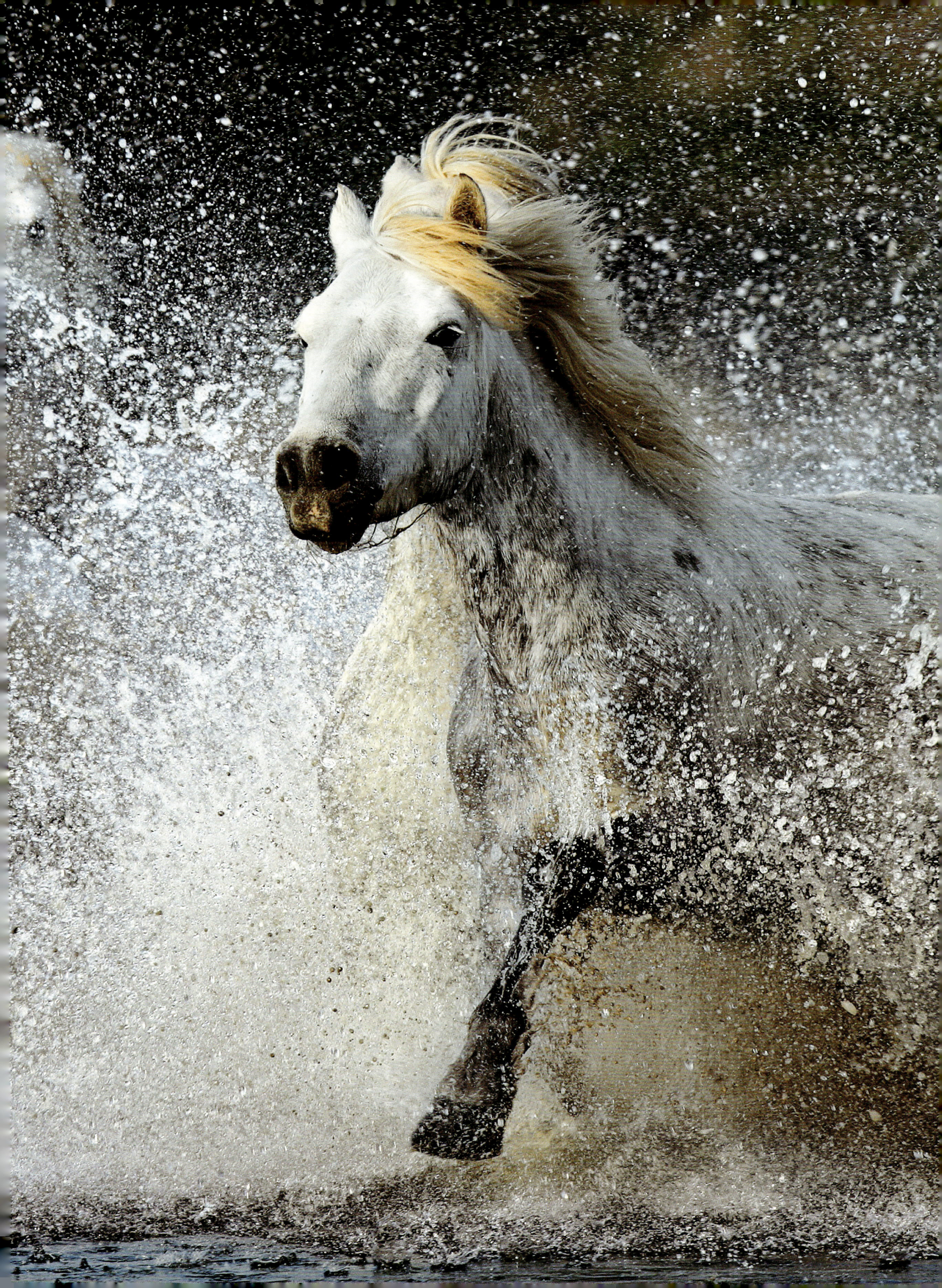

102-103 • The life of horses in the wild consists, as well as the mutual aid of the herd, of living spaces, territoriality and competitiveness, so that the dominant male is respected and feared, as we see in this revealing photograph.

104-105 • A herd of Camargues fords a brackish lagoon at the first light of dawn.

106-107 • This famous picture of the Camargue Pony shows it in its most typical behavior and environment, that is, galloping in a marsh and sending out sprays of froth.

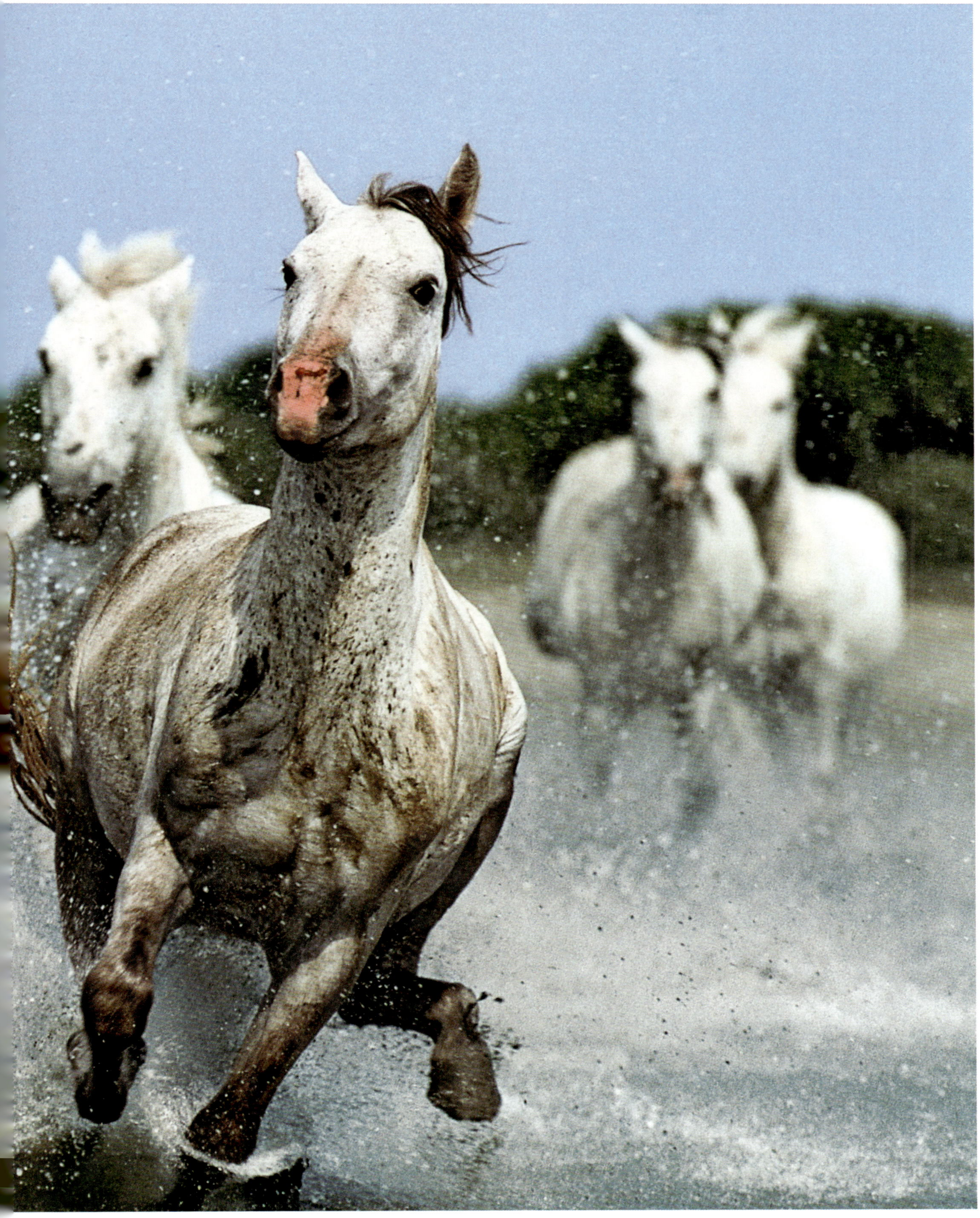

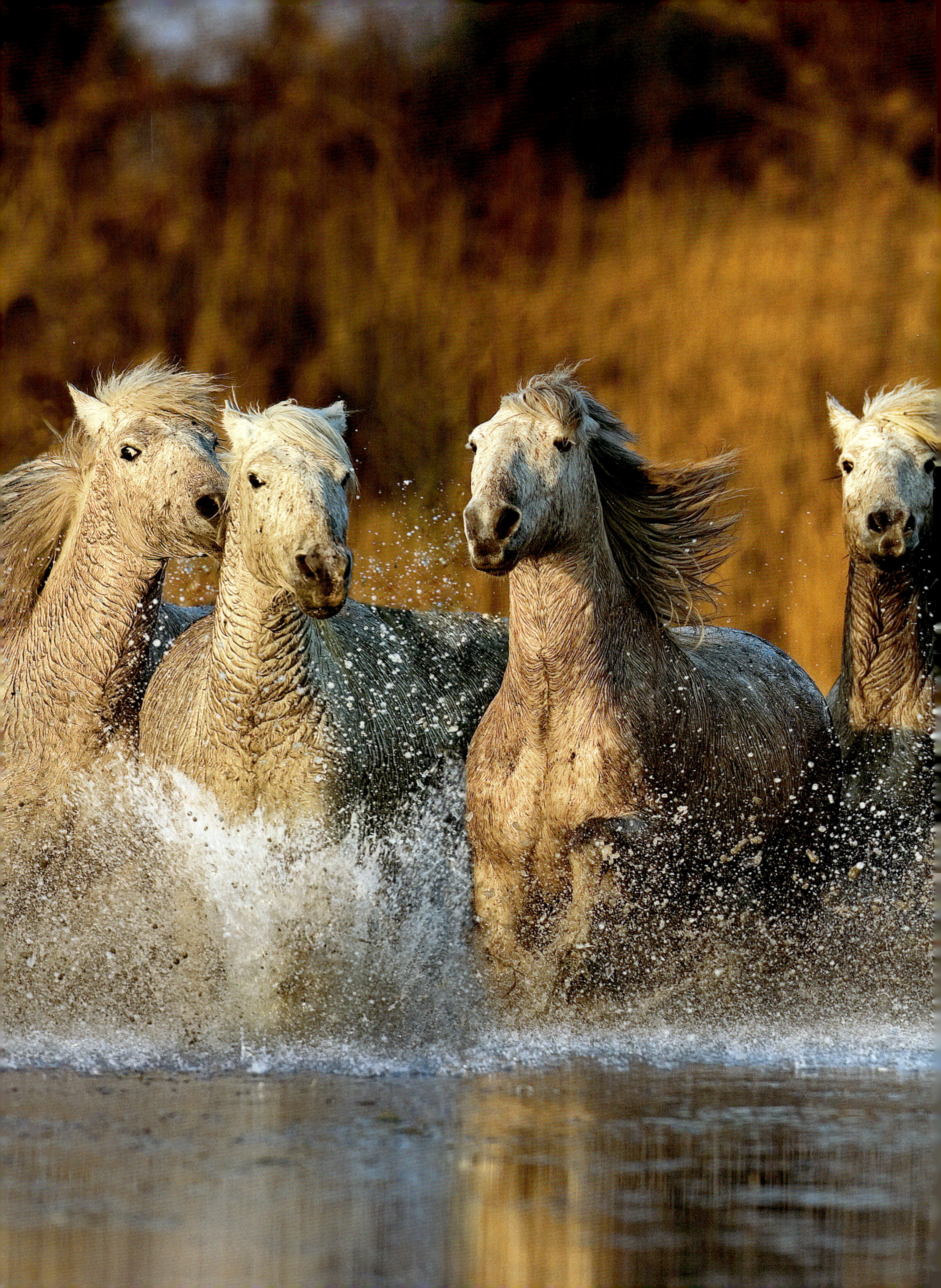

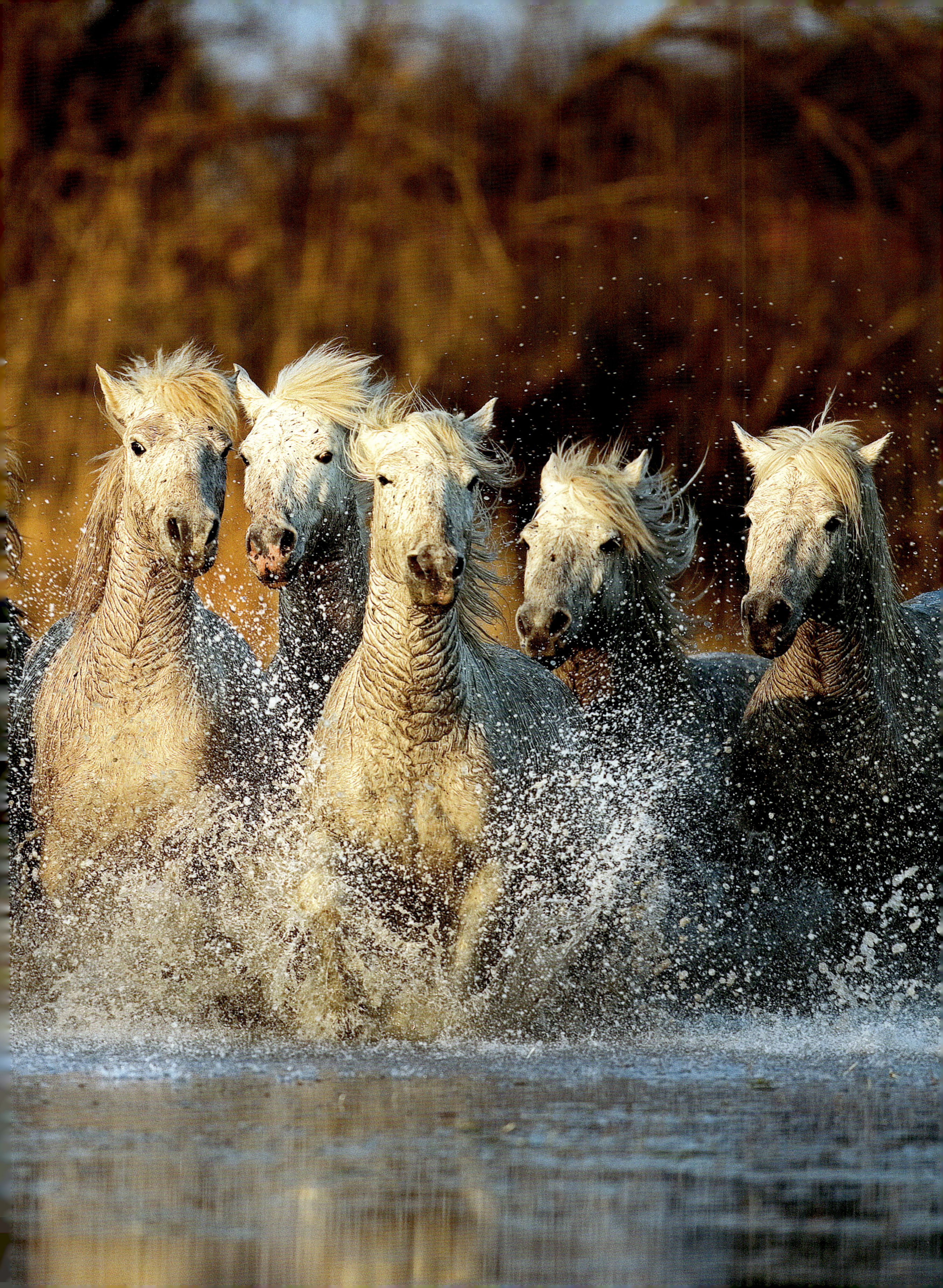

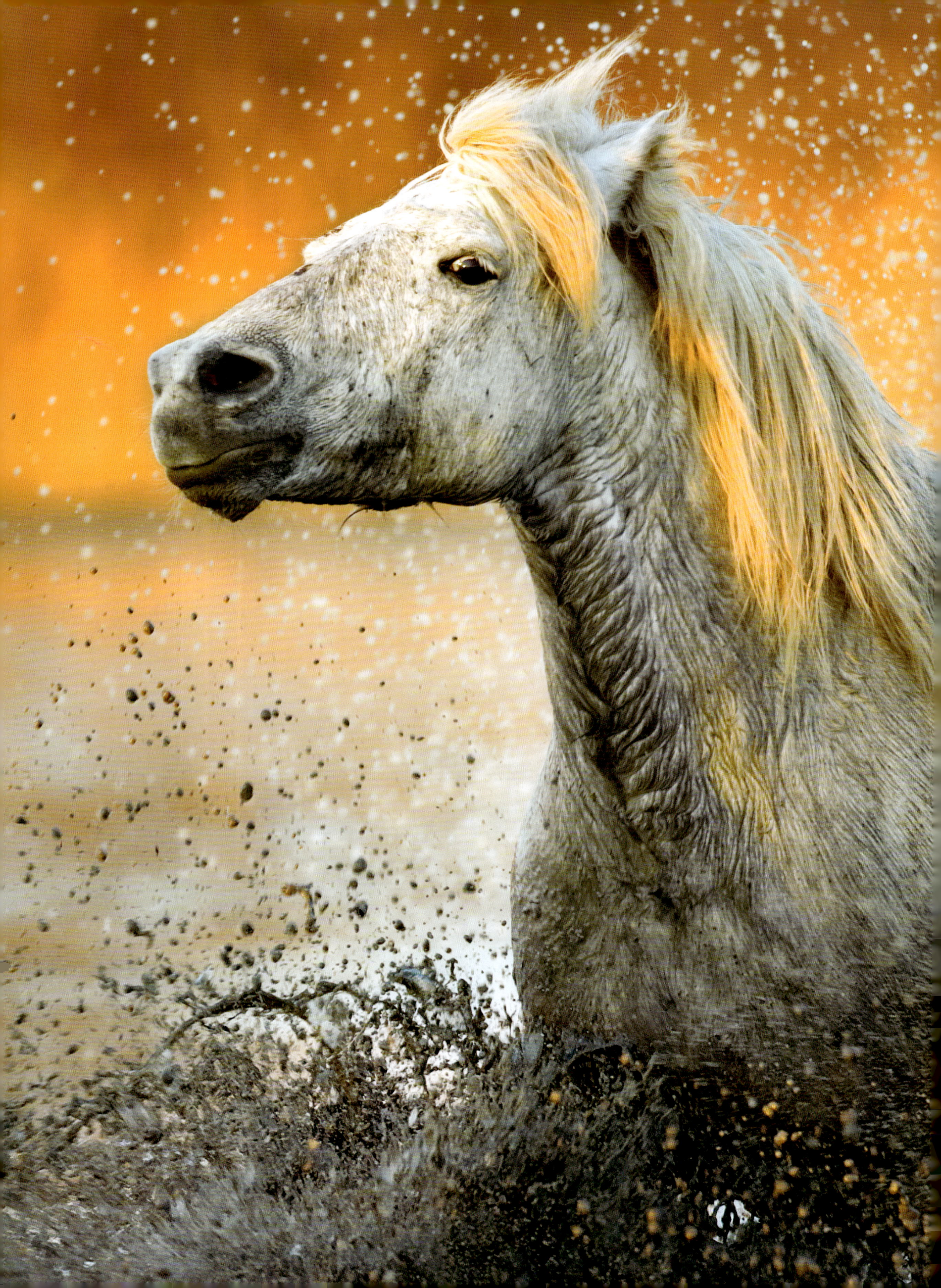

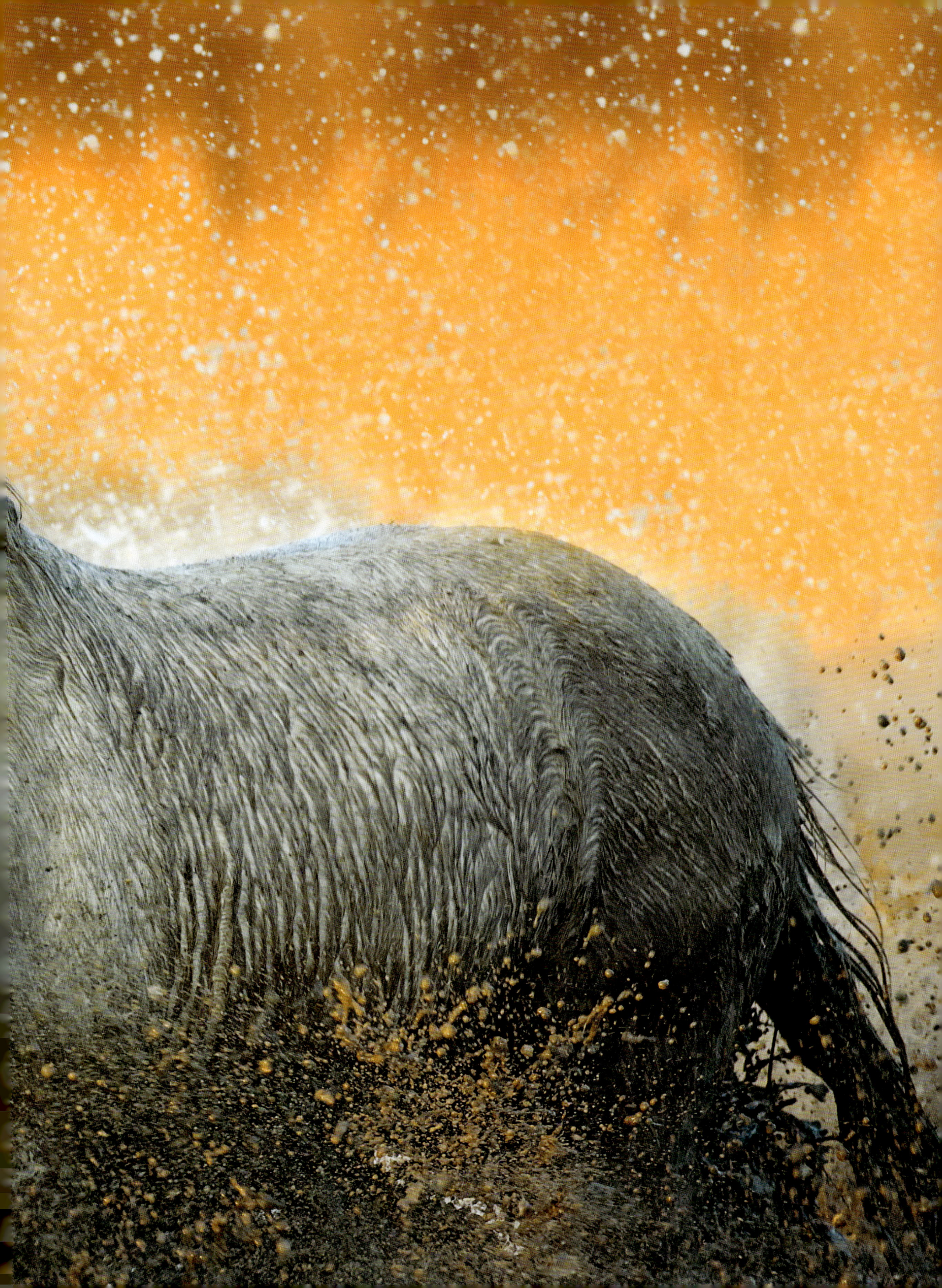

THE LORD OF THE BUSH

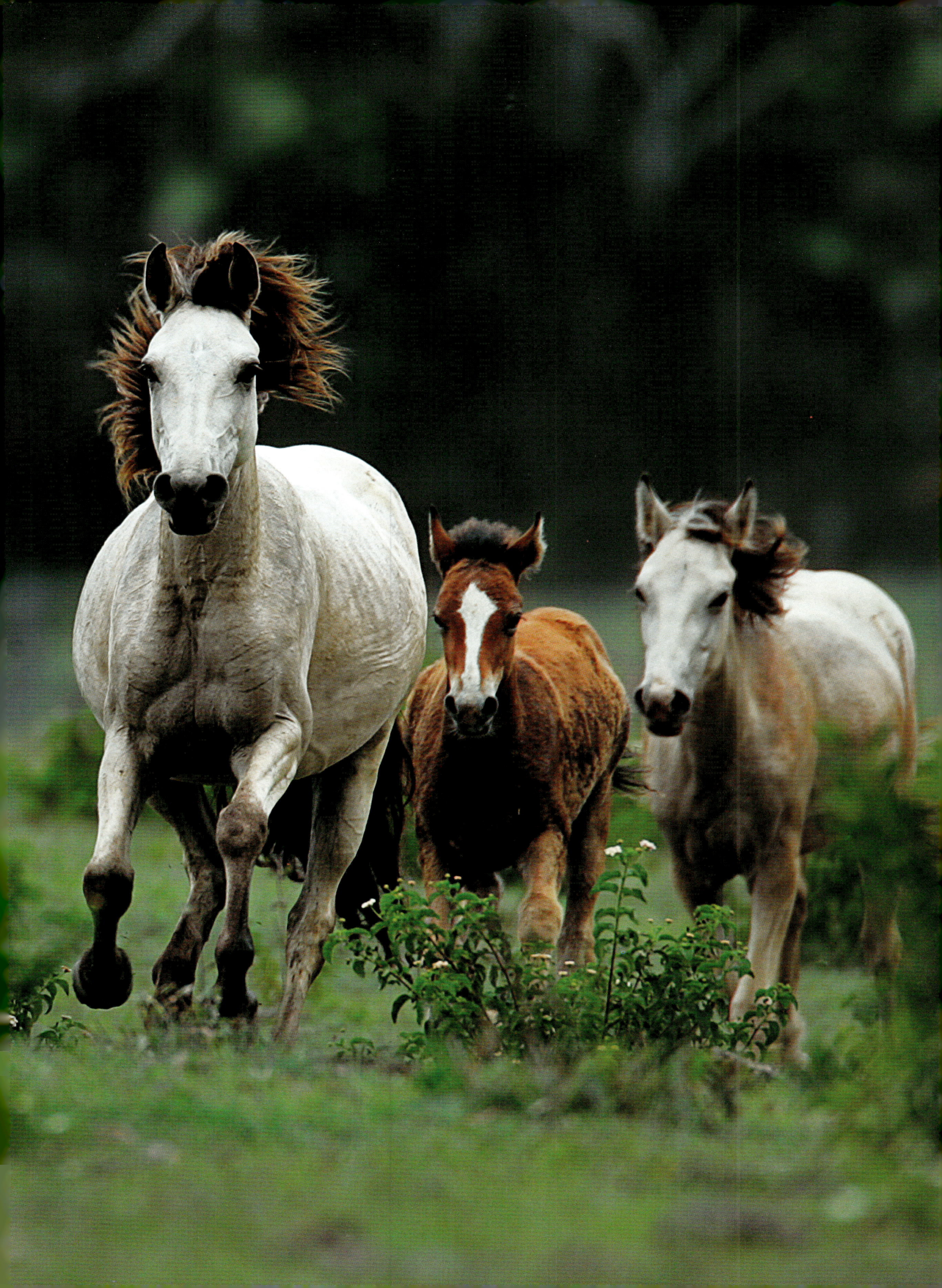

Horses are an integral part of modern Australian culture because they made a vital contribution to the birth and development of this immense country-continent. Australians are traditionally very attached to their identity and distinctive features, including their often-unique species and breeds of animals.

The most famous of these animals is the Kangaroo. However, although Australia is also known as 'the land of the kangaroos,' horses have played a more important role in its history as they were the key to its colonization.

Many of the horses used by the colonists and by gold prospectors in the nineteenth century escaped or were abandoned and returned to the wild. They were called Brumbies (there are various theories about the origin of the name) and, thanks to the huge open spaces and favorable climatic conditions, they bred and multiplied enormously, so much so that they became a danger for agriculture and have been subjected to a number of systematic extermination campaigns (also due in part to their unsuitability for domestic use or 'service' as their rebellious nature makes them extremely difficult to tame and train).

The Brumbies have had to overcome all sorts of difficulties in order to survive, including the danger of extinction, which was only relatively recently avoided when the government passed a law to protect the species, now considered a national asset. Today they live protected in National Parks in many areas of the country, above all in the Northern Territory and Queensland. They are also a popular tourist attraction.

Brumbies did not originate from just one breed – Colonists and gold prospectors in the nineteenth century came from all over Europe, South Africa and the Far East (the British Empire had an influence on every continent) bringing their own different horse breeds and types: working, riding, pack-saddle, pureblood racing, ponies from Indonesia or the British Isles and more. Colonists could not have crossed the Blue Mountains behind Sydney and the other inaccessible territories without horses to transport all their goods. Over the course of a century and a half (the nineteenth century and the first half of the twentieth) when Australia was being colonized, some of these horses who either escaped or were abandoned, found the conditions that they needed for survival in the local environment. Often these conditions were the bare minimum, but they were sufficient to assist firstly in their adaptation to living freely and then to the consequent transformations in morphology and characteristics. These horses crossbred with each other whilst living on the margins of cultivated land, next to deserts and mountains and had to learn how to defend themselves from predators and herbivorous 'competitors' in order to find food.

When James Brumby, a former sergeant who had become a farmer, left his property in Mulgrave Place, New South Wales, to go to live in Tasmania, it seems that he abandoned a number of horses that were already used to living in the open and eating what they could find from the land. Legend has it that the origin of the name Brumby lies here, while other theories argue that it is a derivative of the word 'baroomby,' which in the Aboriginal Pitjara language means 'wild.' Yet others argue that the origin of the term Brumby is to be found in the name of a stream and small gold diggers' village in Queensland from which huge numbers of domesticated horses escaped when it was abandoned. The fact is that the name Brumby definitively entered into common parlance when, in 1880, a Melbourne newspaper used the term for the first time to mean 'wild.'

The Brumby does not have a defined standard morphology and has very variable characteristics both in terms of the color of its coat (in almost all possible colors, though bay is dominant), and for its size and wither height.

In general it is long-limbed, of medium-height, well shaped and with a well-developed musculature. Its neck sits firmly on its torso and supports a proportionally sized head, which is never overly heavy. The Brumby has rather thin but strong limbs with very hard hooves. Mother Nature has given these characteristics to an animal that has to be able to cope with bad weather, including torrid heat, wind and rain, to be tough and when necessary to run quickly, at times eating little and drinking when possible. It is also able to fight predators that threaten the herd. This fight for survival has made the Brumby a very brave but difficult character, so much so that it is not worth capturing to domesticate and ride or to harness to a gig.

Today there are around 400,000 Brumbies, which makes them the largest population of wild horses on the planet and far more numerous than the North American Mustangs. They are very popular and appear in literature, for example in Elyne Mitchell's books for children and adults (whose main character is Thowra, a Brumby stallion), on television with the series "The Silver Stallion: King of The Wild Brumbies", and in cinema with a film of the same title starring none other than Russell Crowe and Caroline Goodall.

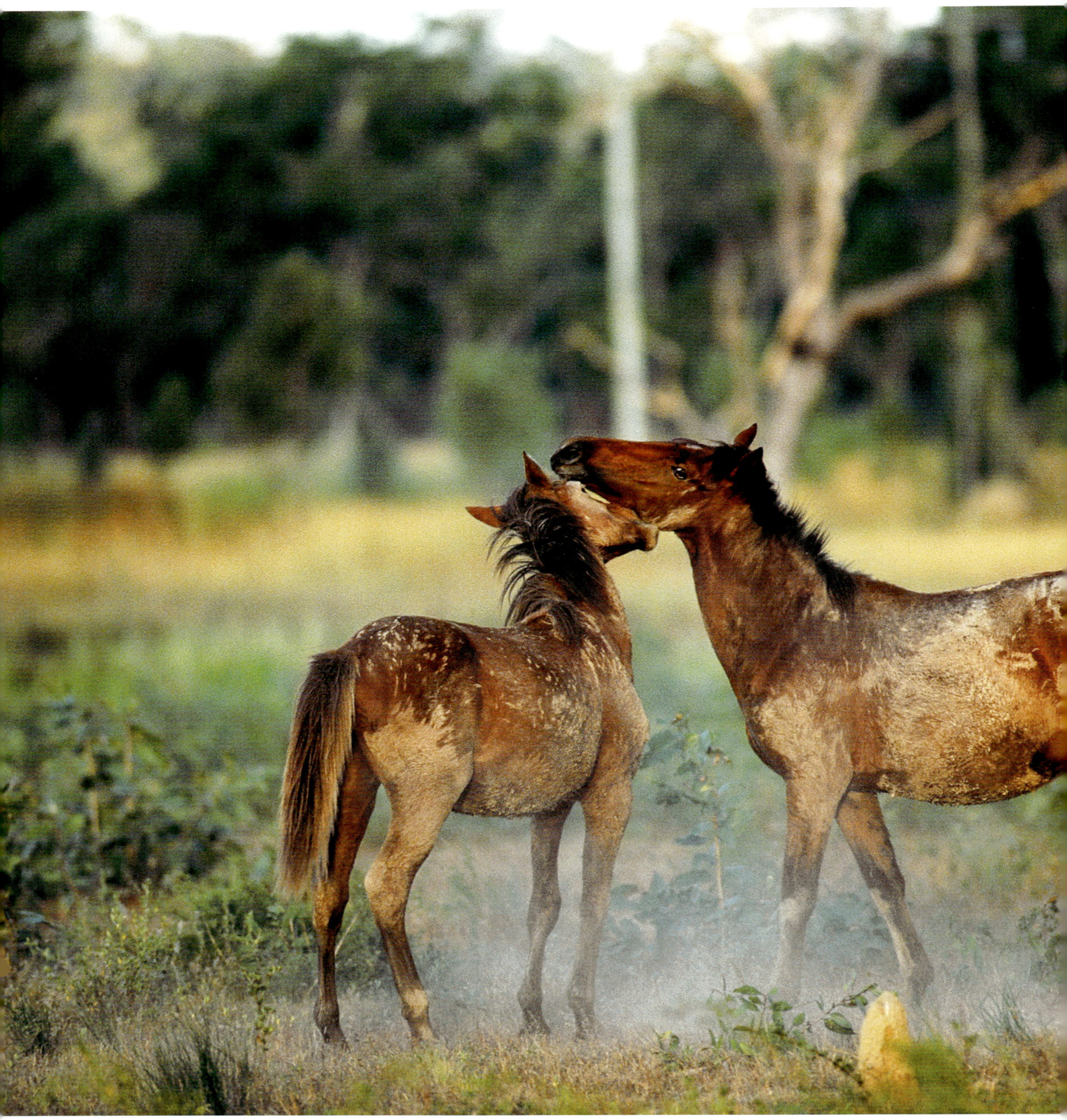

109 • A small family of two pregnant mares and a foal, at the gallop. The color of the foal's coat will change over time to become similar to that of the mother.

112-113 • Two Brumbies have just rolled on the ground 'powdering' themselves with earth, an excellent cure for parasites and also good as a 'dry shampoo' for a clean and shiny coat.

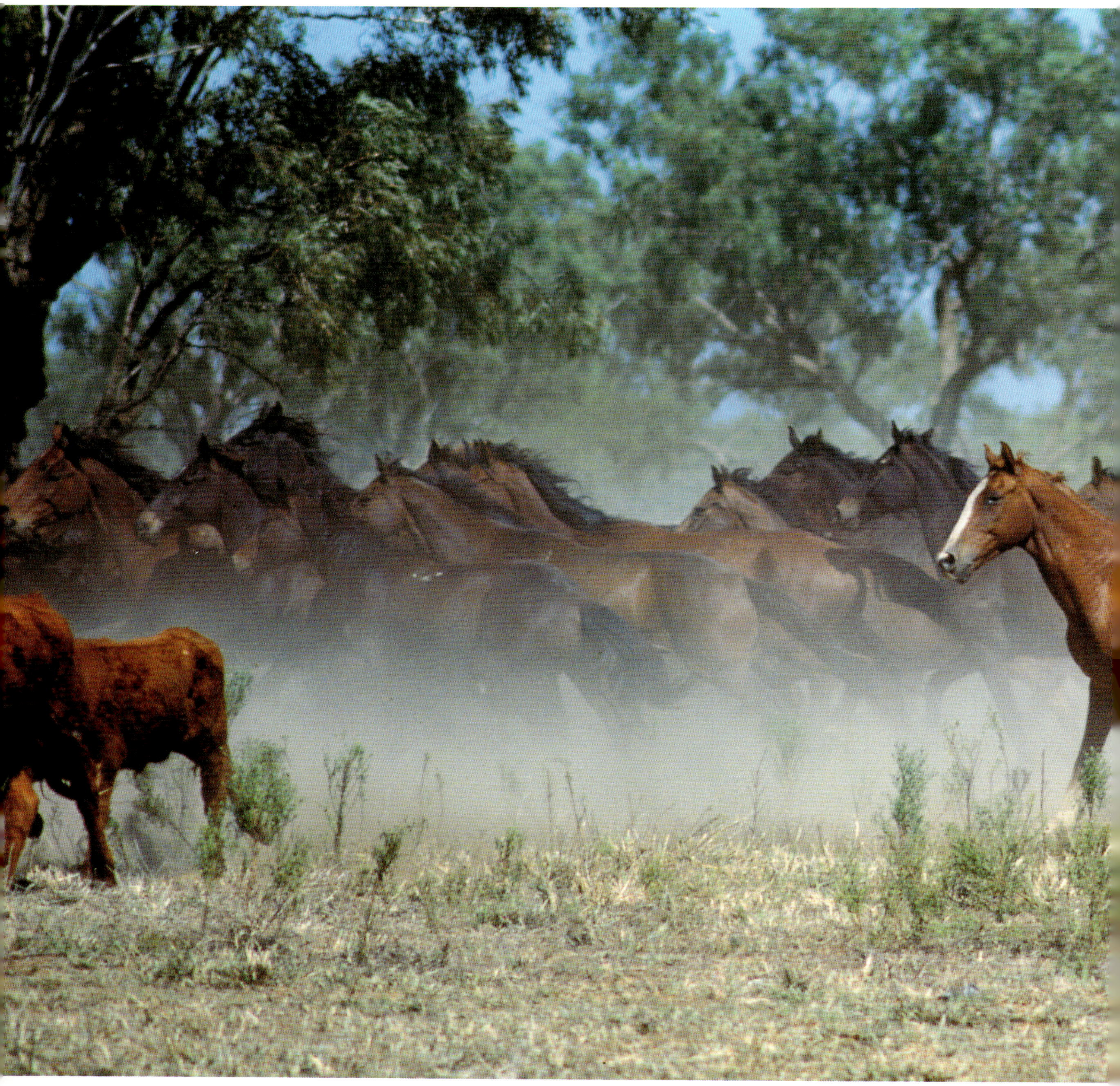

114-115 • Northern Territories: a herd of wild Brumbies during a journey that leads them across a cultivated zone. Wild horses can be a problem for local farming.

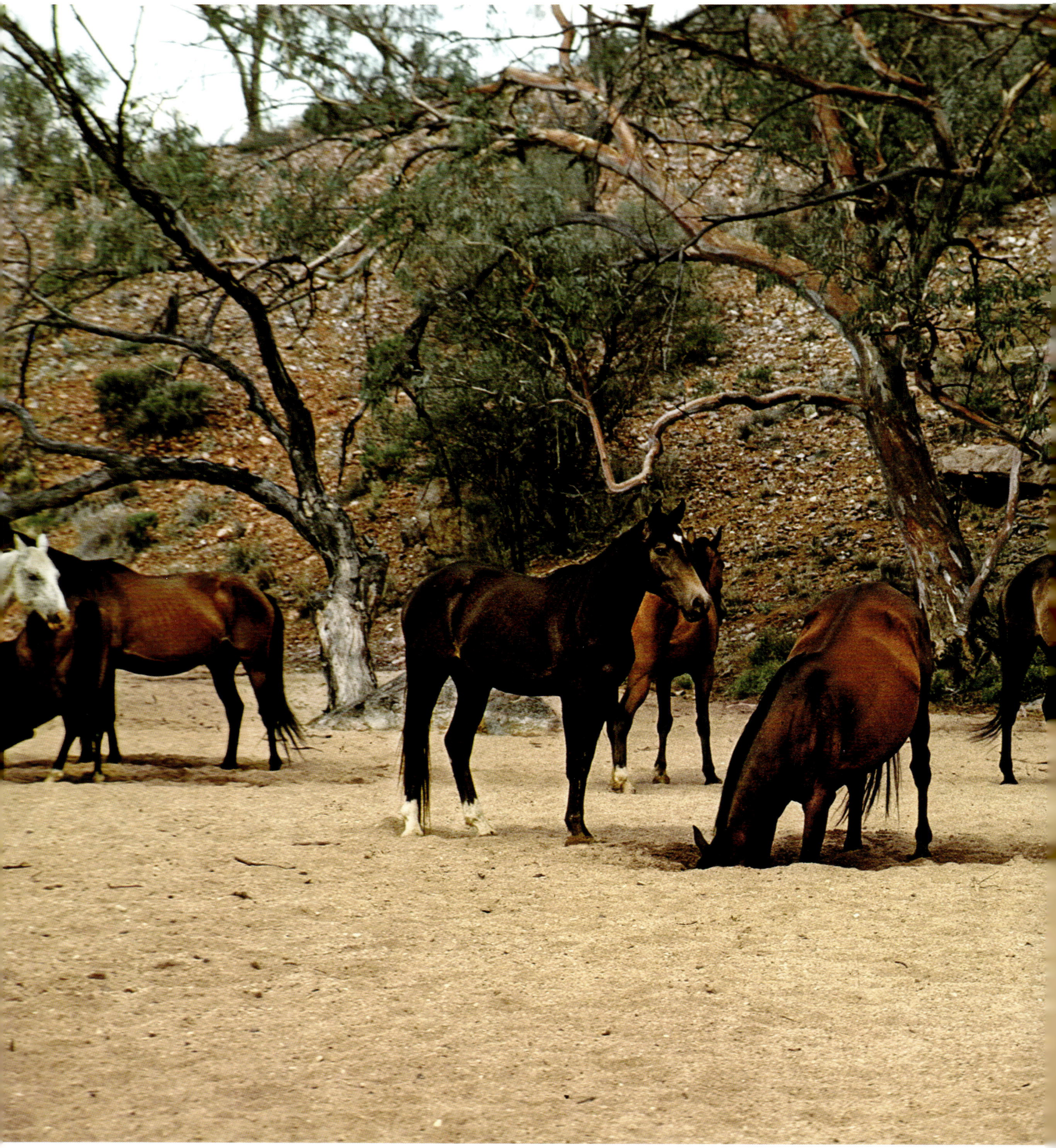

116-117 In order survive in nature the Brumbies have learned how to 'sense' the presence of water and then dig to find it and drink from these wells: this photograph, of enormous documentary value, shows two horses carrying out this practice. • **118-119** These two mares are in a constant state of alert, ready to flee at the slightest danger. Even while galloping, they keep a constant watch over the foal.

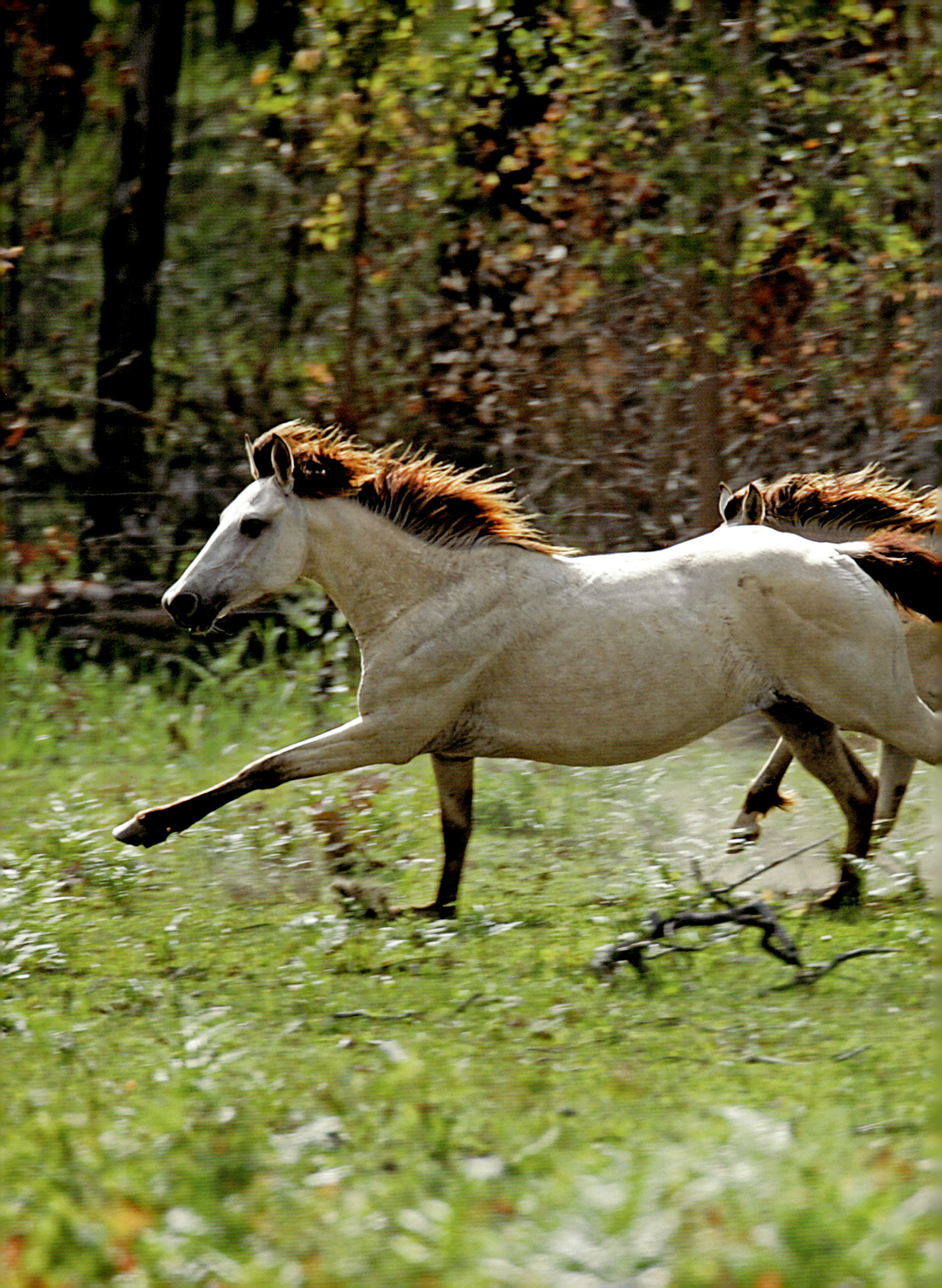

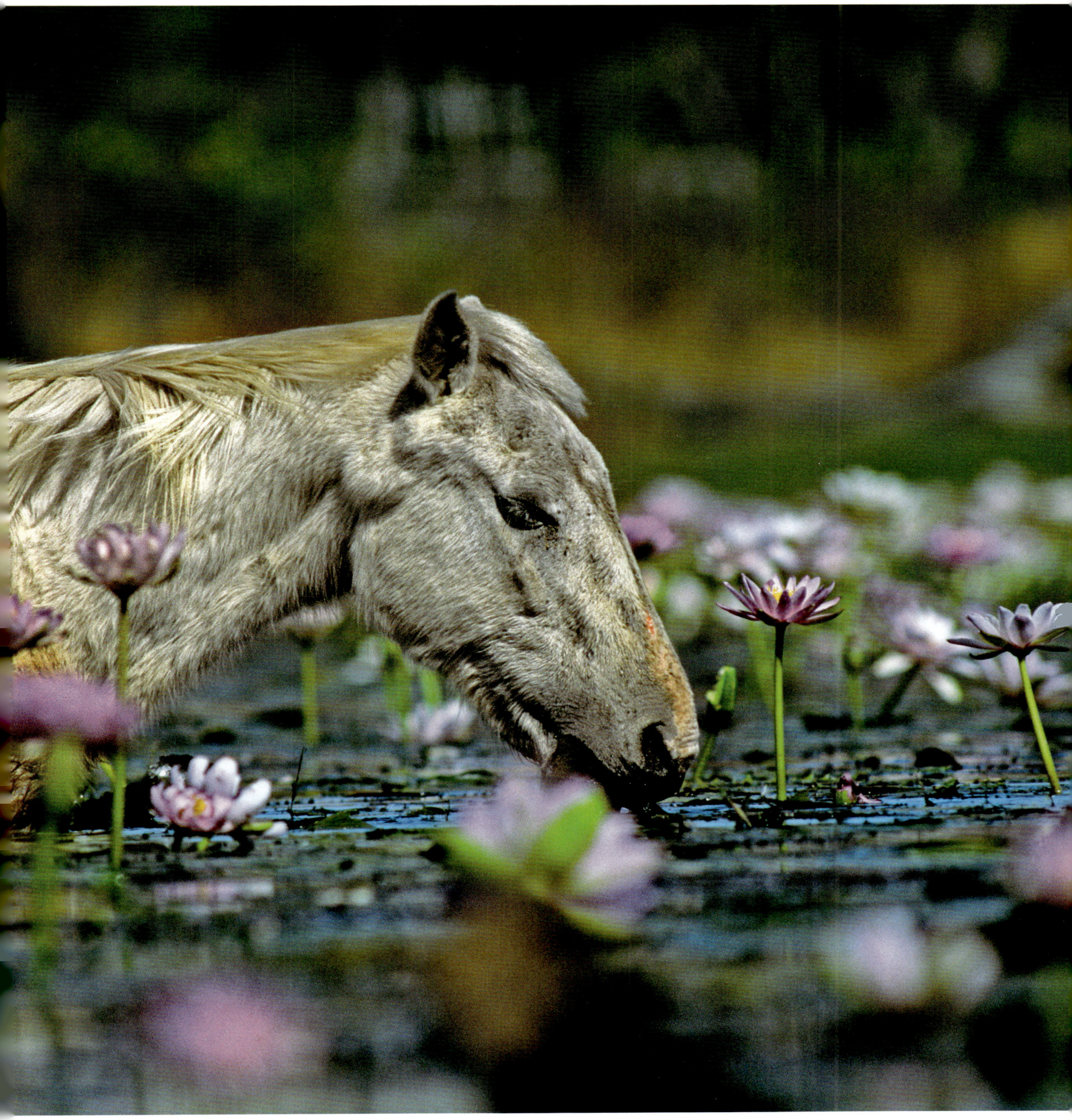

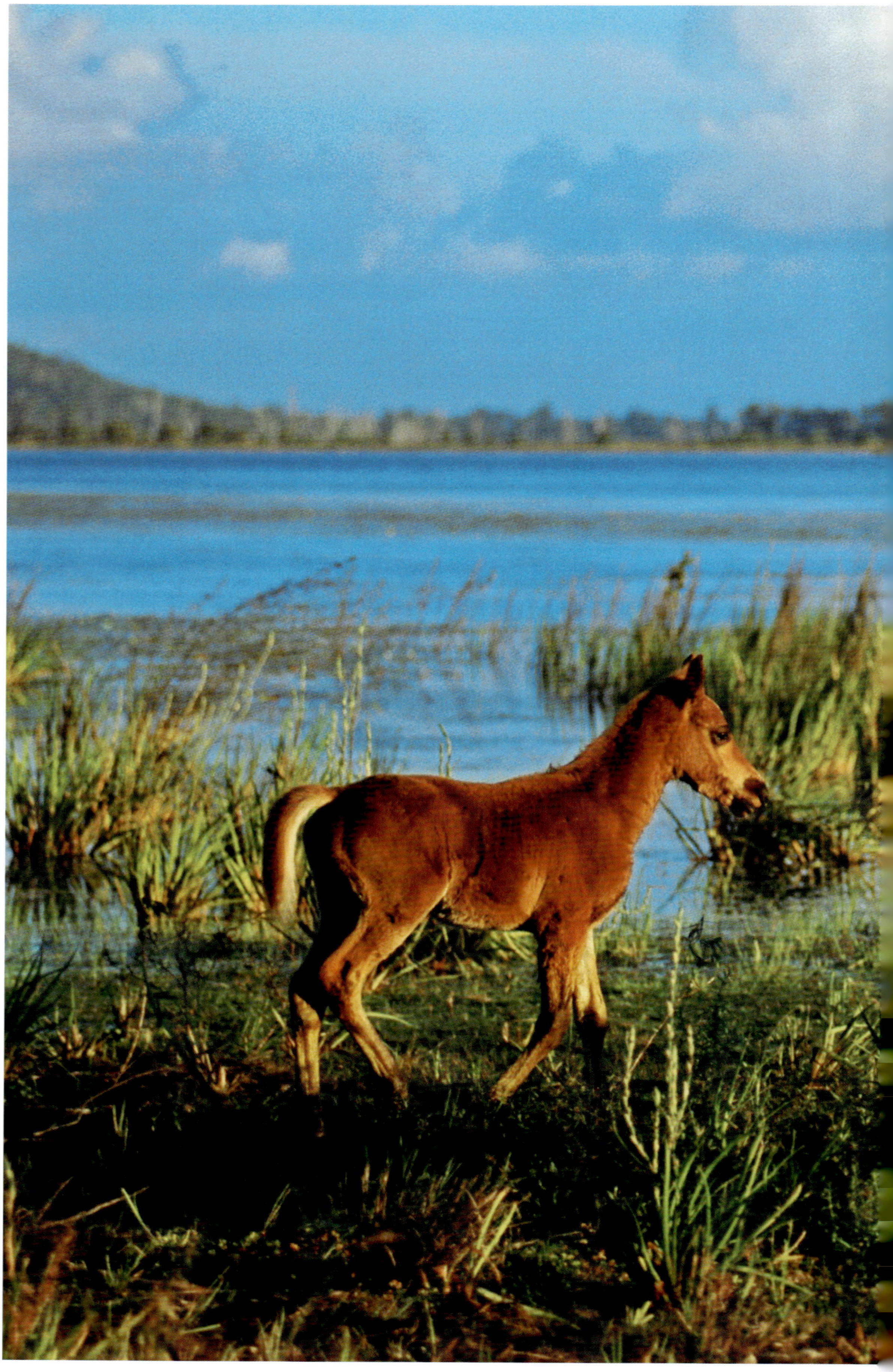

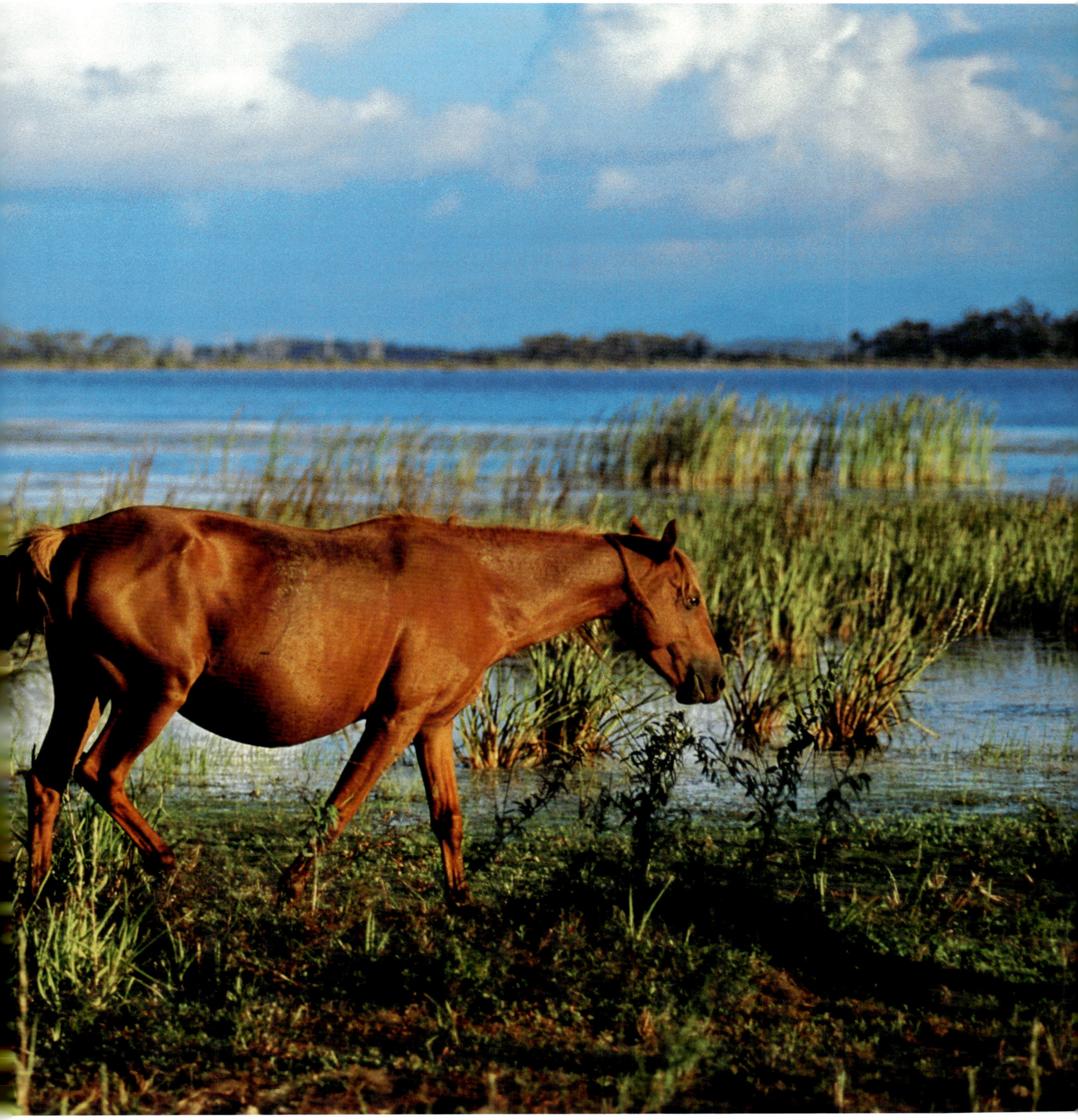

BORN OF THE WIND

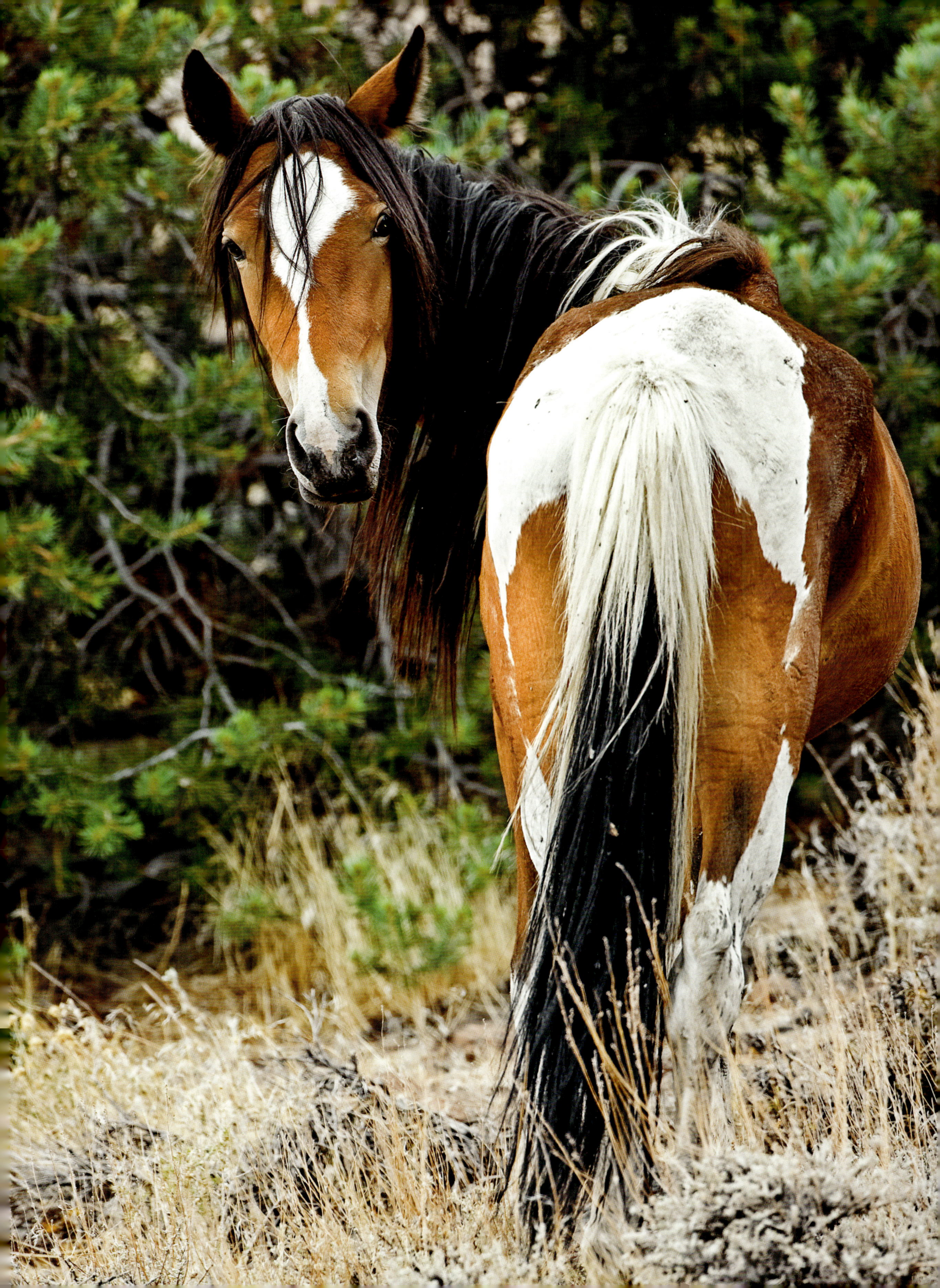

In 1519, when the Aztecs saw the horses of the Spanish Conquistadors for the first time, they were literally terrified. The horses appeared both fearsome and fascinating; half man and half animal, as the Indians saw them, at least initially. They confirmed religious prophecies that spoke of superhuman beings coming from over the sea. A truly dreadful war followed: by rights the few Spaniards led by Hernán Cortès should have had to retreat, but they besieged Tenochtitlan, the capital of Montezuma's empire, not with strength of numbers but rather with 'technological' strength. They laid siege to Tenochtitlan with guns and their unknown and terrifying horses, and with the help of other enemies of the Aztecs who they had already subdued, they perpetrated a terrible massacre. In 1521 the city was razed to the ground and Cuauhtémoc, the last Aztec emperor, and successor to Montezuma, was killed. This is how the Conquistadors and their horses forever changed the history of America.

Today wild horses descending from those that escaped or were abandoned by Hernán Cortès's Conquistadors still roam northwest America. They are the Mustangs: the word is taken from the Spanish 'mestengo,' which means 'livestock raised in the mestas,' a sort of forerunner of the farmers cooperative, which parceled out wild animals to take and rear.

The horses that escaped the Conquistadors adapted back to living freely despite many dangers, returning to the wild and reproducing in surprisingly large numbers for over 300 years. Some of them, wandering in search of new pastures and more hospitable climates, were captured by the indigenous peoples and transformed into 'control' groups that developed particular characteristics.

One representative example is the leopard-spotted horse of the Nez Perce, a people living along the Palouse River (passing through today's States of Washington, Oregon, and Idaho) and from which they took the name Appaloosa, or 'Palouse horse.'

The vicissitudes and privations that these horses had to overcome in order to survive strongly molded and formed them so that today the rugged wild Mustangs do not even vaguely resemble Cortès's sumptuous and baroque Andalusian horses. Natural selection has made them more spare and also less elegant, and they also vary greatly in size, so much so that it would be inappropriate to speak of a standard. However they are incredibly tough and resilient, capable of crossing unimaginable distances eating just scrub or even nothing for days at a time.

As the pioneers conquered the Far West, the Mustangs interbred (either deliberately or accidentally) and with the incoming horses came a further enriching of their gene pool. There is one thing that they have in common with their Spanish forefathers — their great variety of coat colors. Thus, among the free running herds we can see, besides the single colors (bay, chestnut, and, less often, gray), also particular types of coats such as, for example the 'palomino' (washed chestnut) or the Isabella, or dun-color, etc. Then there are also dappled and appaloosa coats: the same coats that are found among horses in Andalucía.

Mustangs were at times captured and tamed for riding, both by Native Americans and pioneers. At first they were used for hunting and raids, but the Indians also demonstrated a great ability as farmers, as well as horse-breakers and riders. Pioneers and cowboys in turn captured and tamed the Mustangs to use them to work with livestock (and at times to sell them to the Cavalry). These Mustangs were then crossed with already domesticated horses and this crossbreeding led to the production of the standard breeds of North America.

The ever-growing Mustang herds were recently subject to intensive culling as they were seen as a 'threat' to grazing land, until the US Congress intervened to safeguard the species (with herds protected on reserves). Subsequently however the authorities have allowed their capture for butchery and meat export.

Mustangs have often played significant roles in American literature and Hollywood filmography: for example the novel, 'The Horse Whisperer' (from which came the famous film with Robert Redford and Scarlett Johansson) or a cult-movie like 'The Misfits,' with the legendary Clark Gable and Marilyn Monroe, and the more recent 'World in Flames' with Viggo Mortensen. The untamed wild stallions, the 'Broncos' (this is also a Spanish term), are the most famous of all. They are often captured and sent to the rodeo, where their free and rebellious temperament is accentuated by a belt that pulls tight around the lower-stomach which would even drive a placid plough horse to buck and kick. Sometimes these rough and temperamental horses, if they can be tamed, become really special partners. Although difficult to manage and 'independent,' once saddled they are brave, hardy and, having a very strong instinct, cooperative like few other horses in the world.

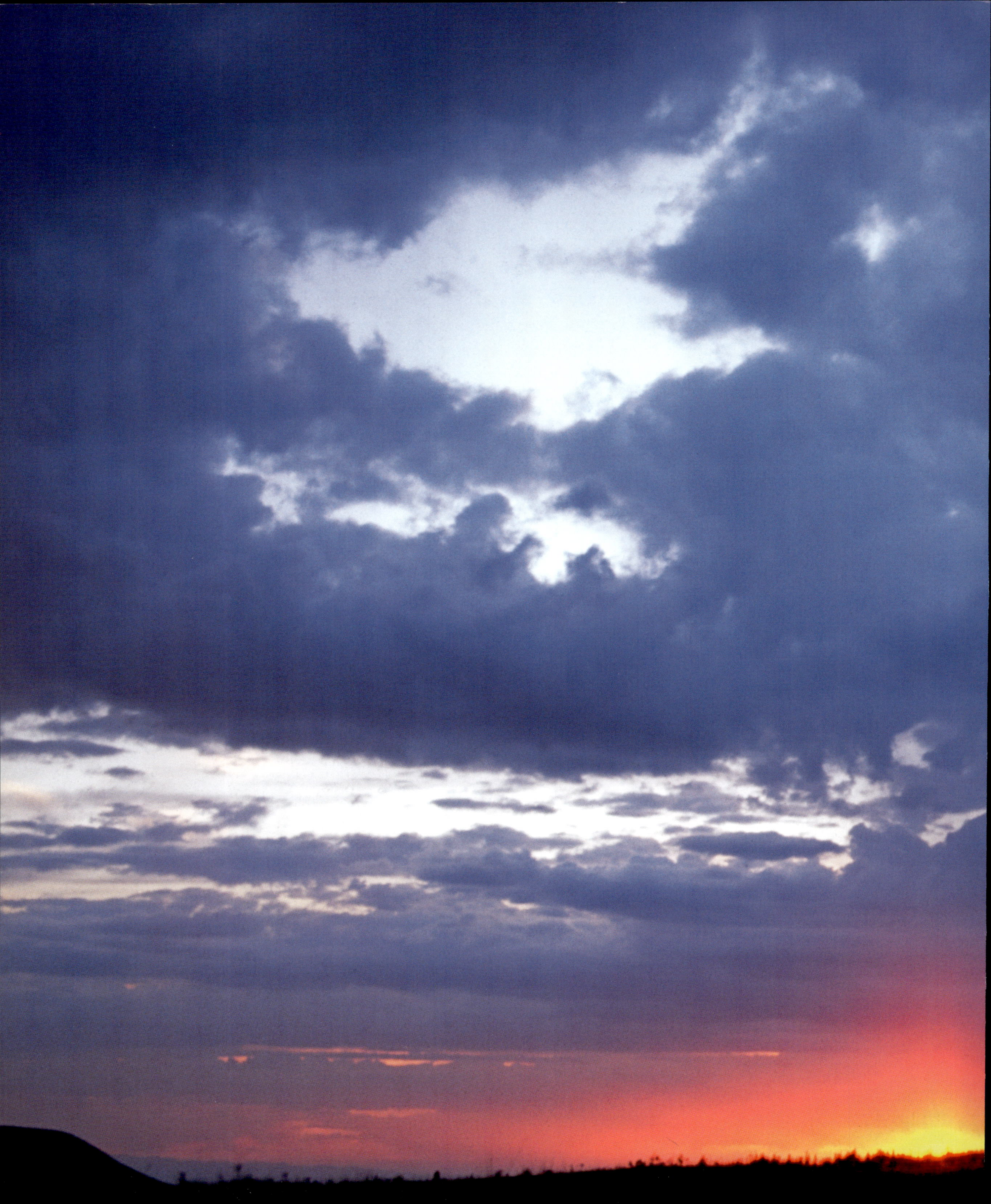

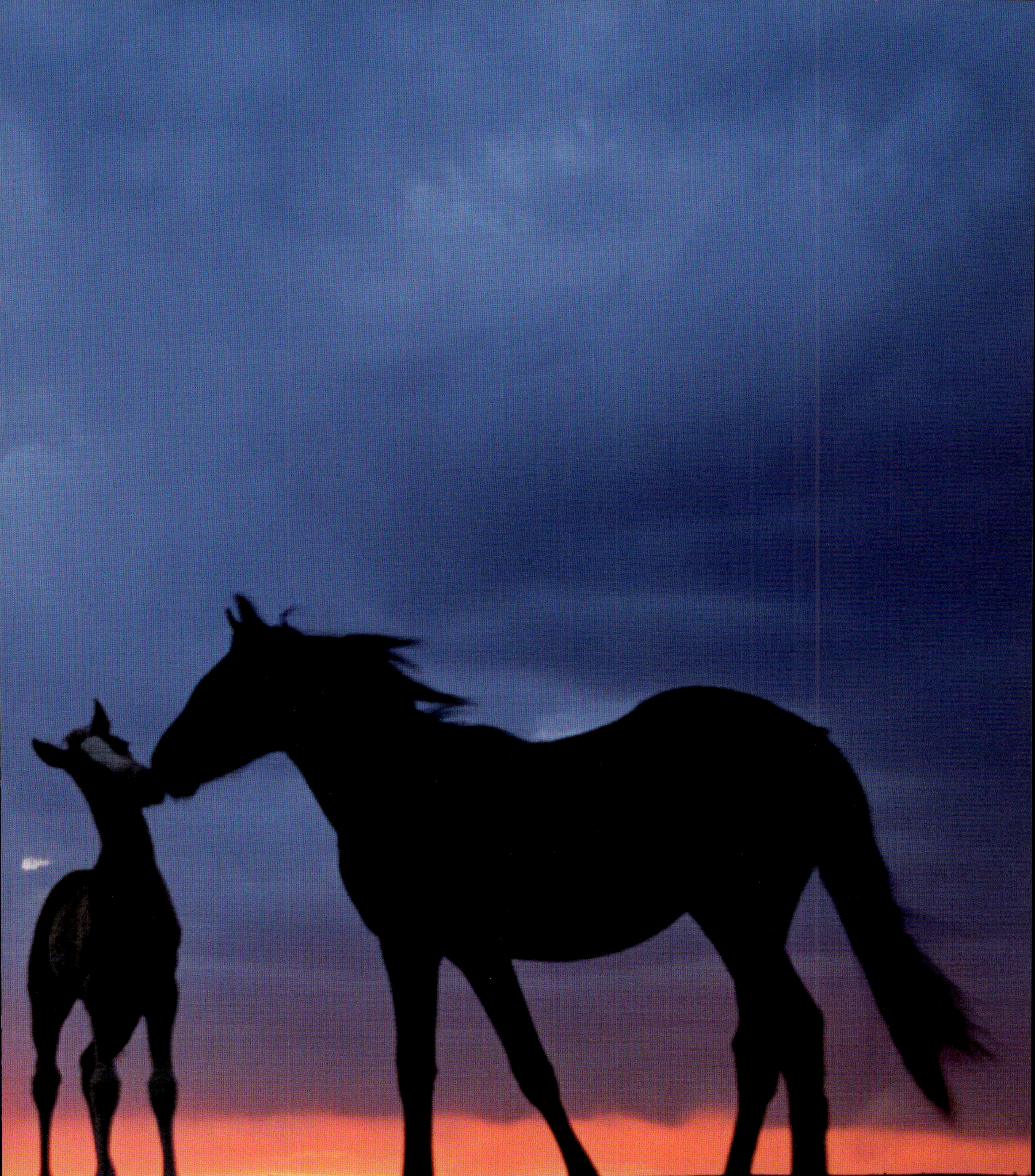

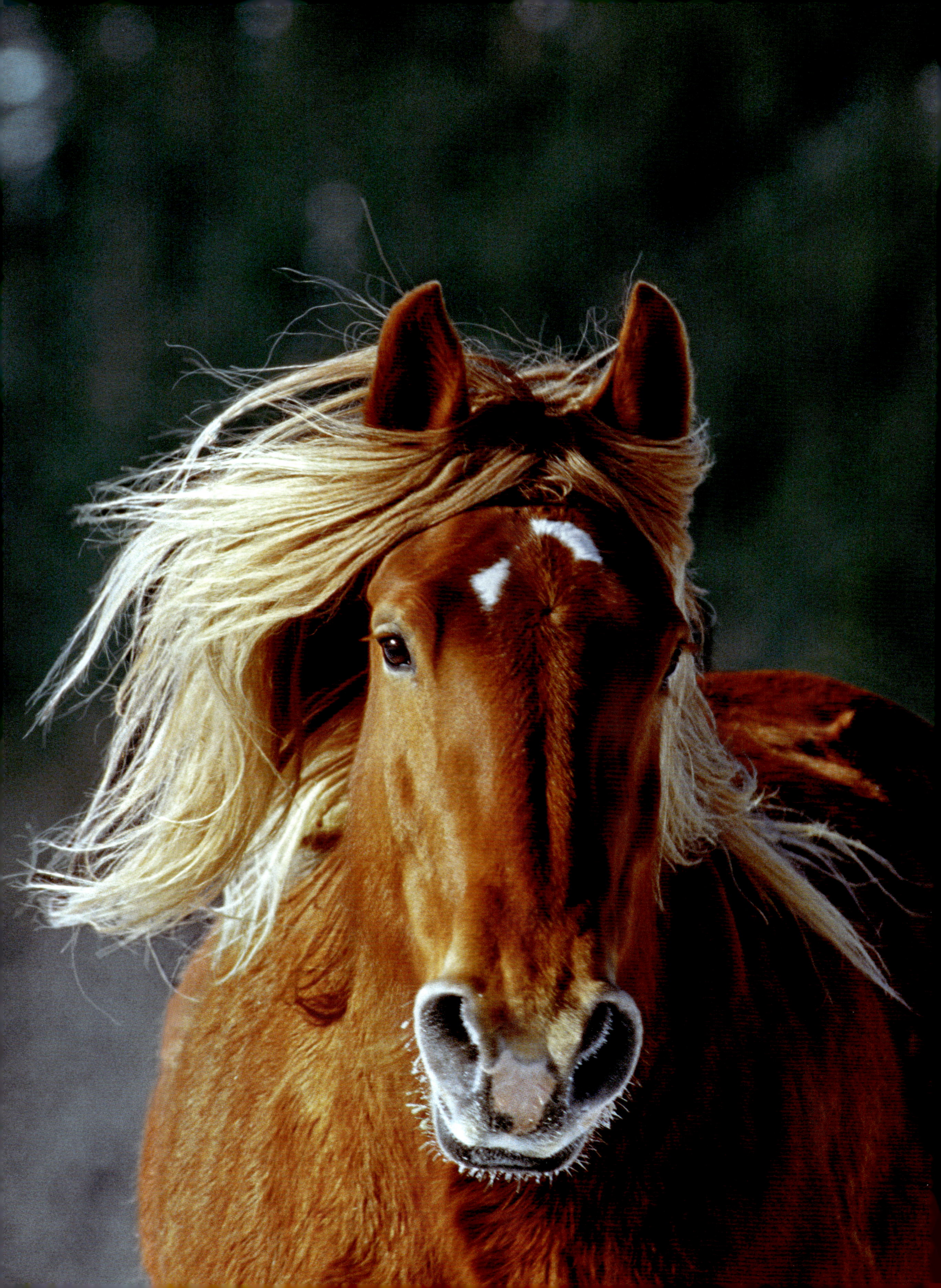

125 Dappled horses conjure up images of the horses of the Native Americans. There are still many Mustangs living free in the wild. • 128-129 Mother and son silhouetted in the Montana sunset. • 130 A foreground shot of a lively chestnut stallion.

132-133 • The wild beauty of a black stallion, pictured in a well-chosen pose in the Prior Mountains, in the State of Montana.

134-135 • The fantastical and almost surreal countryside of the Grand Teton National Park in Wyoming is a particularly suitable environment for wild Mustangs.

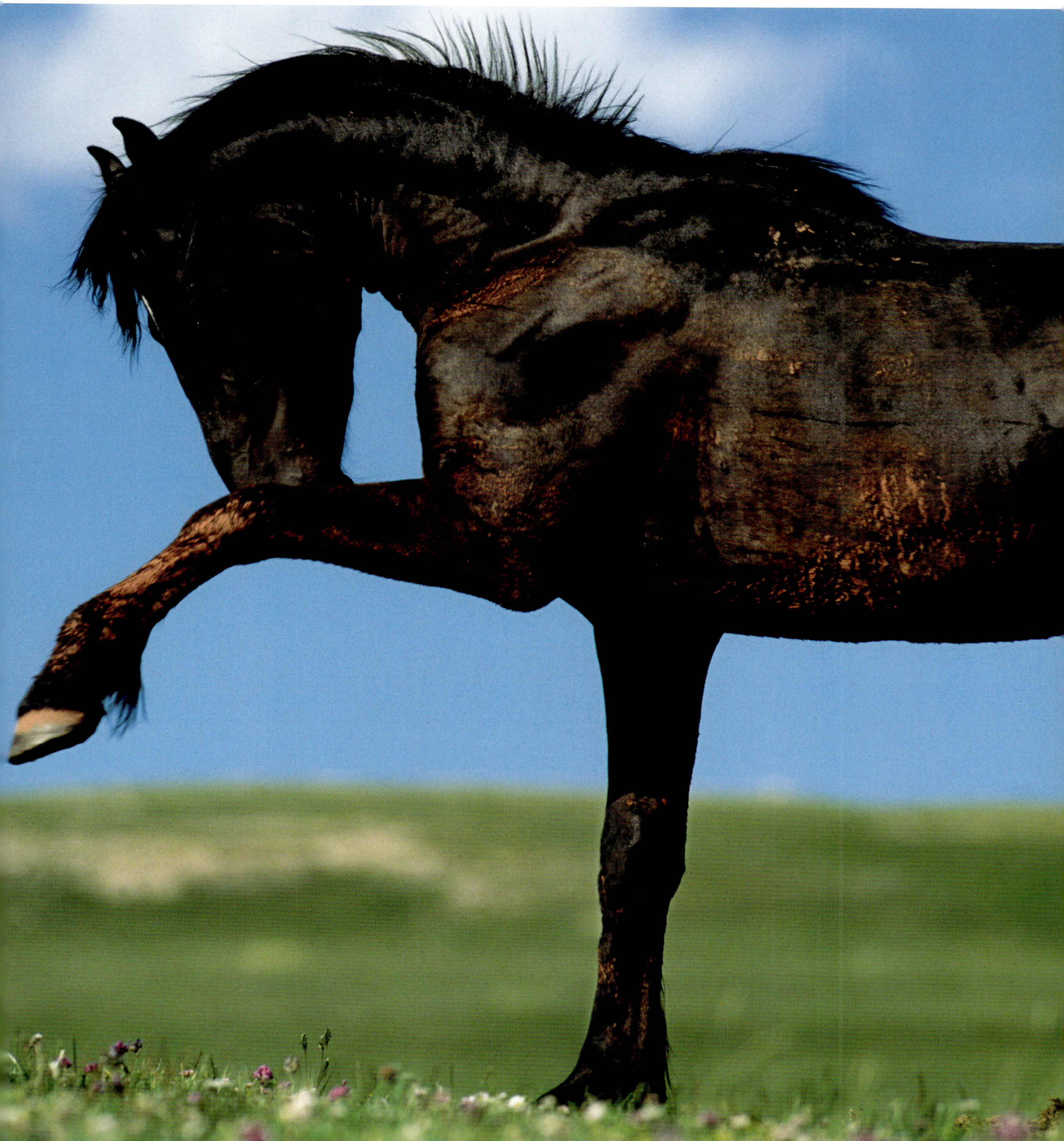

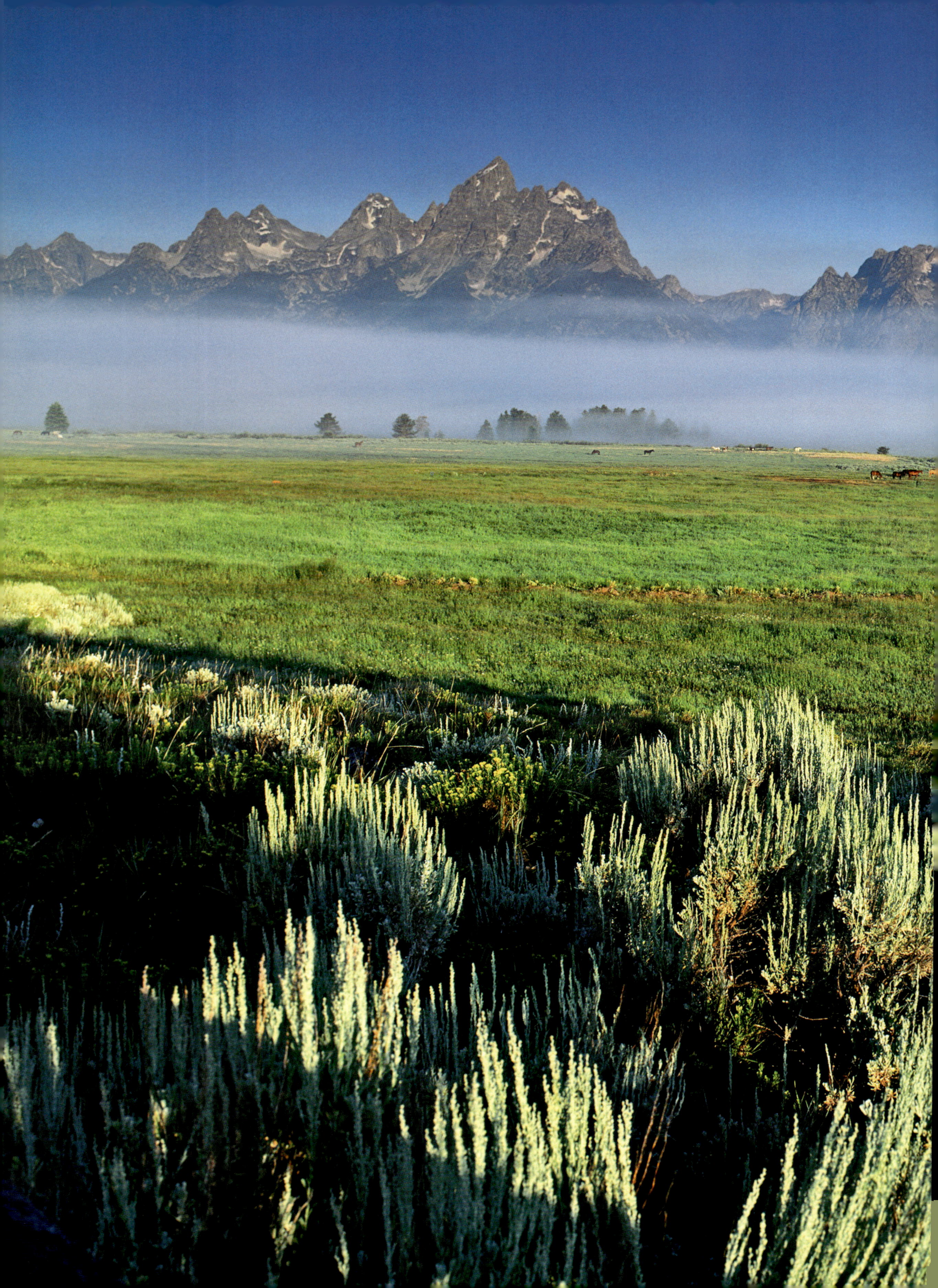

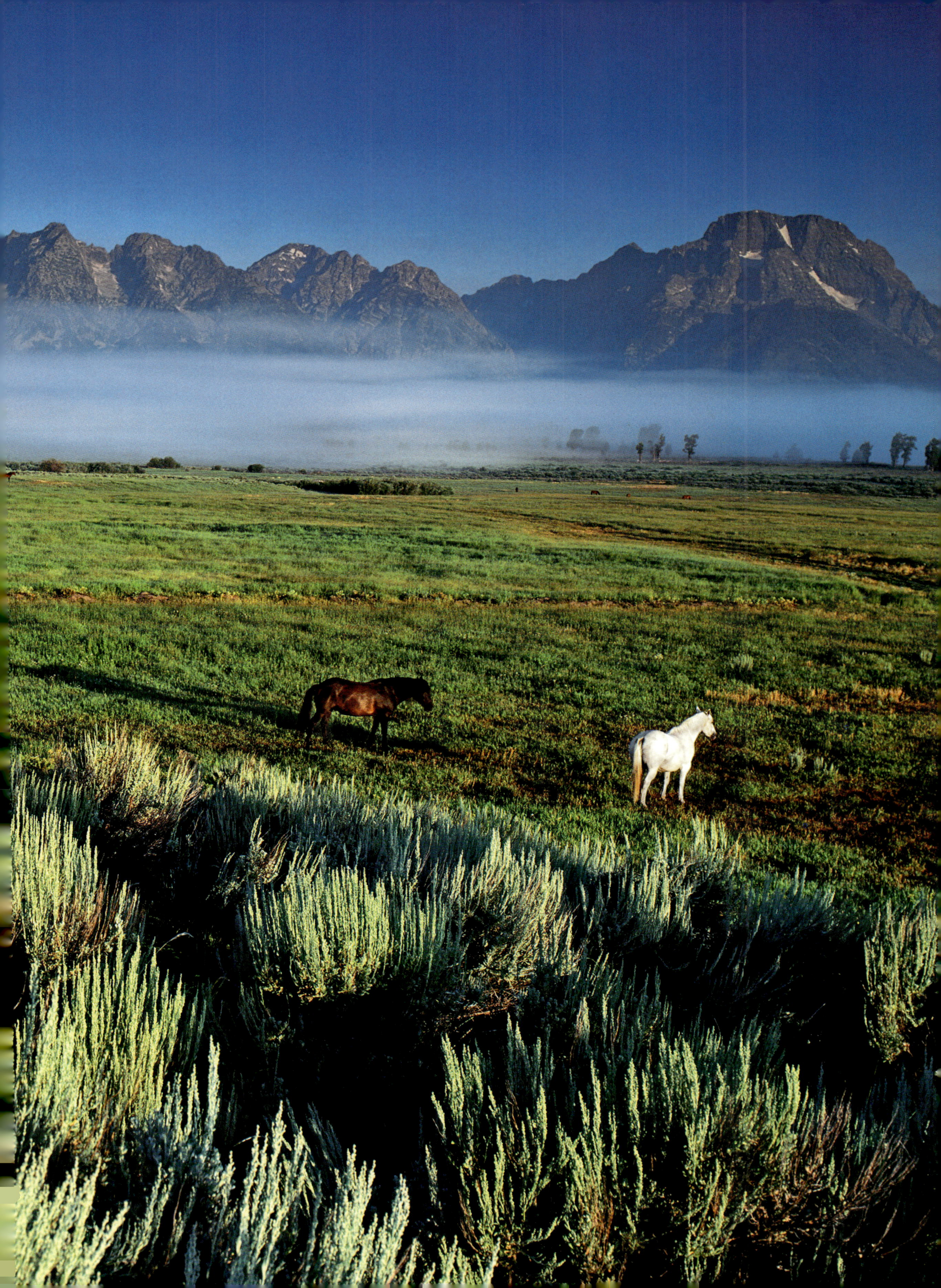

136 • A wild Mustang gives vent to the exuberance that, together with its strength and hardiness, has made the breed famous the world over.

137 • A horse with an iron gray coat enjoys the tidbits that grow in the spring fields.

138-139 • Given that predators usually attack from behind, the backwards kick is an instinct innate to all equines from when they are foals.

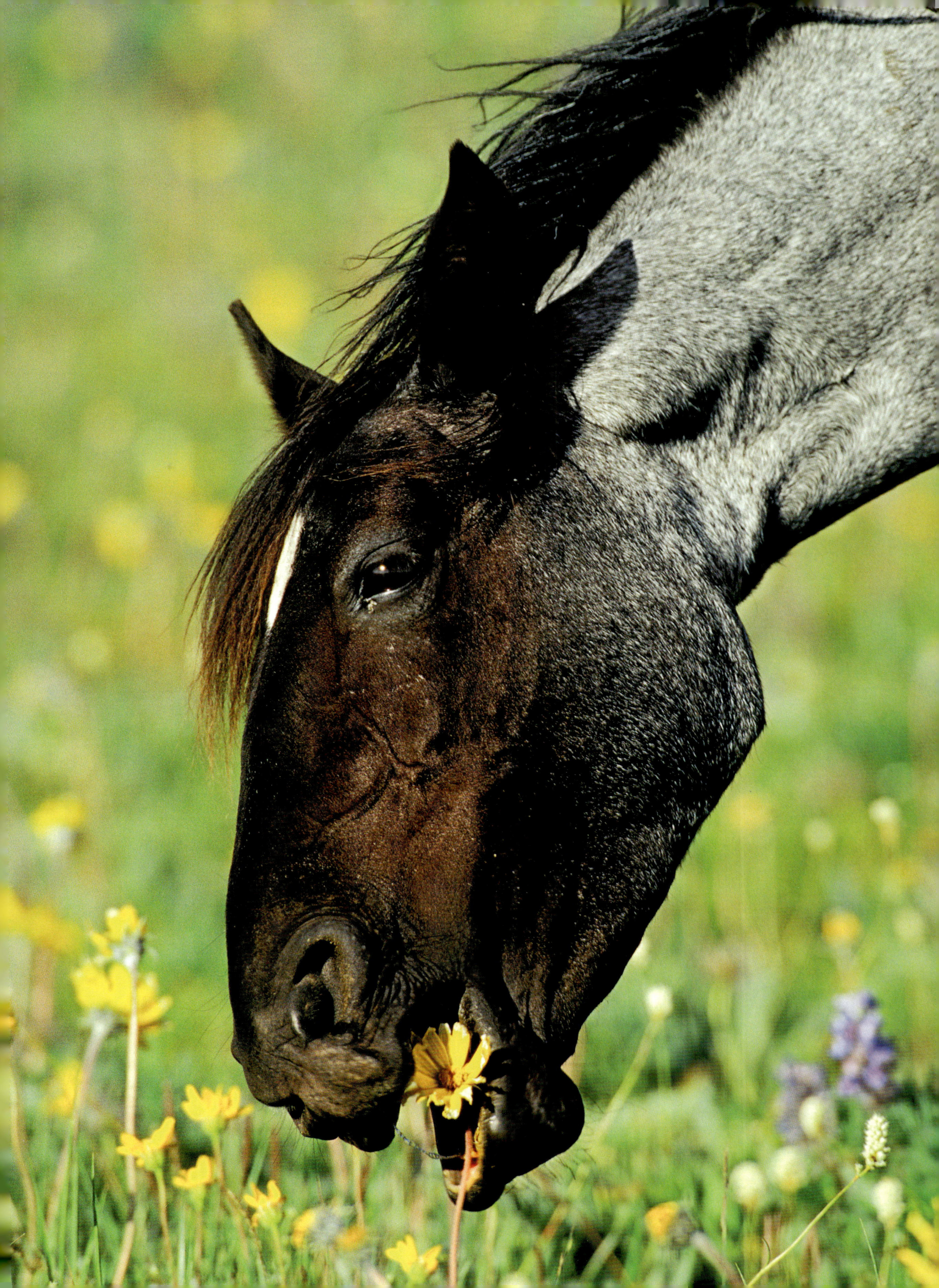

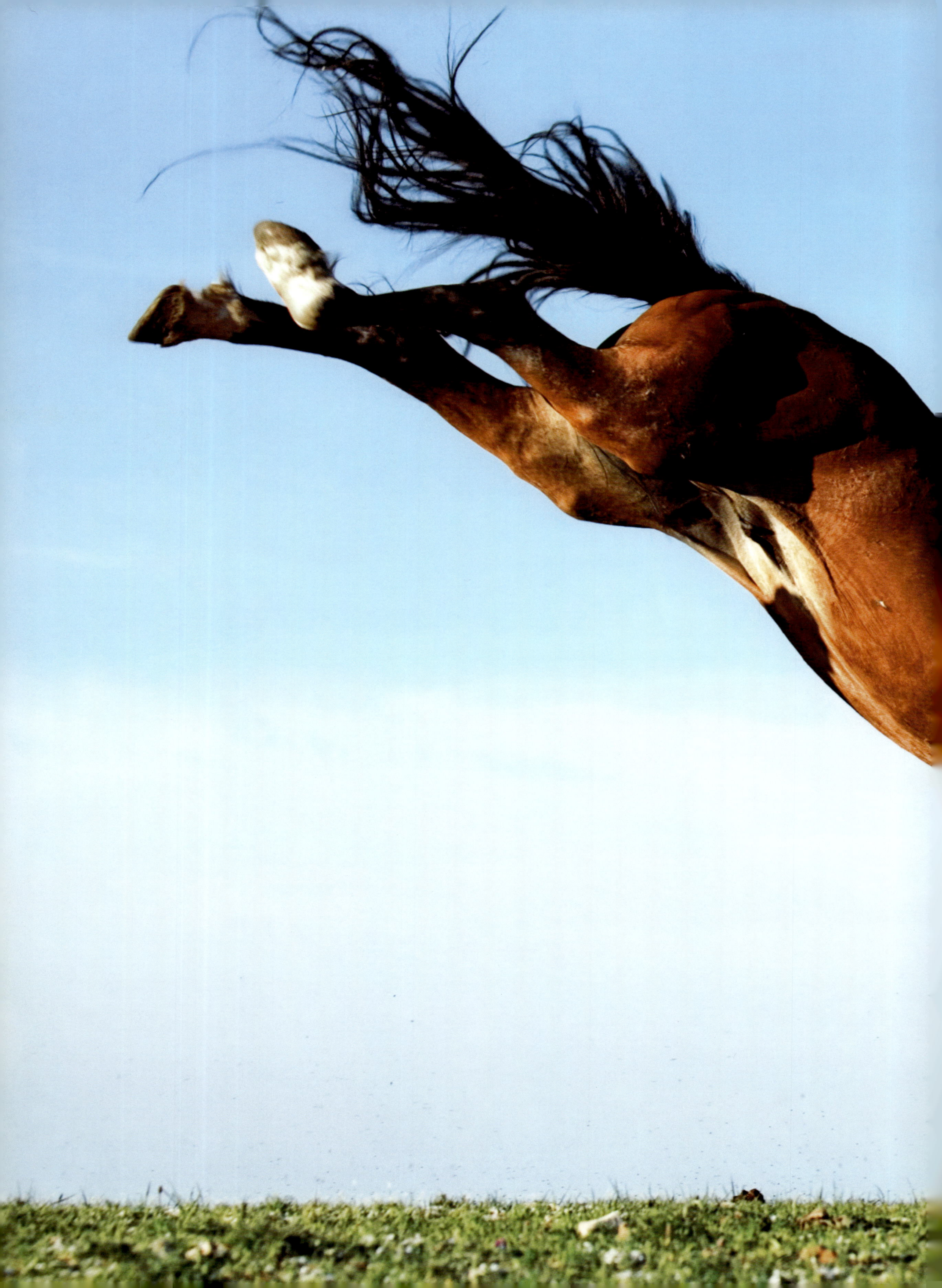

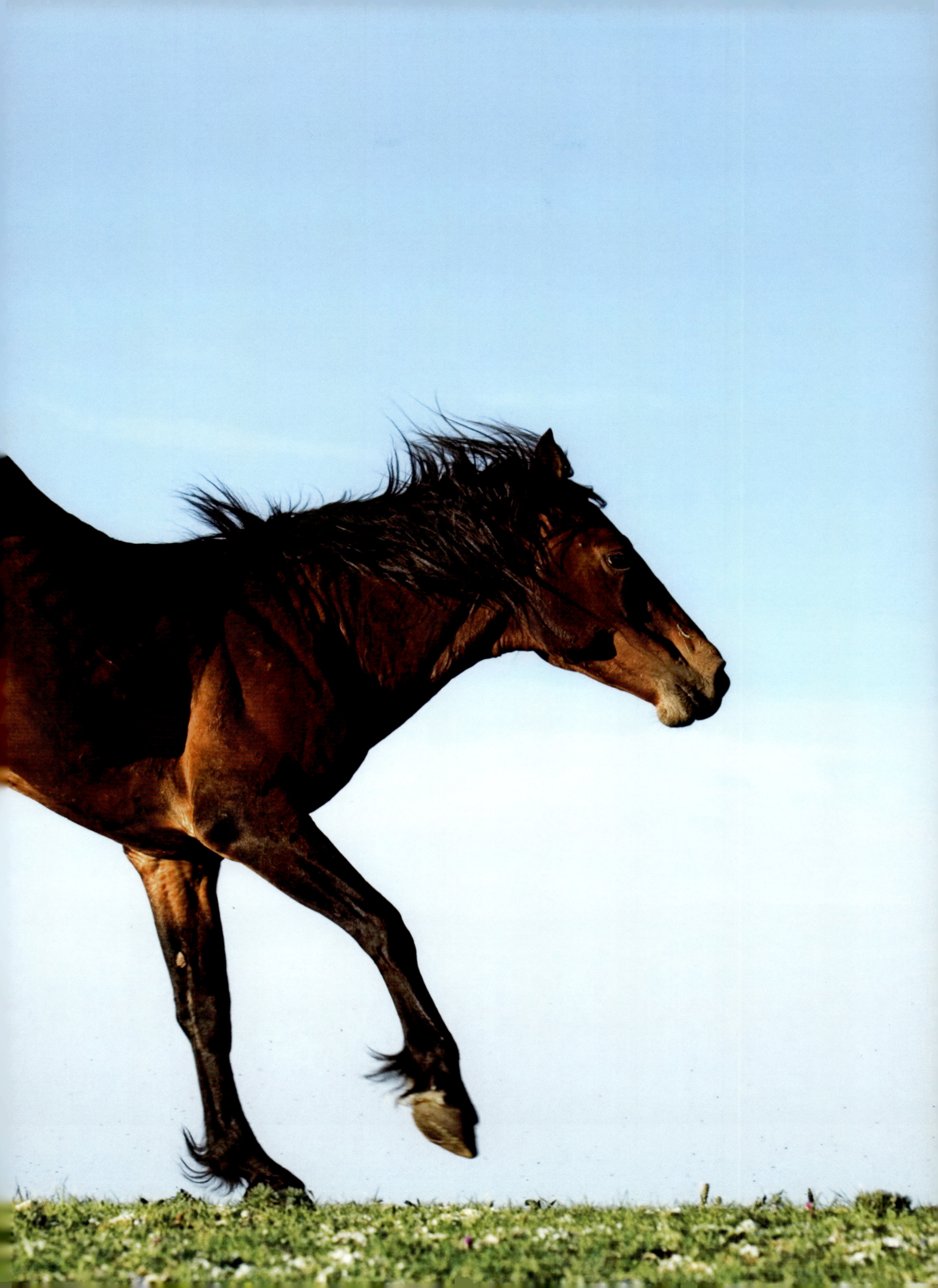

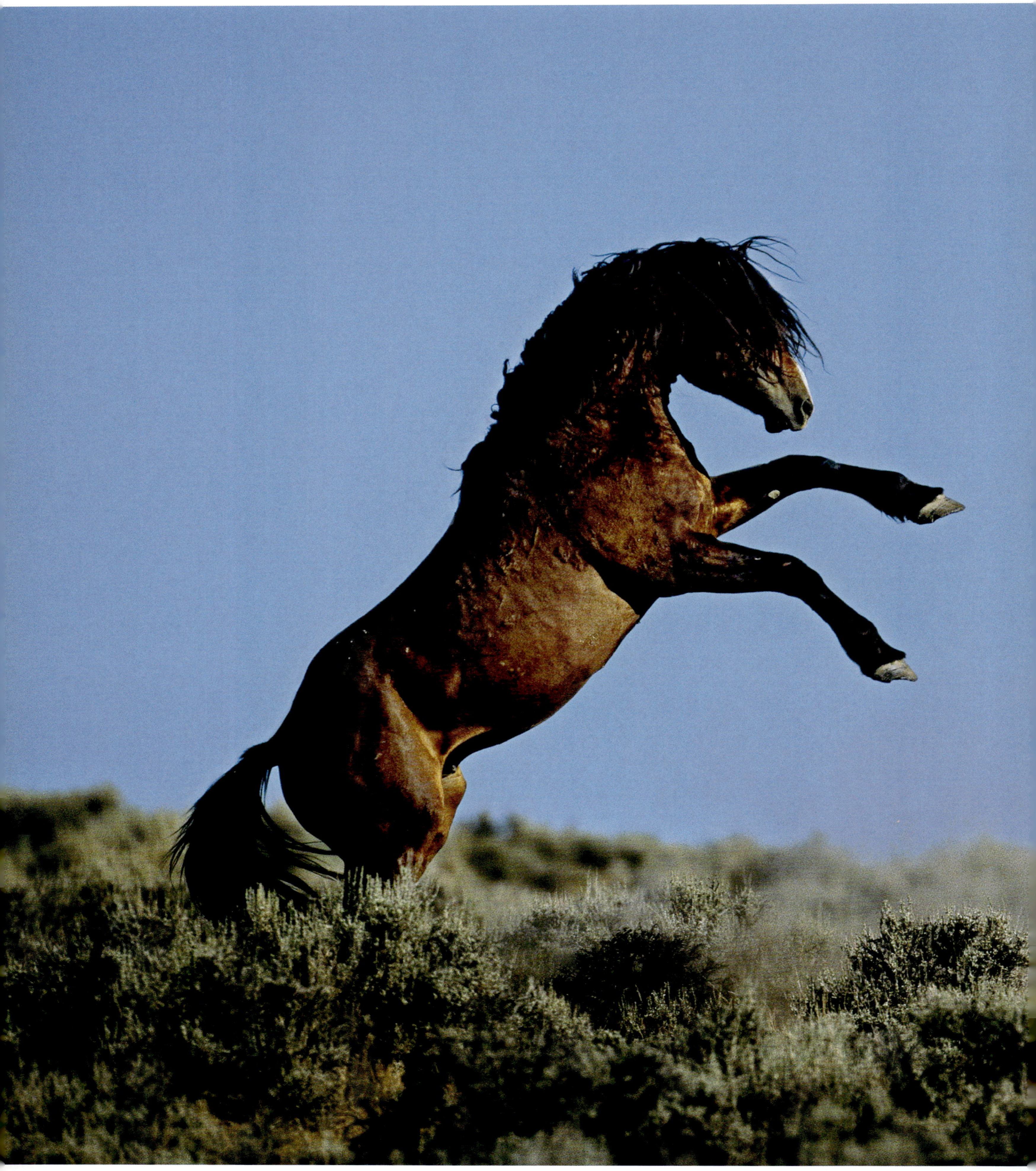

140-141 • In the frequent conflicts between wild horses, sometimes it is the bravest and not the largest that prevails, but here it is immediately clear who is going to come off best.

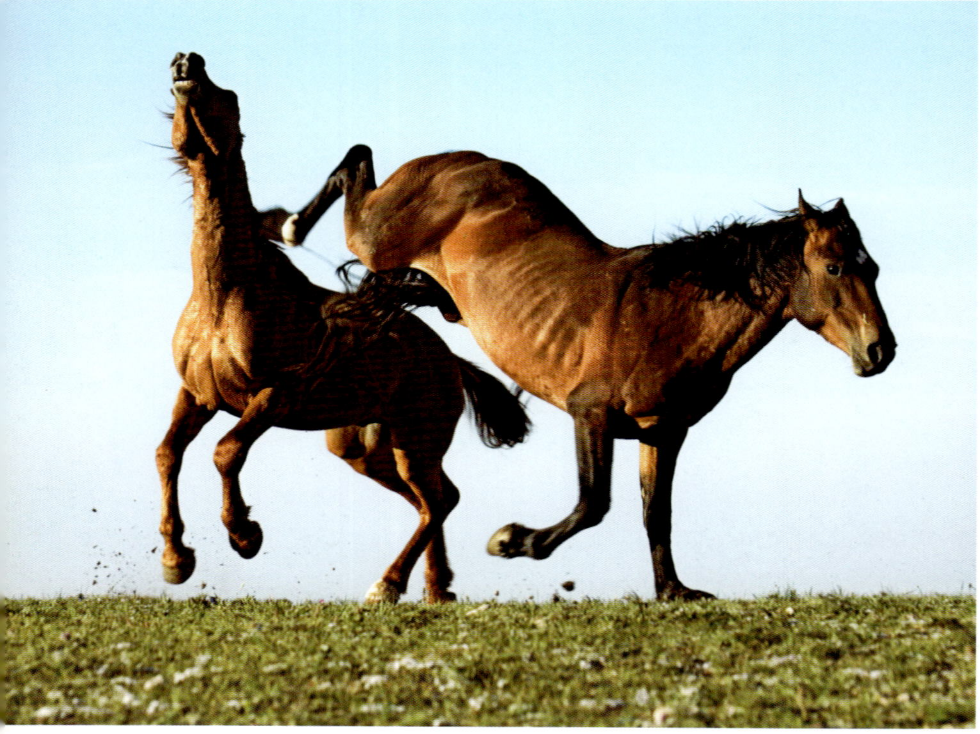

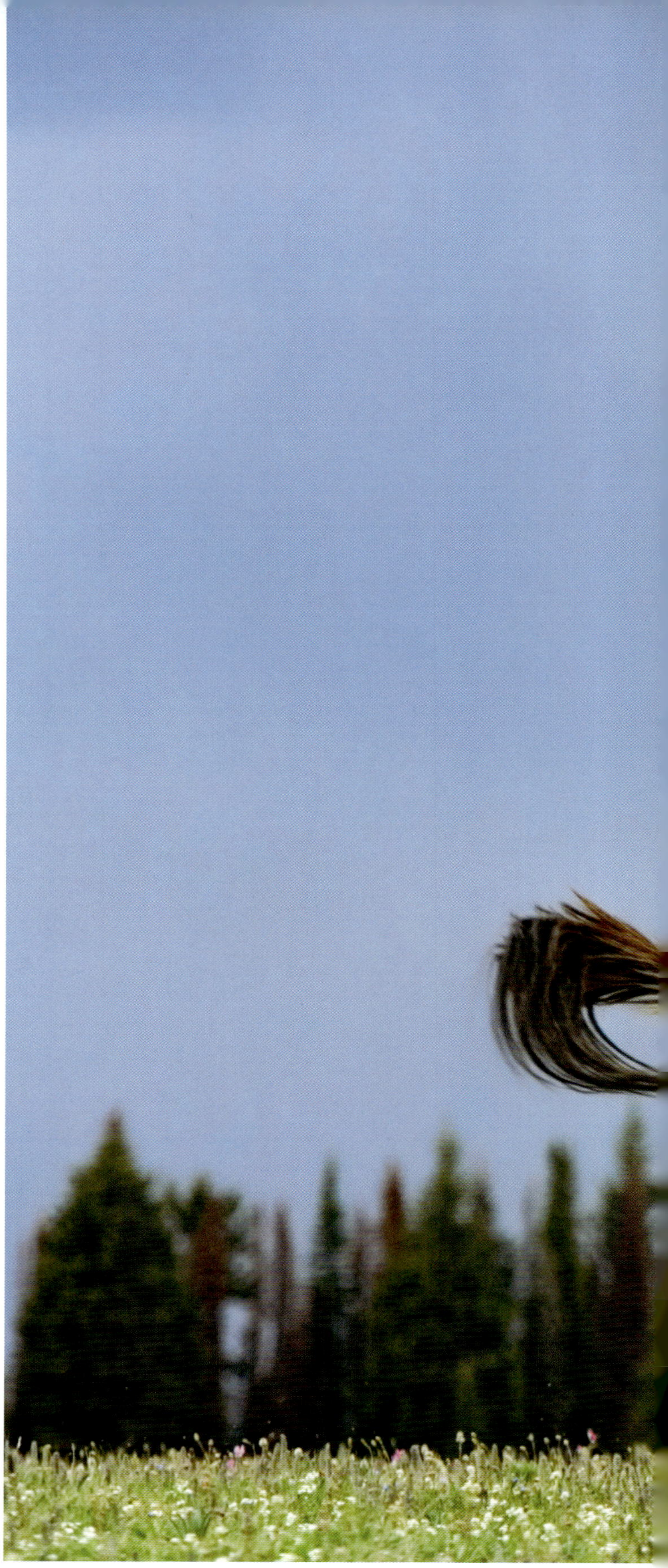

142-143 • When stallions fight they have various 'weapons' available. Indeed they can kick with one or both hind legs, or rear up to strike with the front ones. Both methods can be lethal.

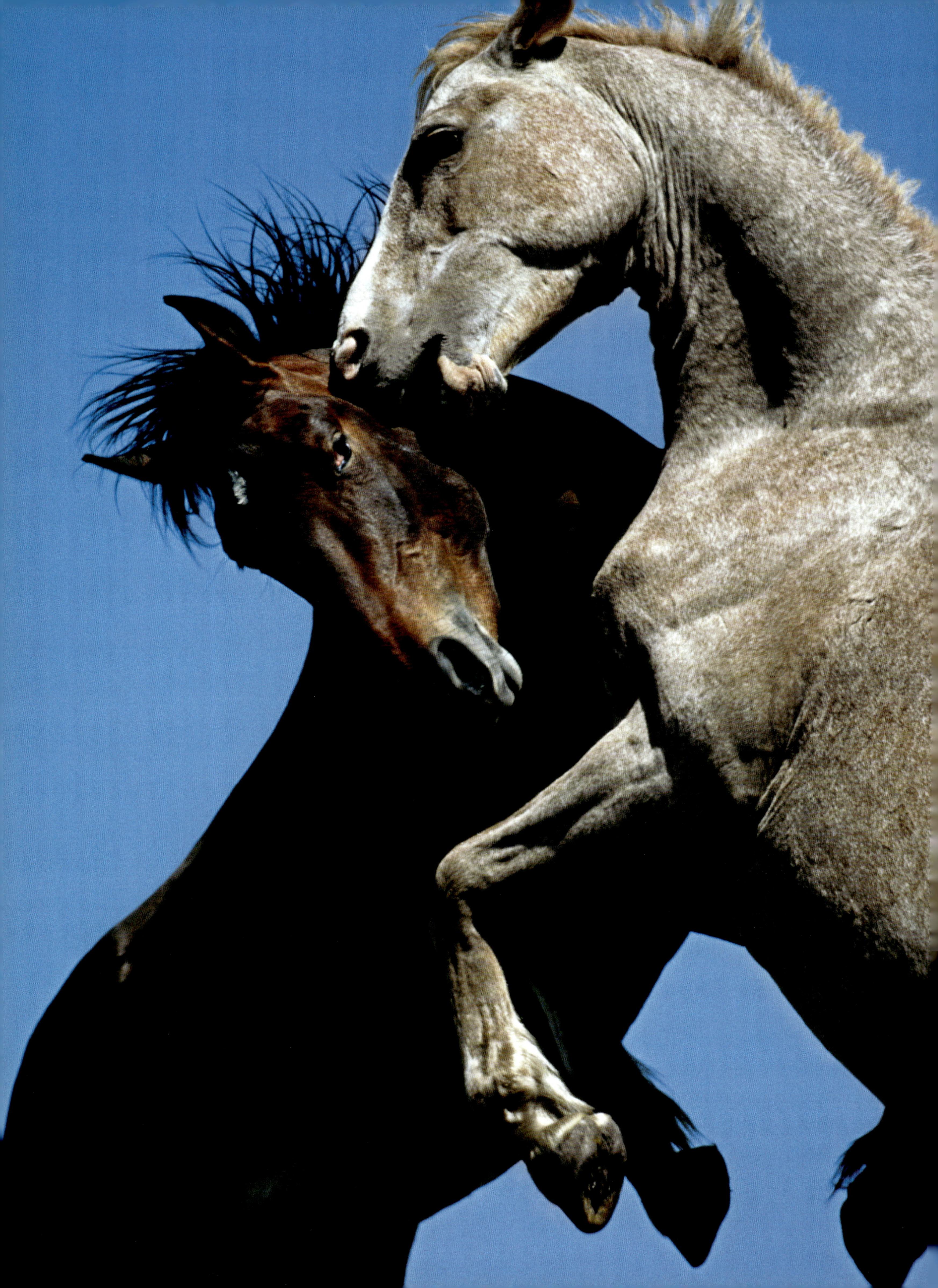

144 • They also fight with their teeth, as in the picture, which shows how a pair of Mustangs attack and defend themselves.

145 • To give an idea of a horse's strength, if a Mustang were to bite an average sized man; it could easily lift him off the ground and throw him a few meters in distance.

146-147 A pair of foals playfully imitates the violent movements of the stallions. • 147 This small foal is particularly concerned with the complicated operation of scratching an ear. • 148-149 and 150-151 Two splendid pictures of Mustang foals born in the wild just a few days before and photographed in the flowery fields of the Rocky Mountains and North Wyoming.

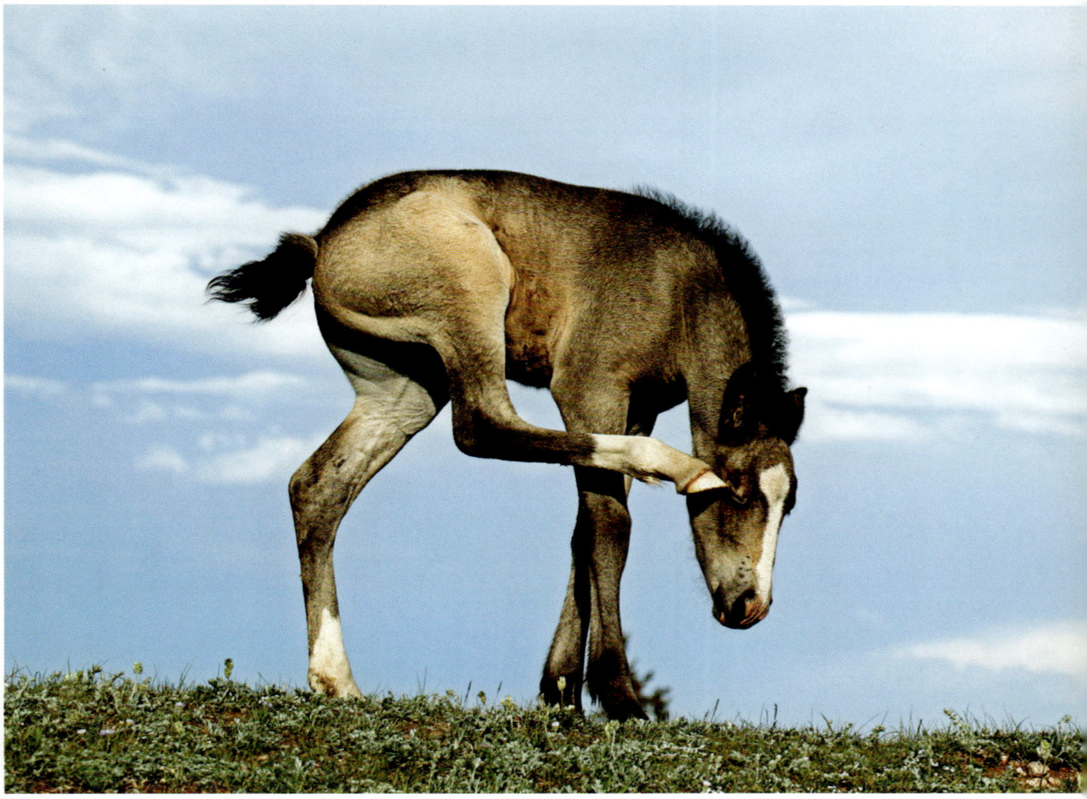

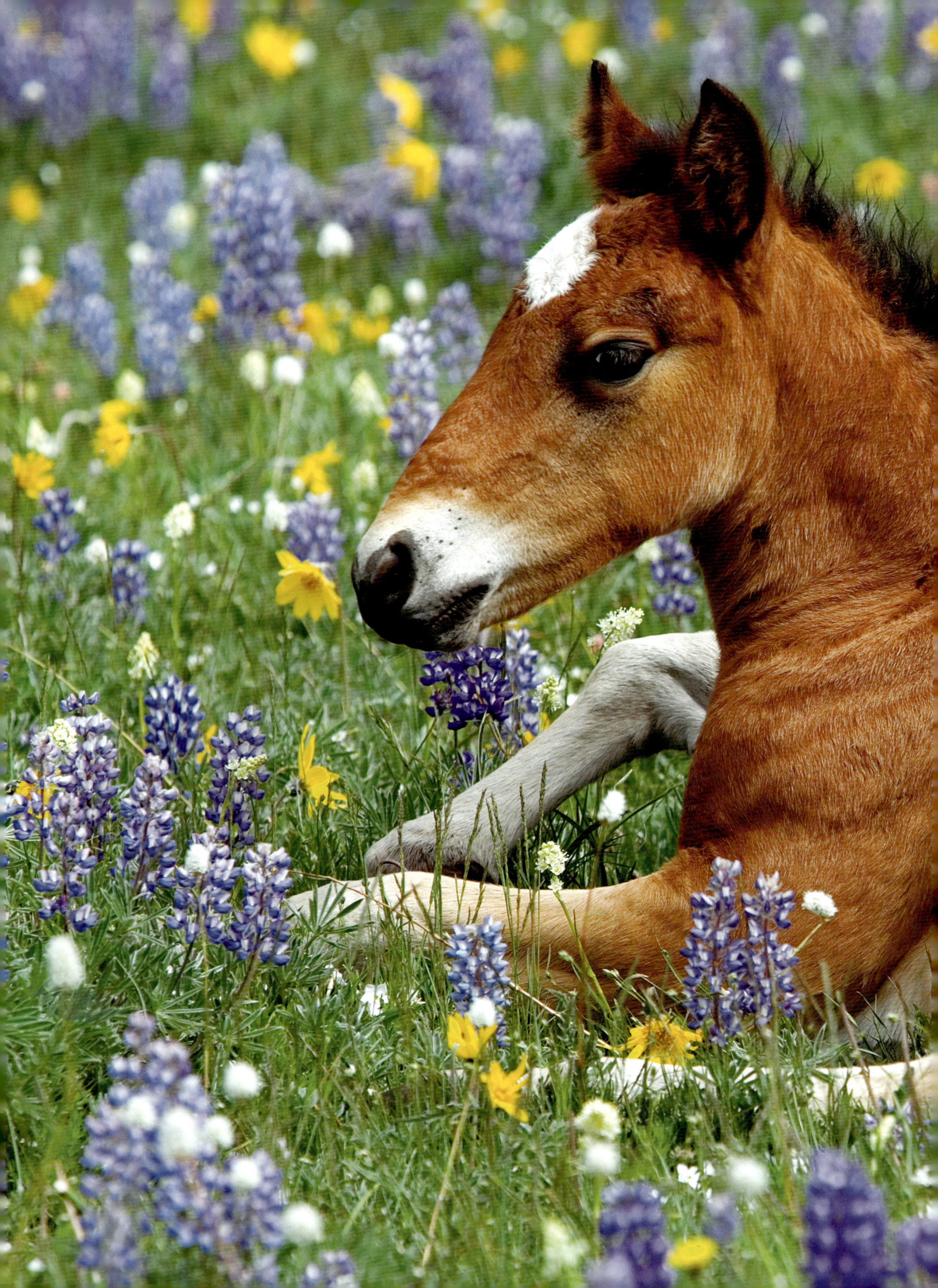

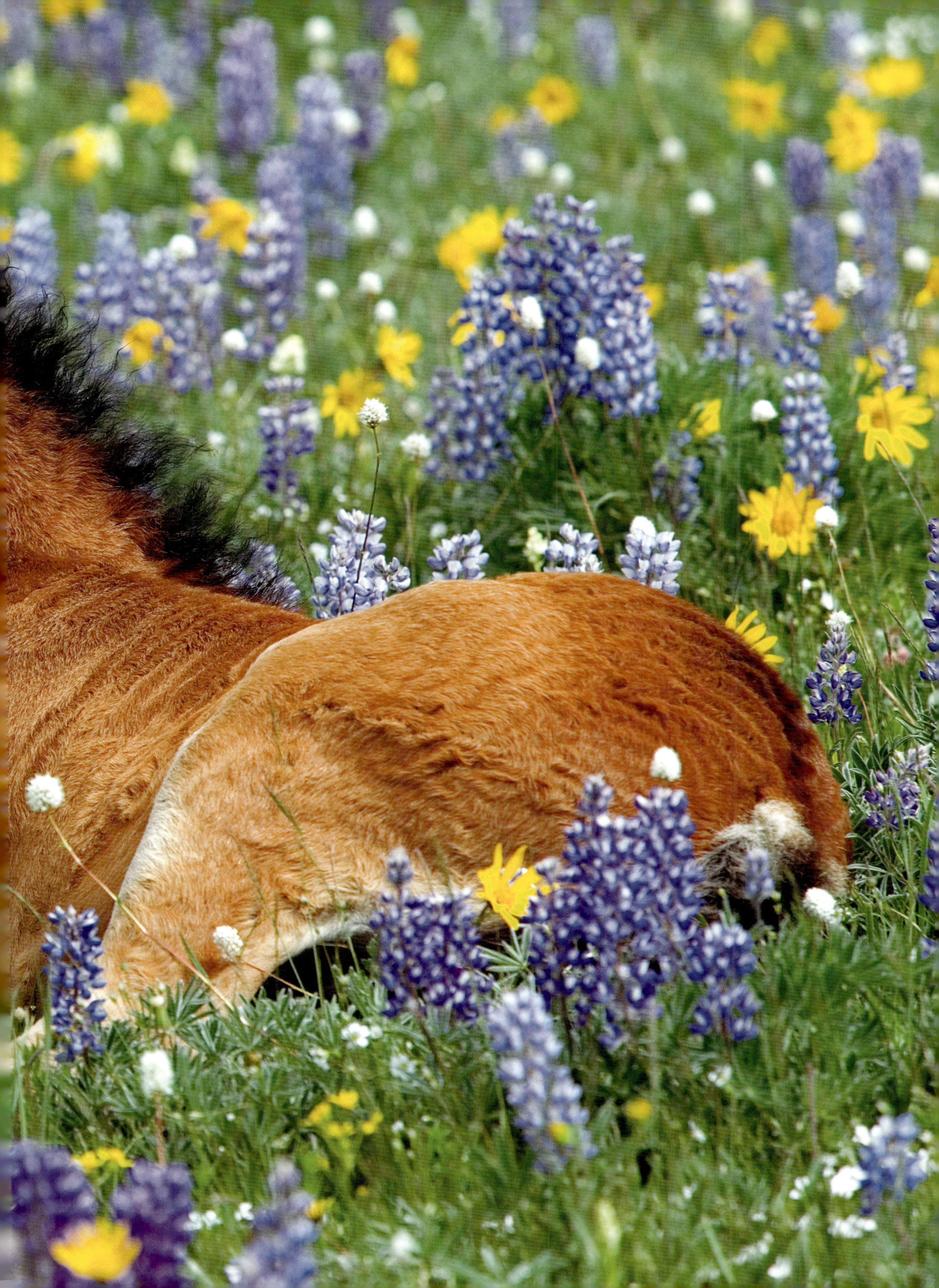

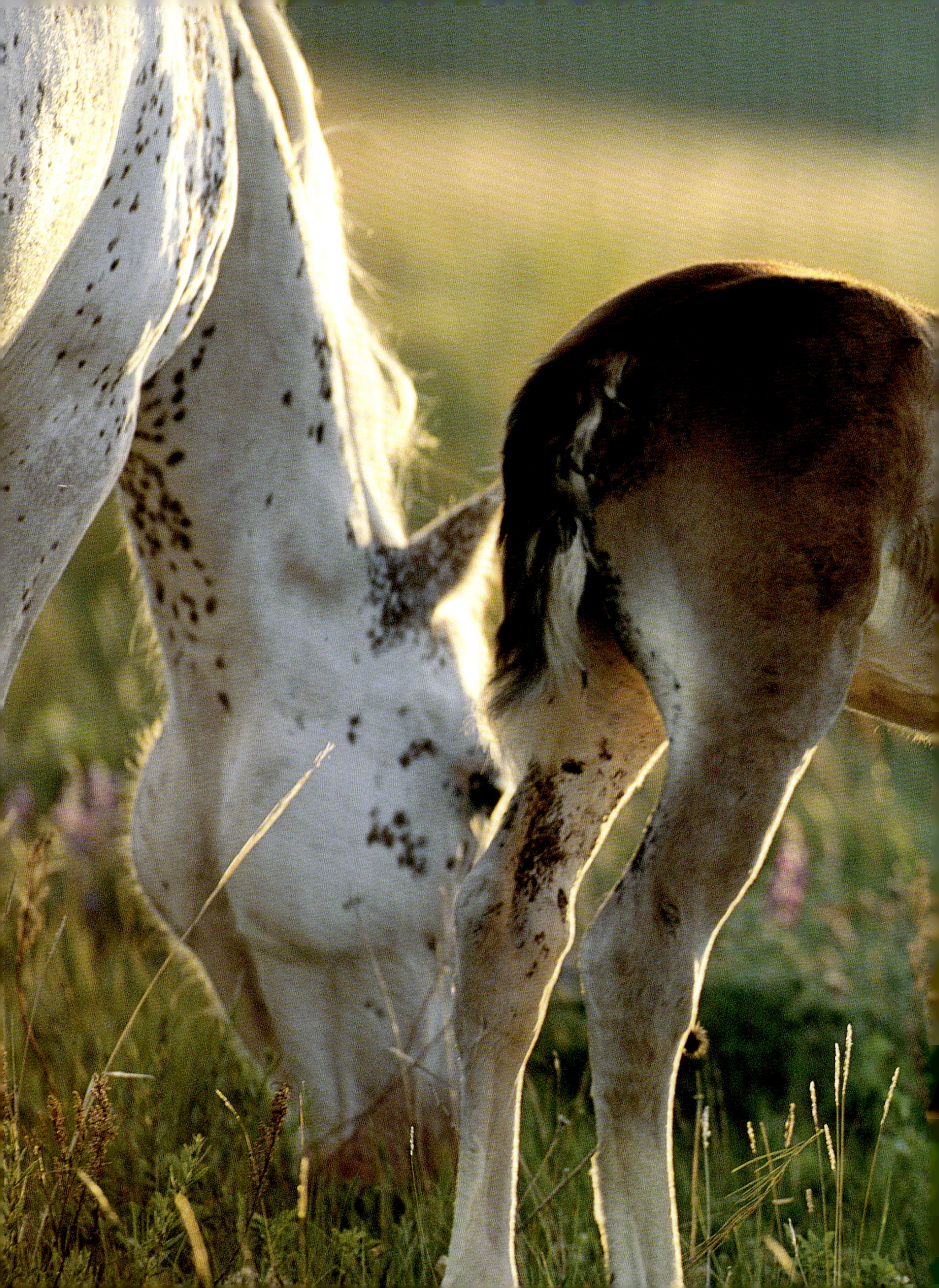

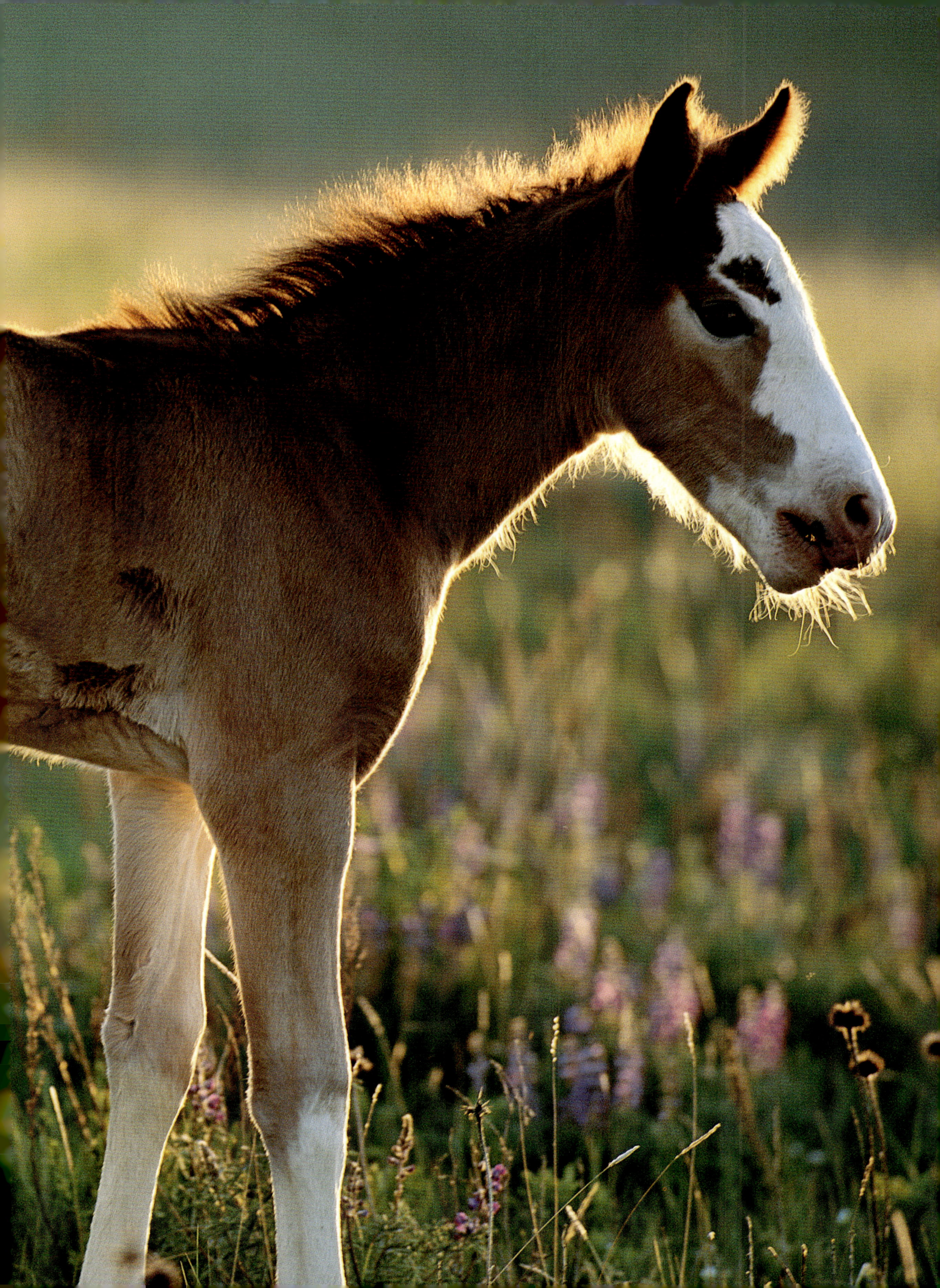

152 • McCullough Peaks: these photographs show a Mustang mother and her foal that, just a few minutes after birth, is trying to stand up and coordinate its very long legs.

153 • The foal is already walking, which is also an innate behavior, necessary in order to avoid becoming the victim of predators.

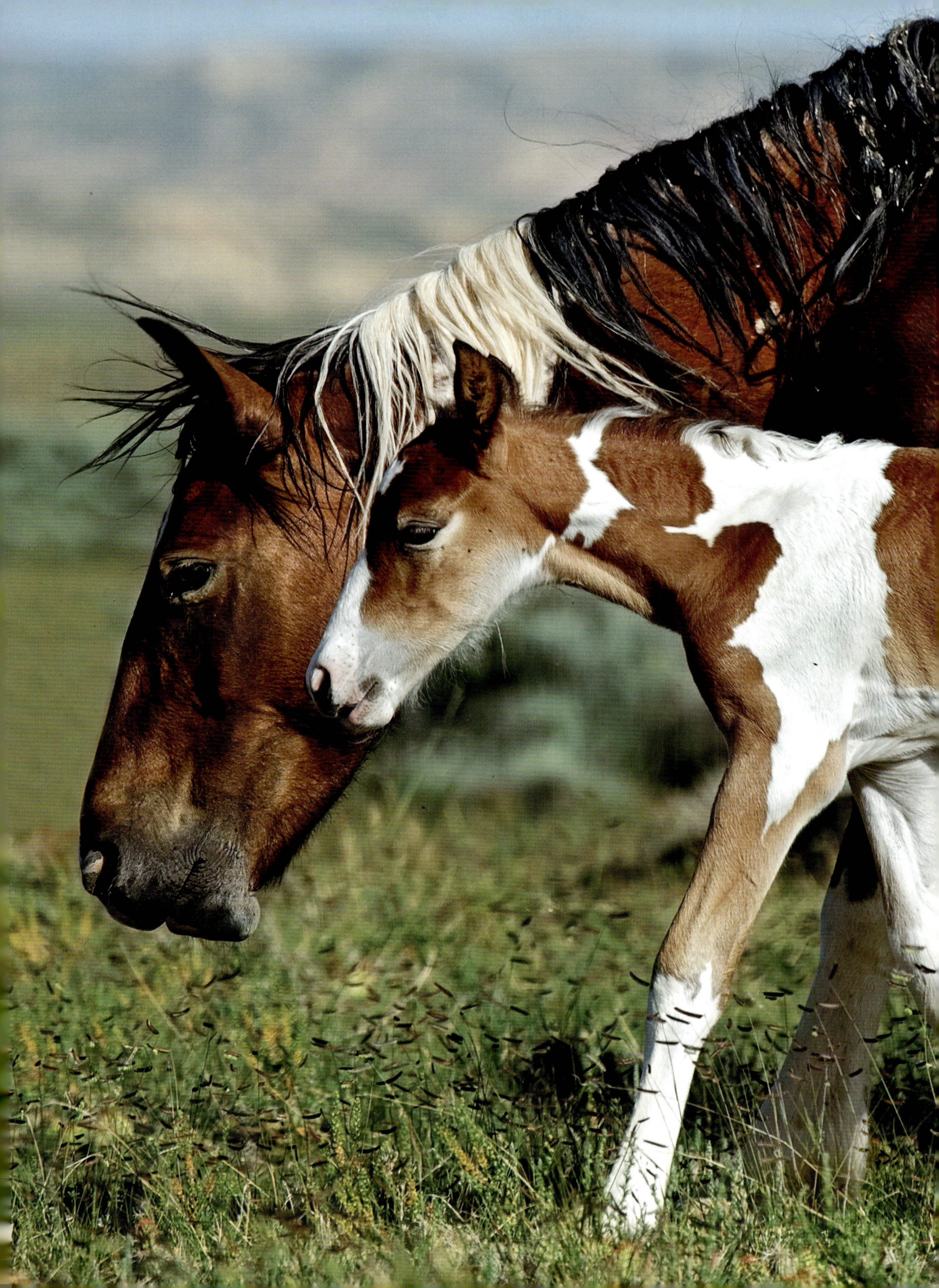

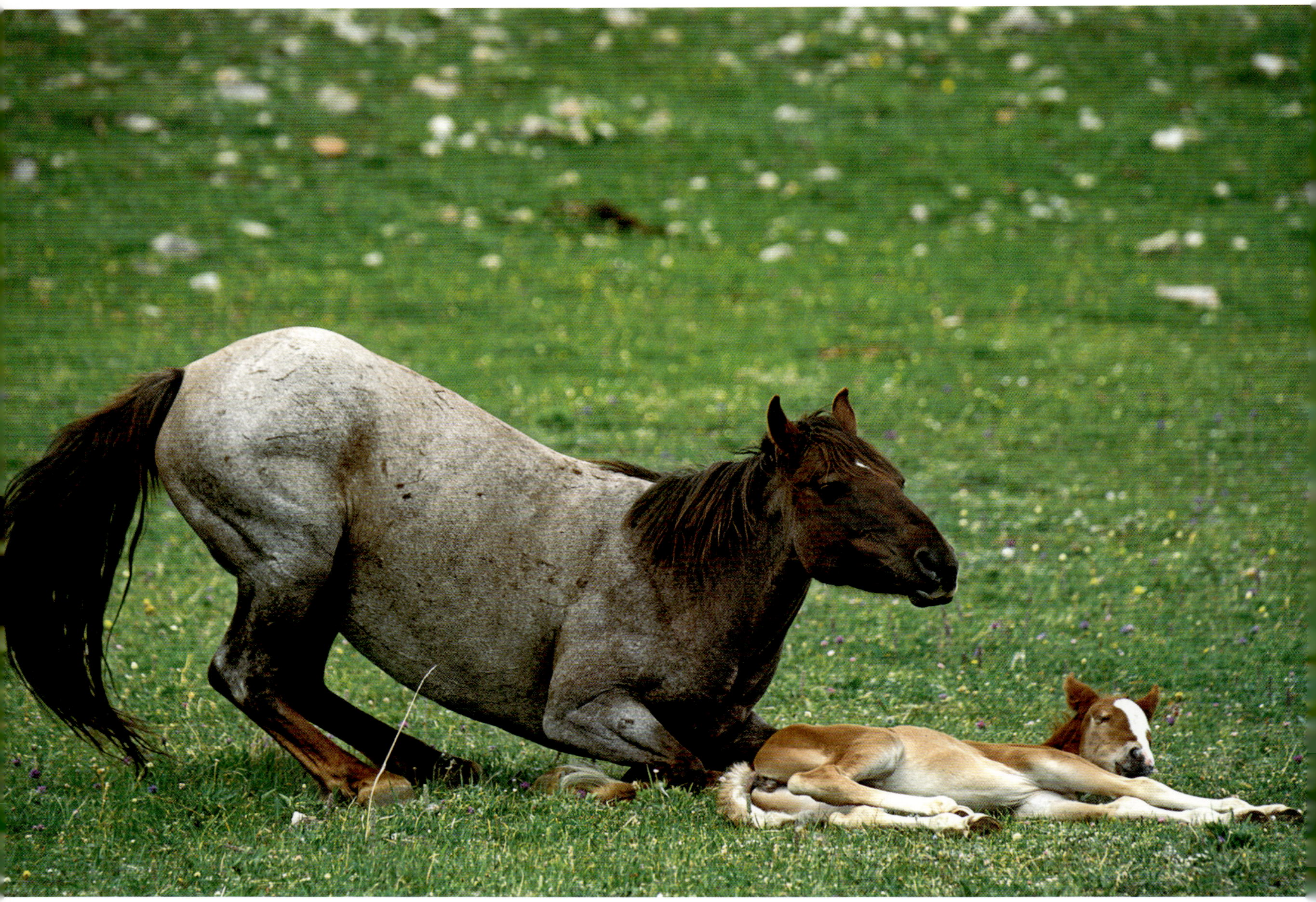

154 • More Mustang mothers and foals in the Rocky Mountain: a female lies next to her foal who is sleeping placidly on the grass.

155 • A mare keeps a close eye on her little one, who looks as if he wants to get up at any moment.

156-157 • North Dakota: a splendid, young Mustang mare with a dappled iron gray coat teaches her daughter to gallop in the high grass. The foal, born golden chestnut, is a few months old.

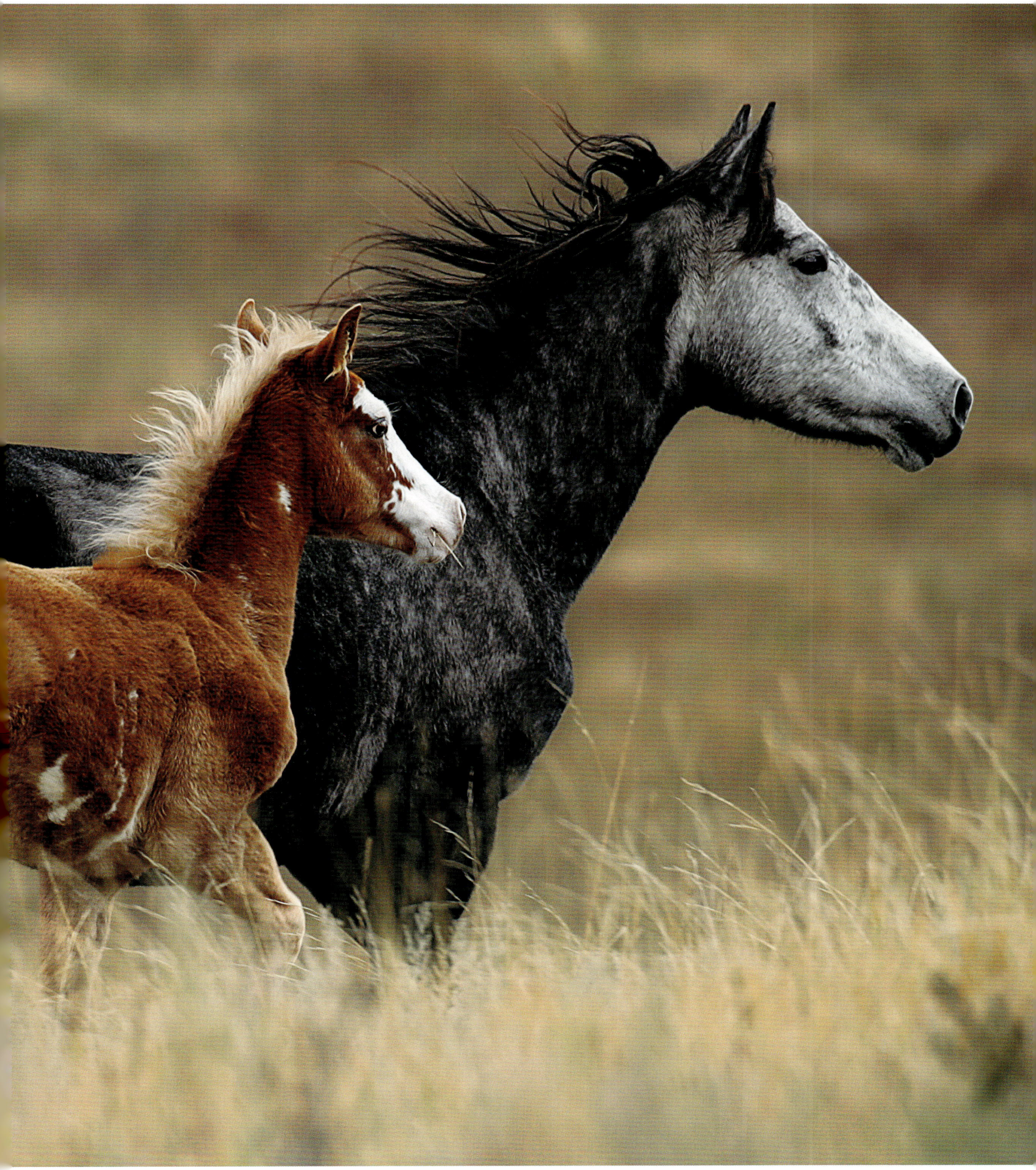

158-159 and 159 A Mustang mare and her foal just have their winter coats and tough constitution to get them through the cold winter of the Rocky Mountains. • 160 and 161 It is not easy to find food during the winter and this is why these two horses are happy to eat icy shrubs and brambles. • 162-163 A splendid example of a Mustang Paint — a horse with a dappled coat — galloping on the snow on a beautiful sunny day.

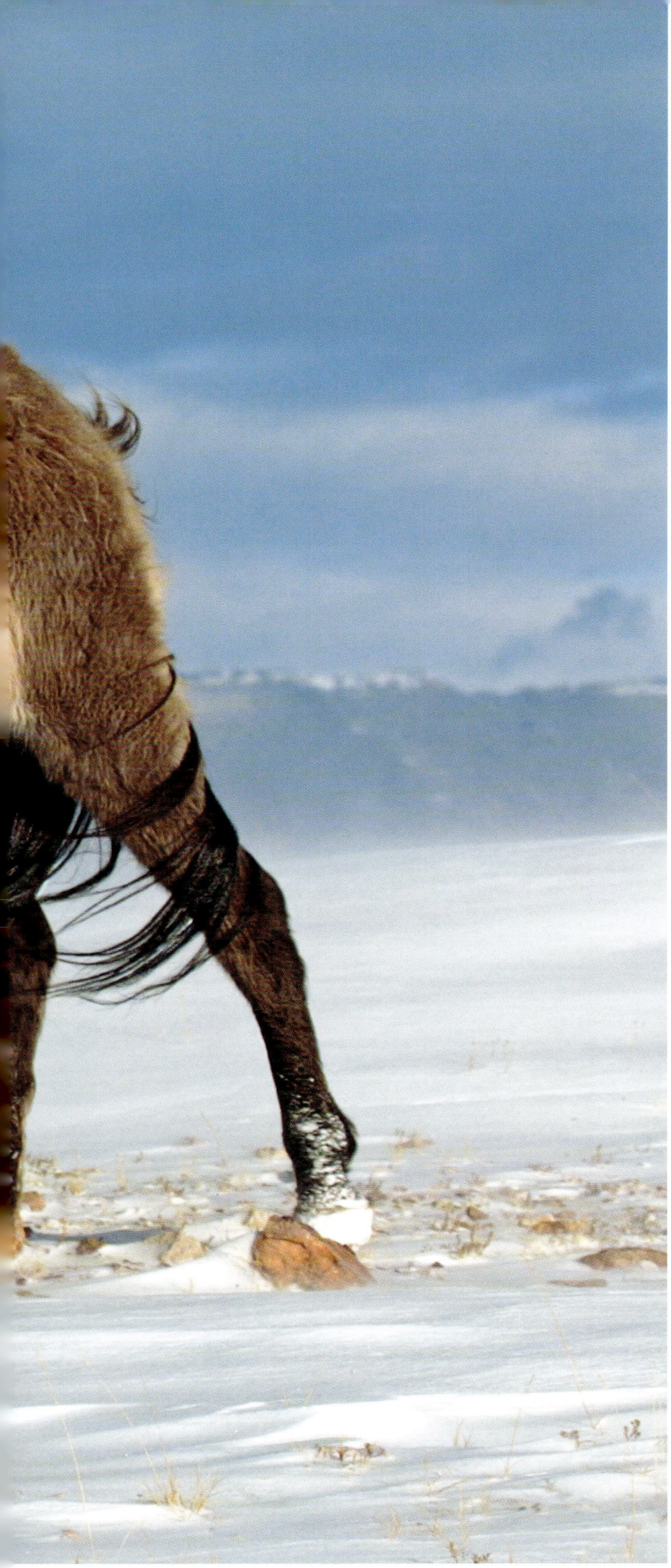

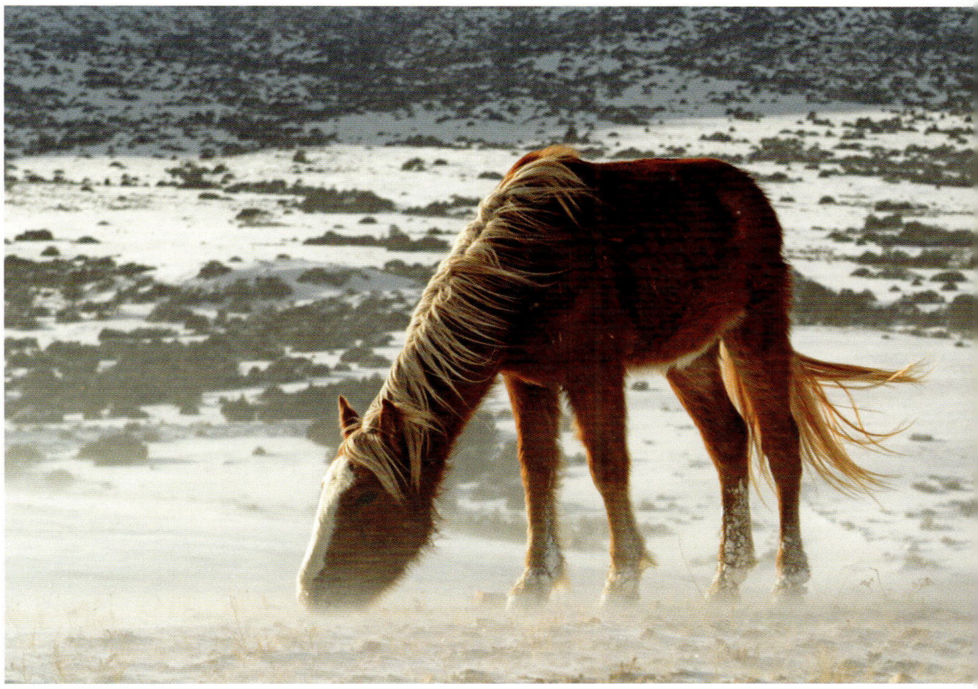

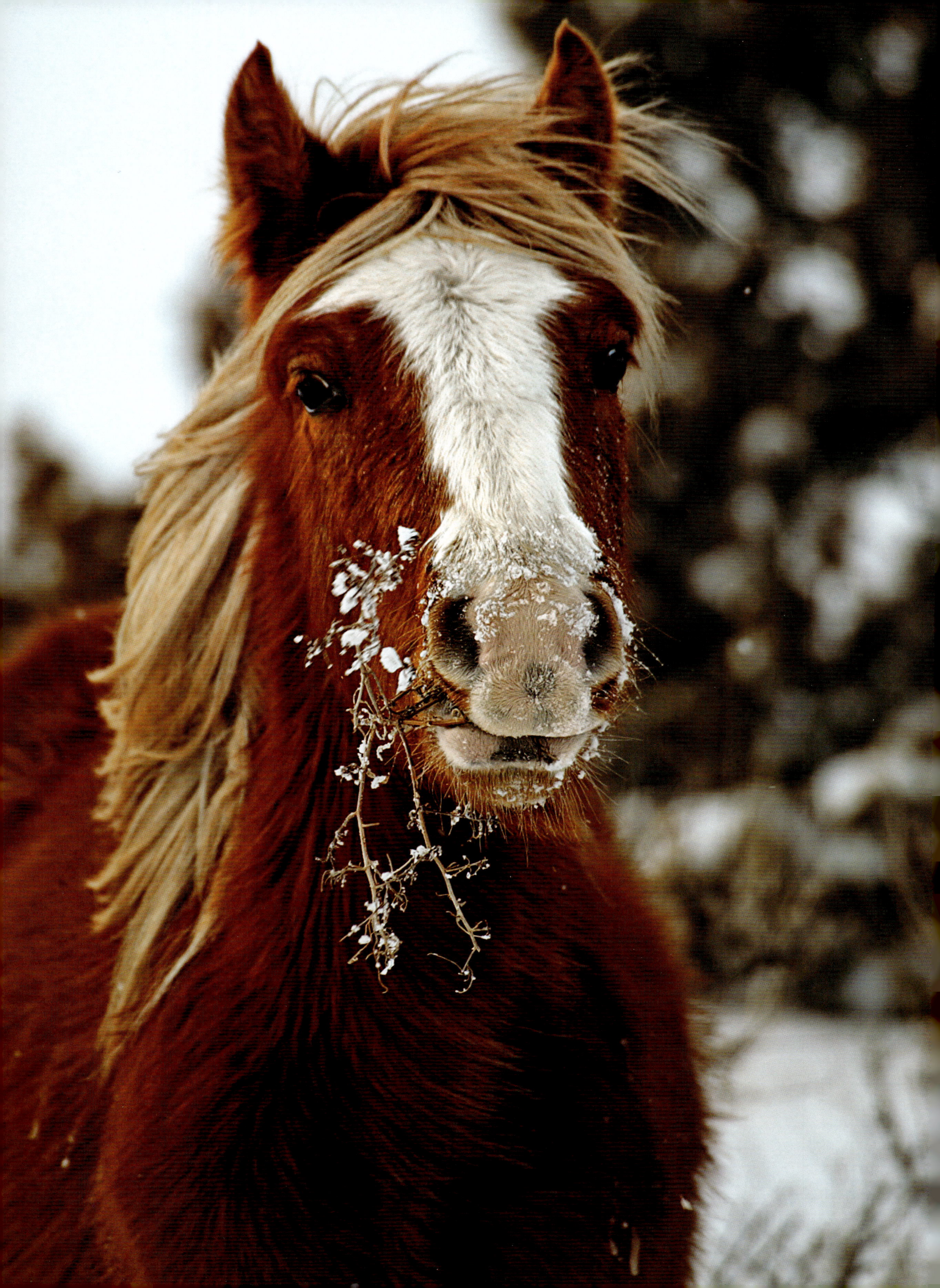

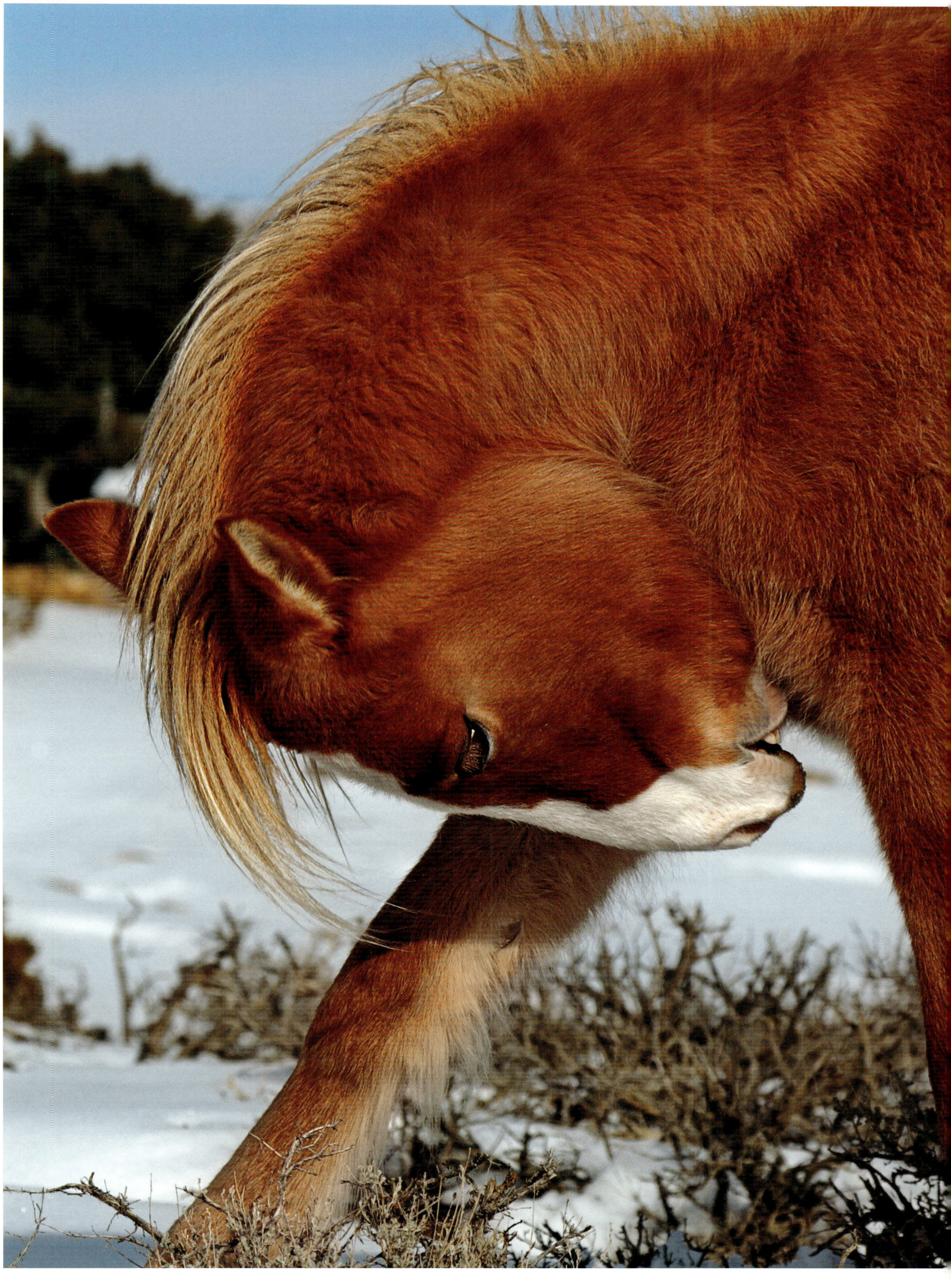

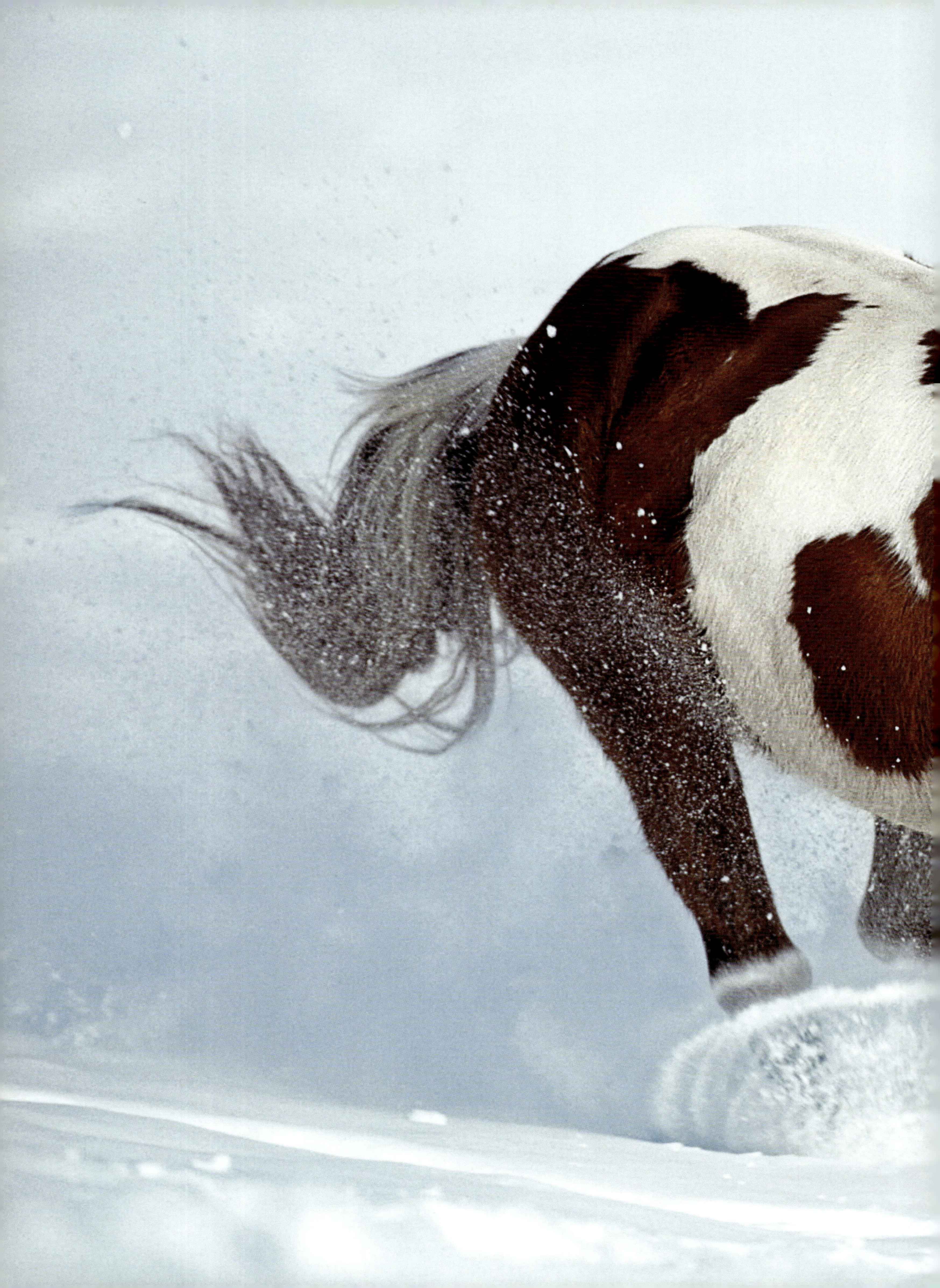

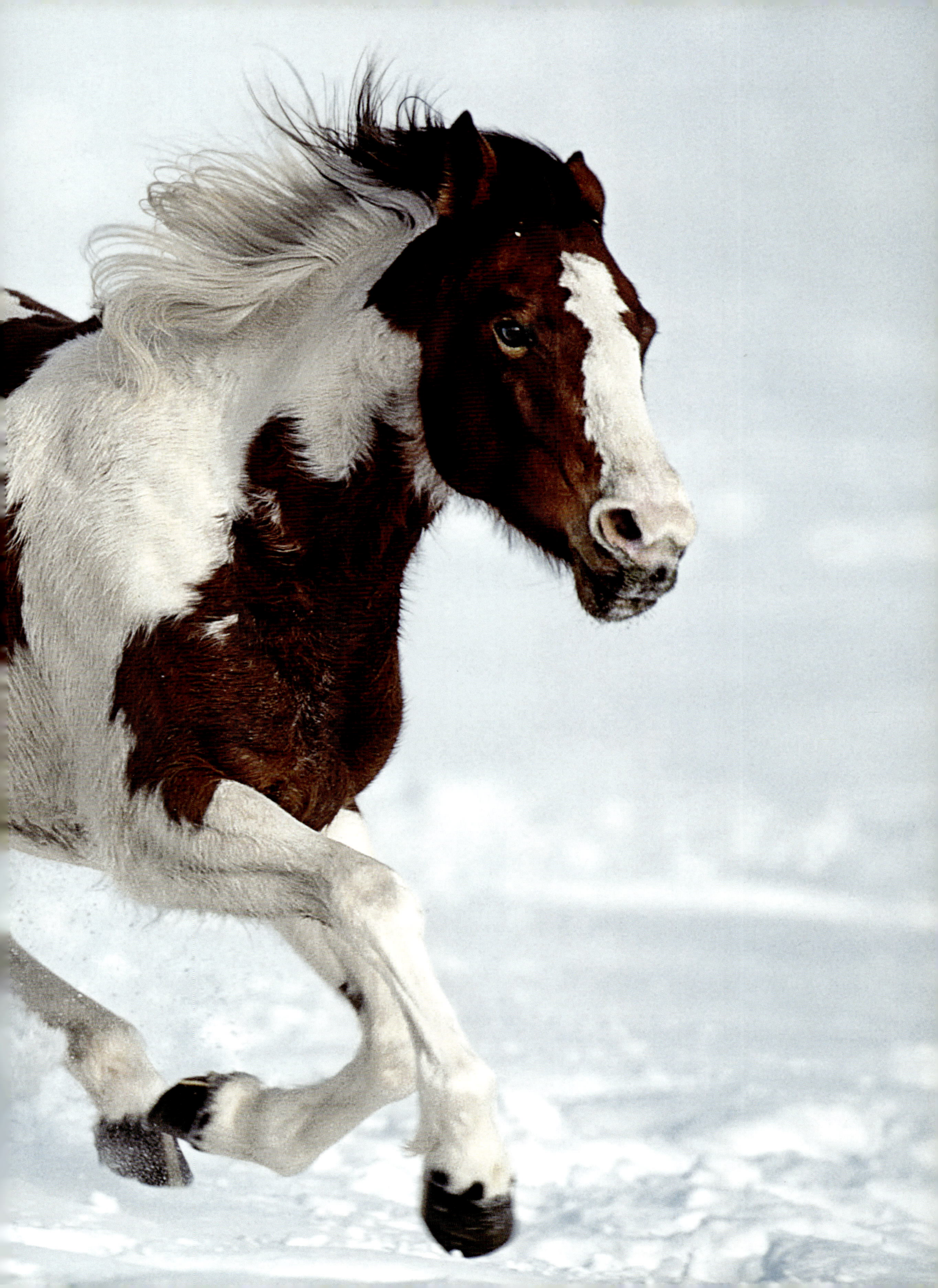

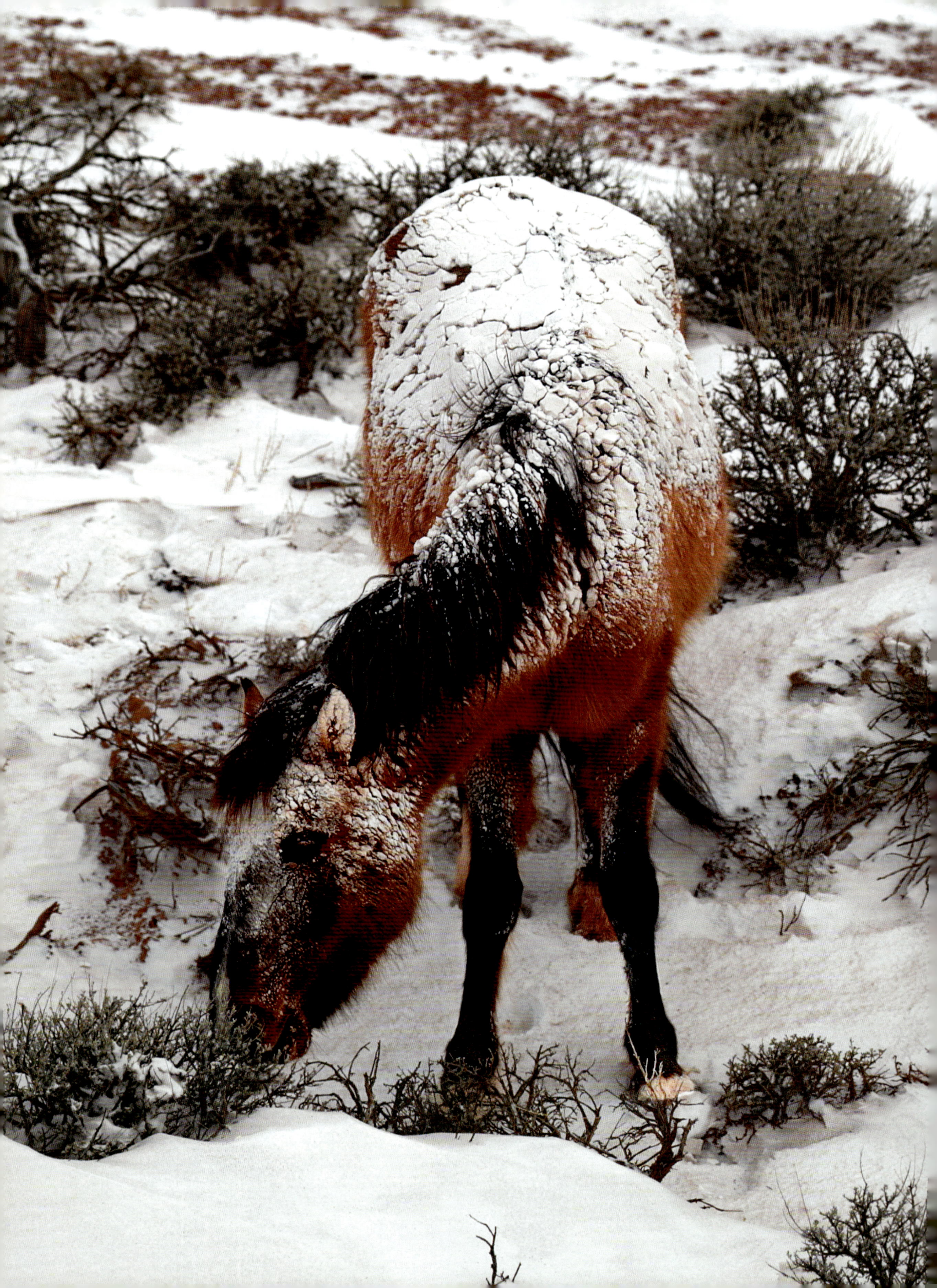

164 and 165 • In colder periods the icy blizzards trap the snow in the thick hair of the coats of the wild Mustangs, which wander in search of little dry shrubs to eat.

166-167 • A herd of Mustangs with a range of colors and tones of coat, probably of Quarter-Horse origin judging by the morphology, have been photographed on the Missouri snow.

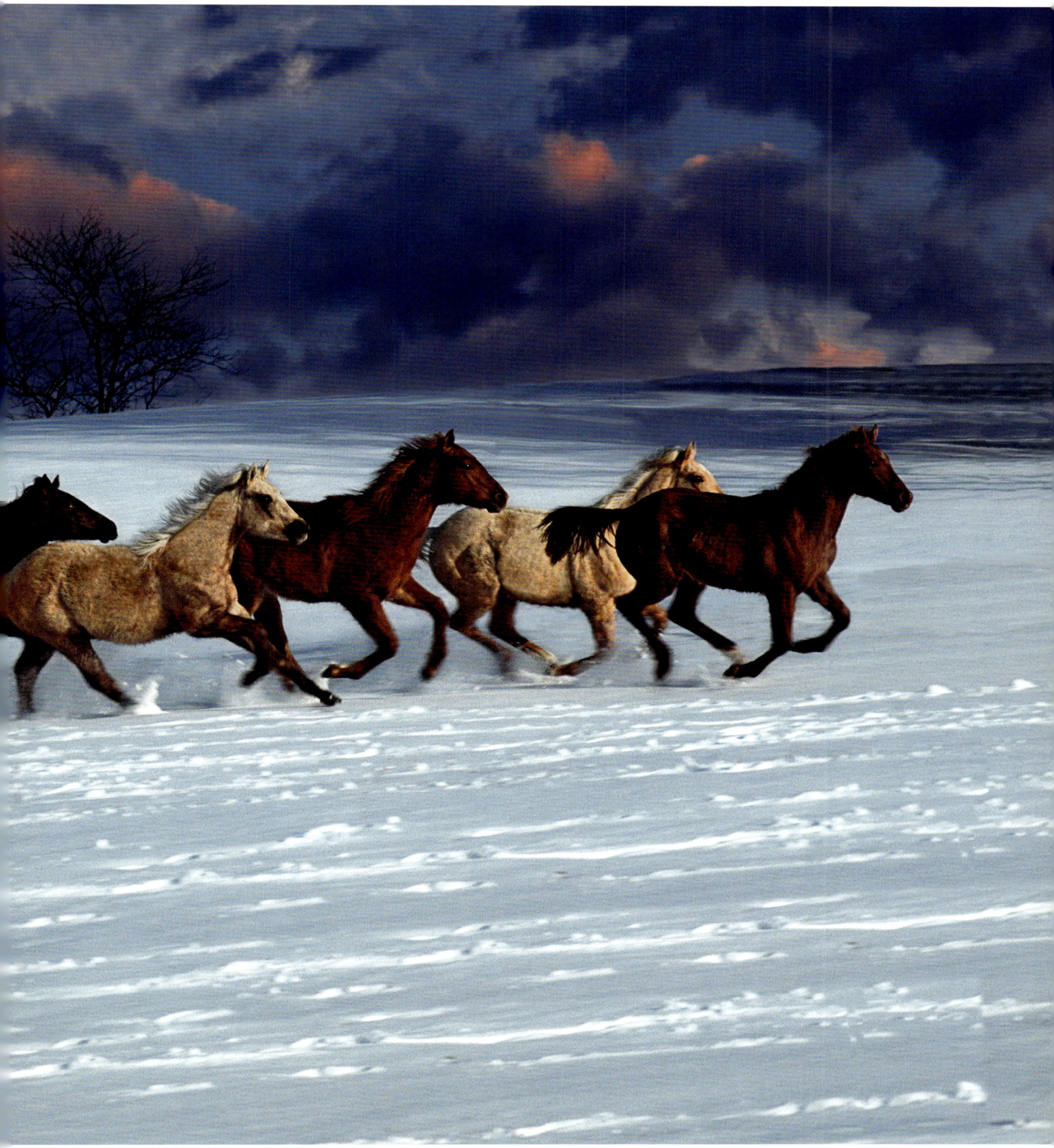

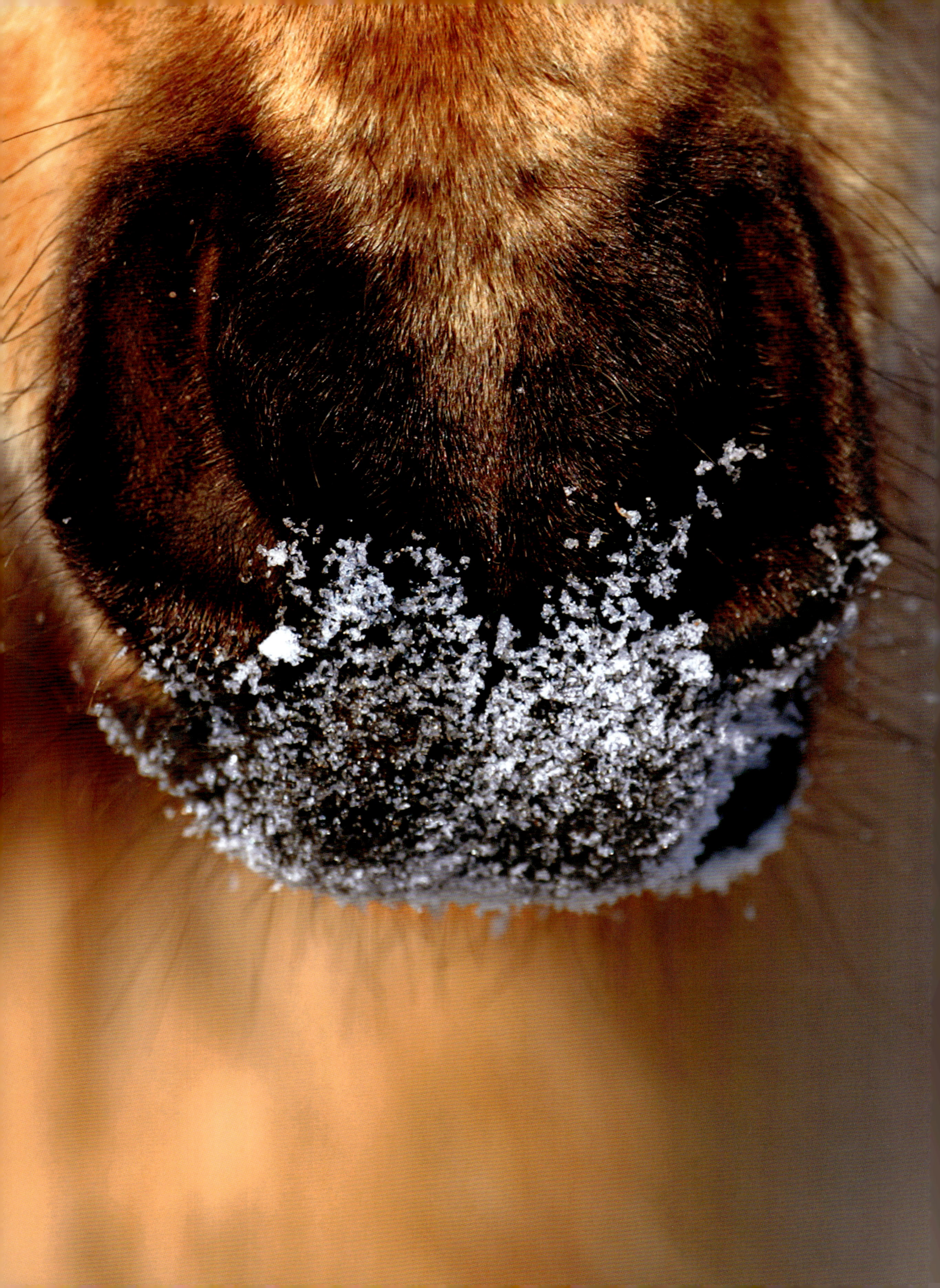

168 • The upper lip and nostrils of a Mustang encrusted with the snow that cakes their nostrils when the temperature falls below zero.

169 • A small group of North American wild horses shelter from the wind behind a dip in the ground, the females 'covering' the smallest foal, the dark one, in the lee of the two with the appaloosa coats.

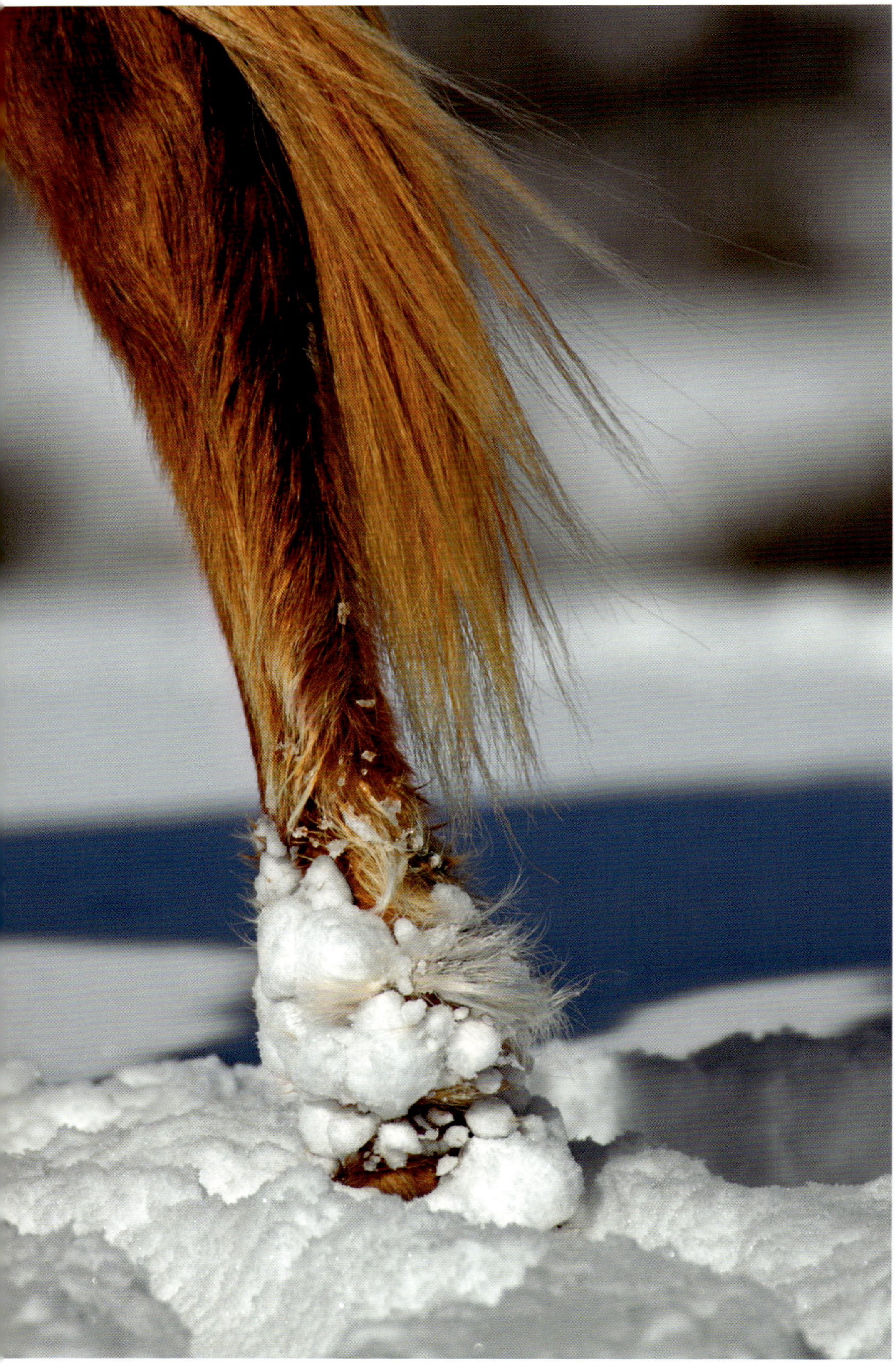

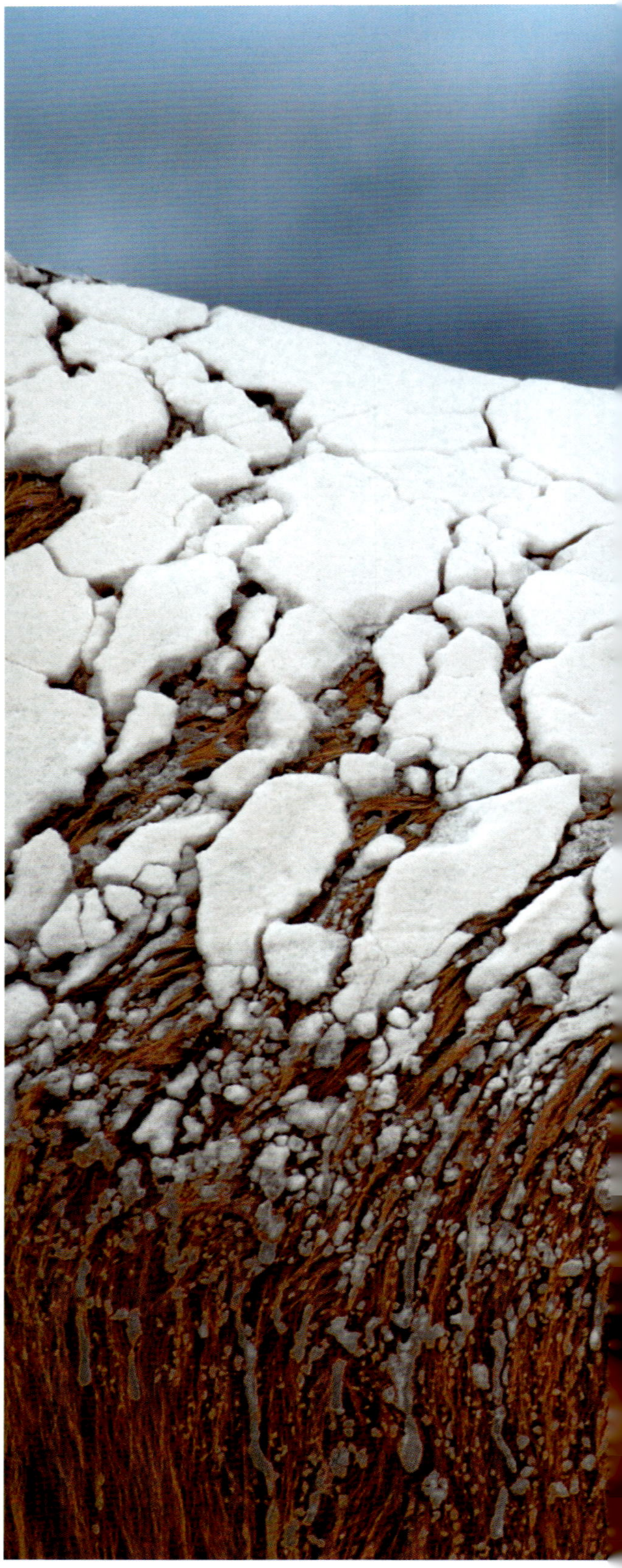

170 and 170-171 • Two details of the hard life that the Mustangs face in the winter, to survive in the wild.

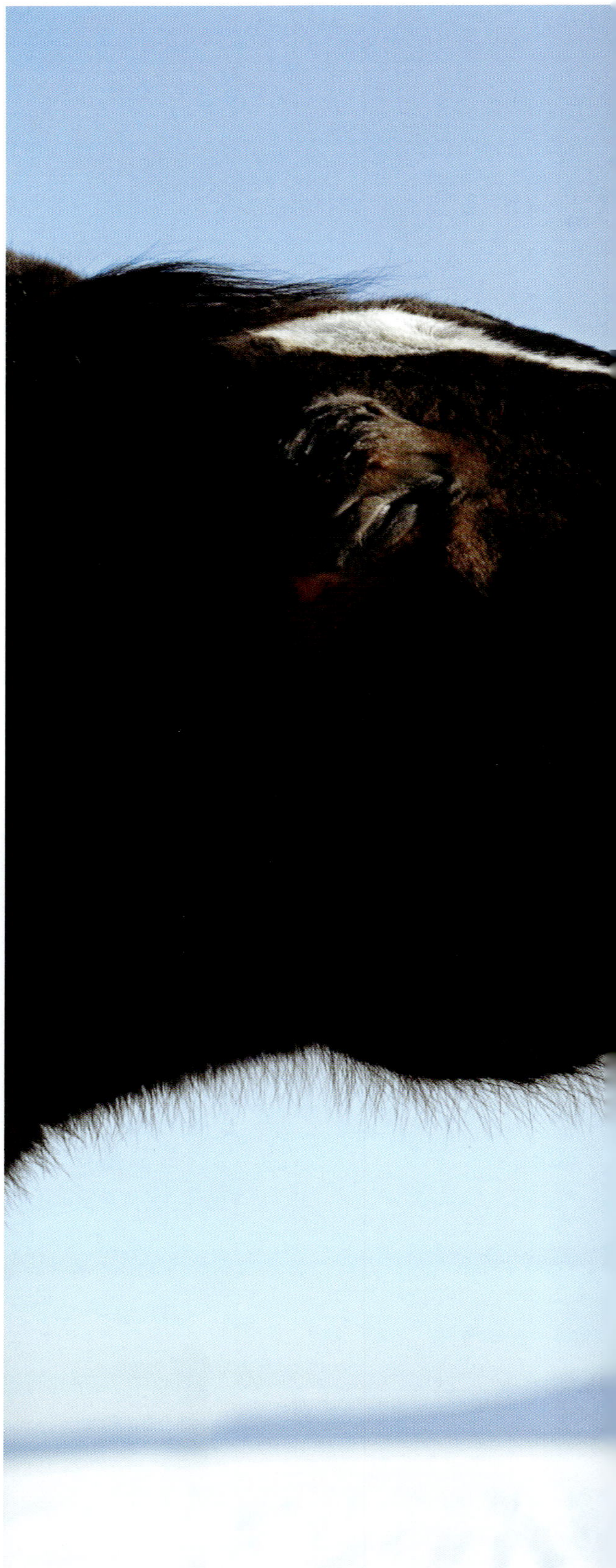

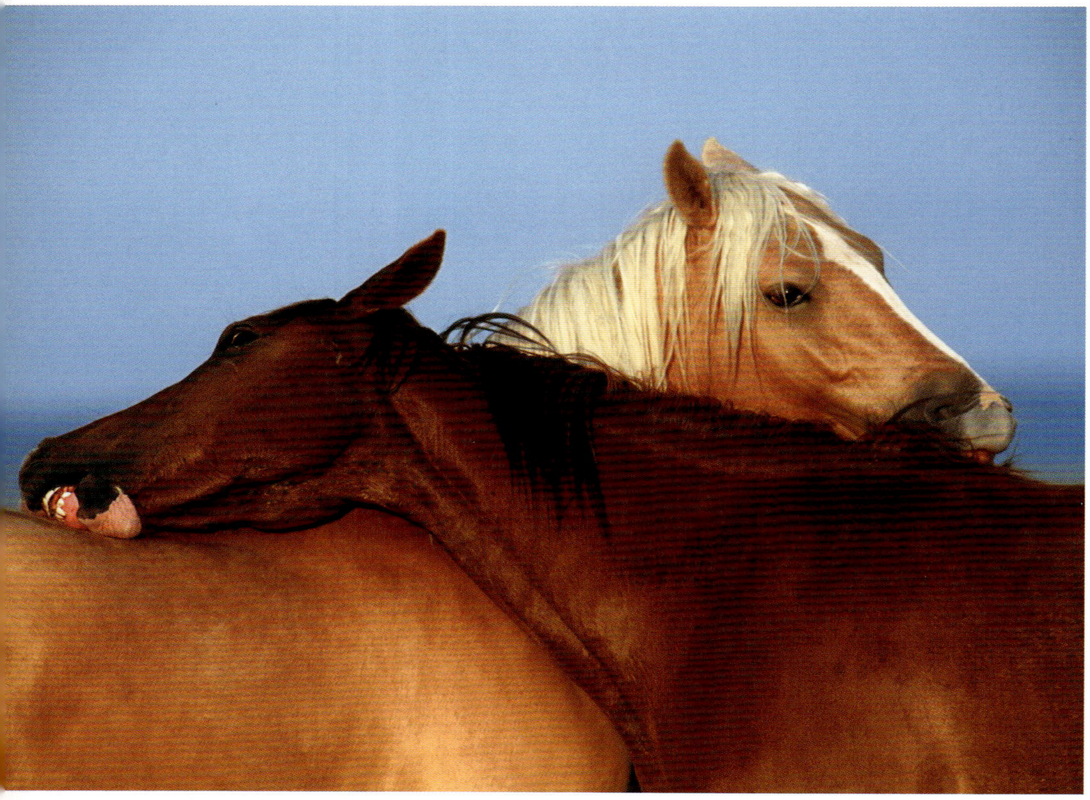

172 and 172-173 • When the sun comes out the horses become more playful and affectionate again, as if to congratulate each other upon having survived another winter.

174 • The lazy yawn of this gray Mustang reveals the typical teeth of a male, with very sharp 'tushes' between the front teeth and the molars.

175 • The roan blue stallion uses the 'flehmen' to capture precious information about his harem from the air around him.

176-177 • With the arrival of spring, warmth and affection increase even between the rough and combative wild Mustangs.

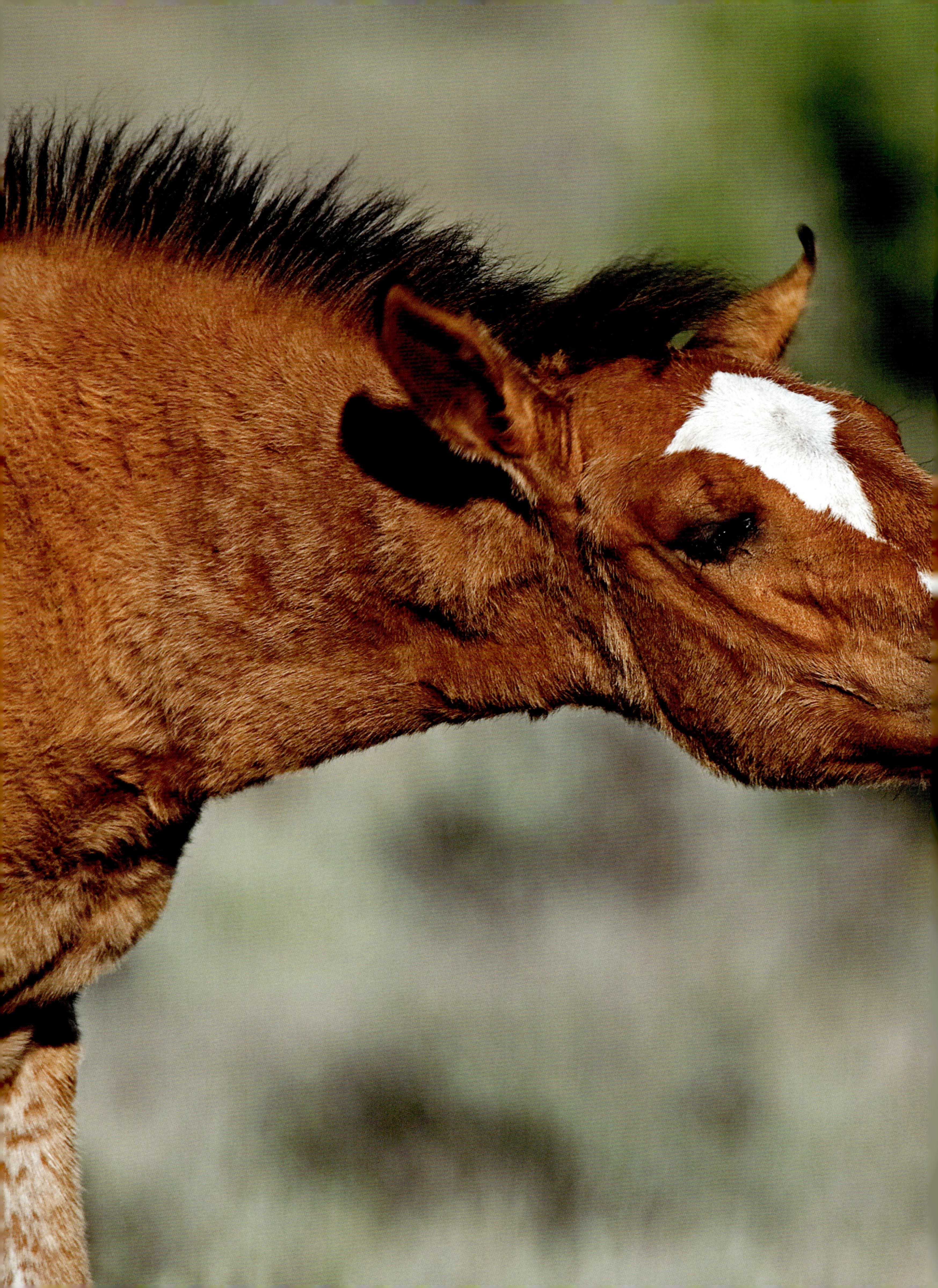

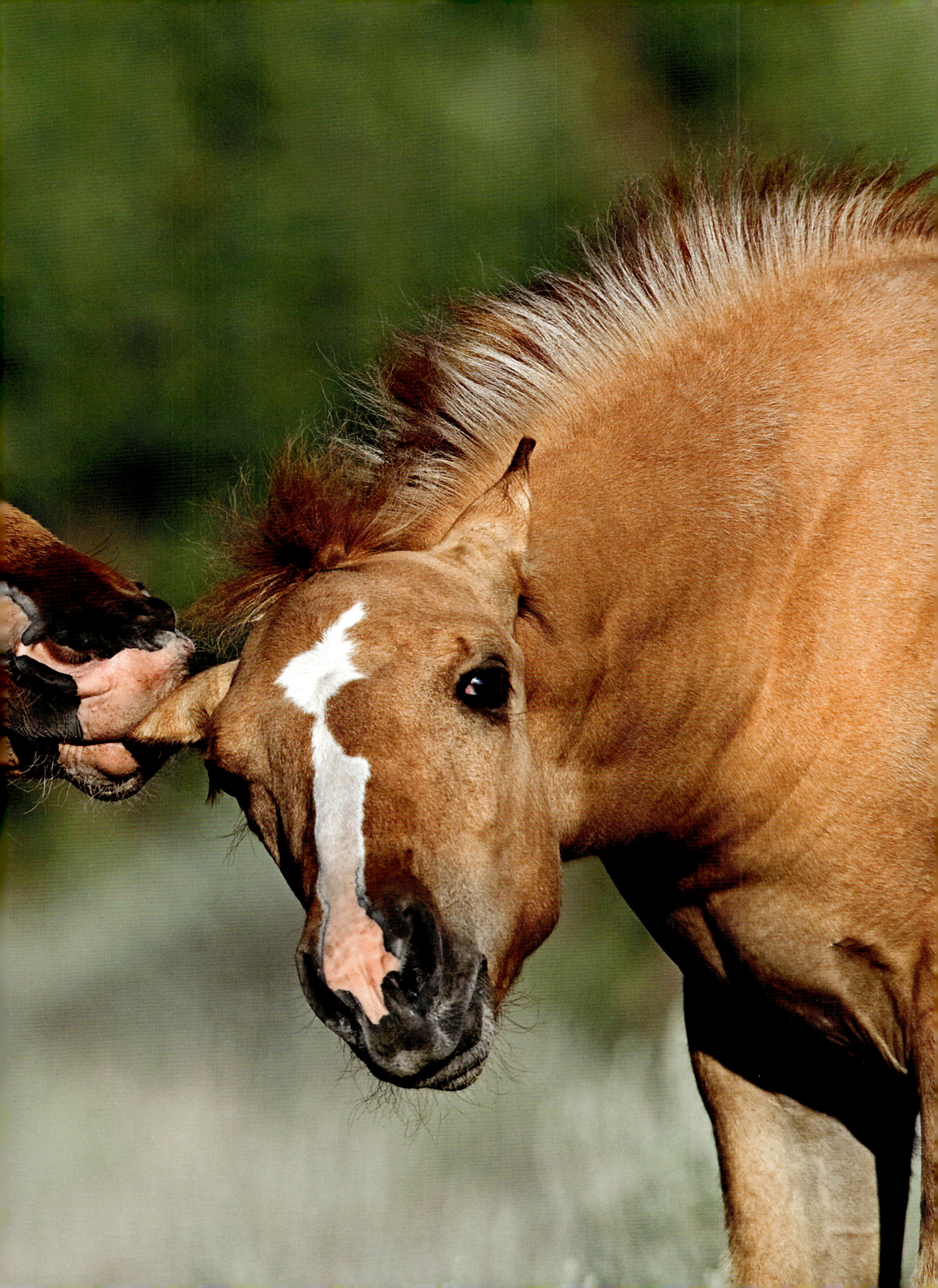

178-179 and 179 • Now that summer is here a mud bath is used to remove impurities from the coat and to protect it from parasites and insects.

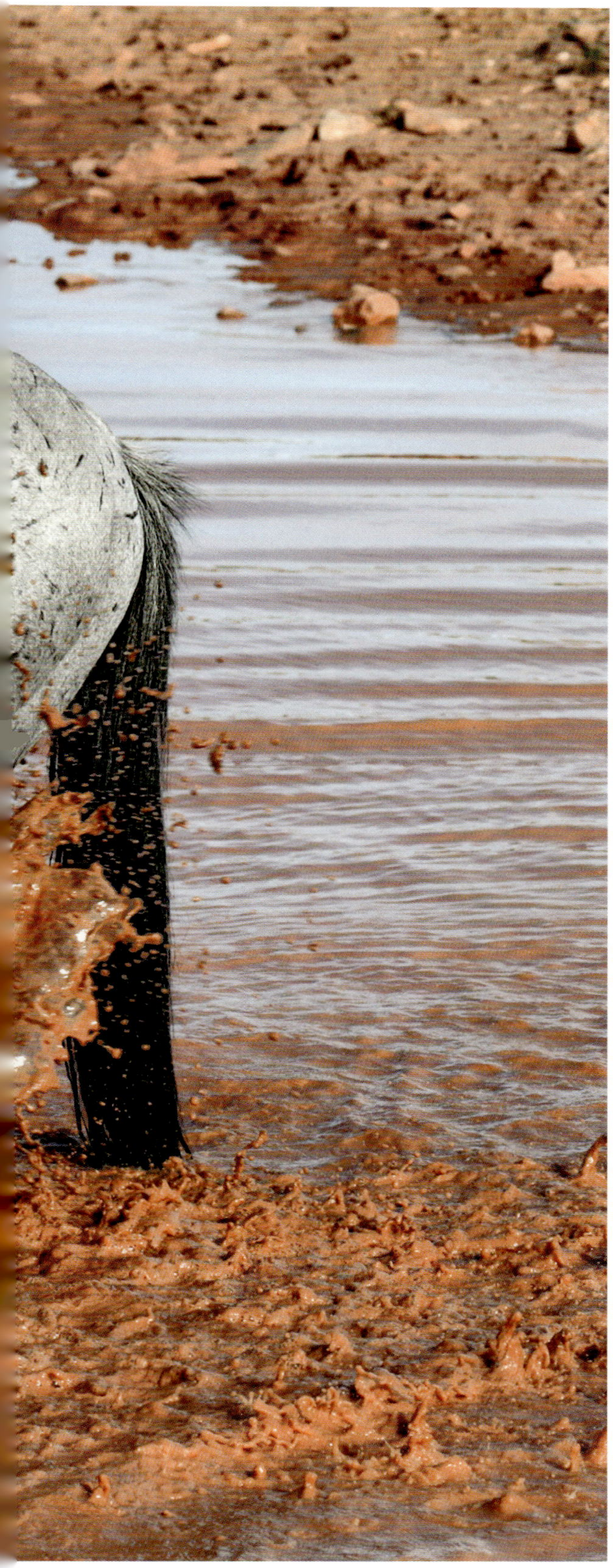

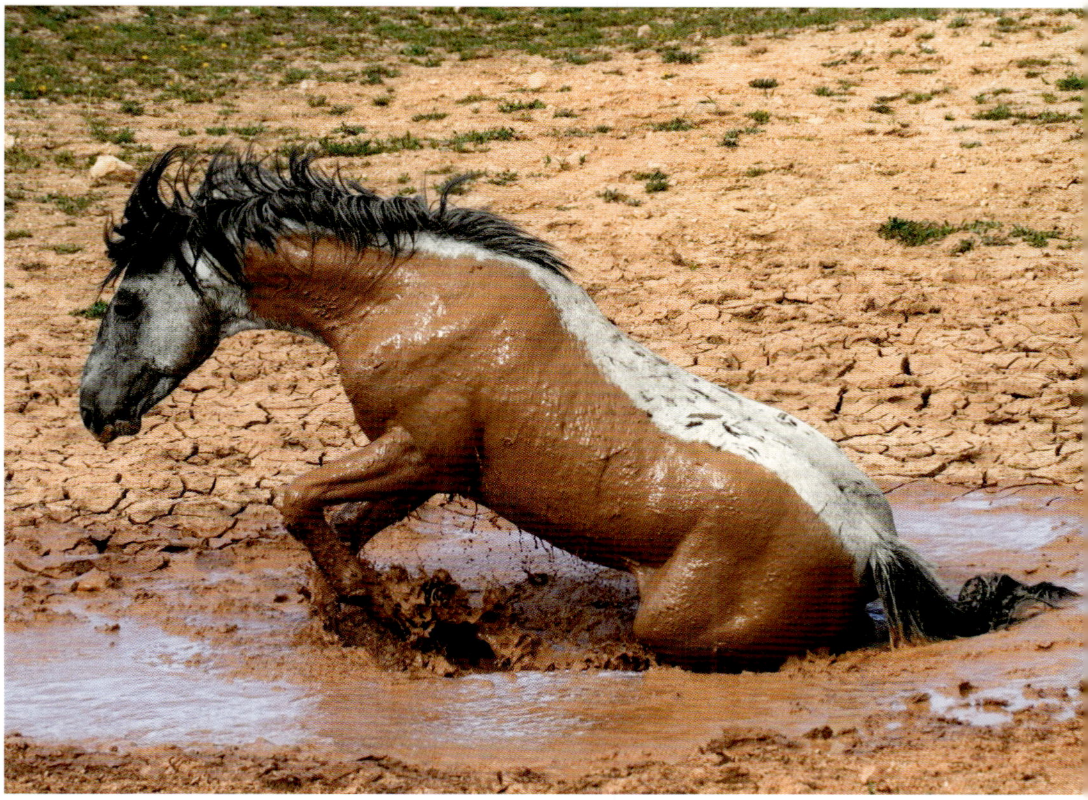

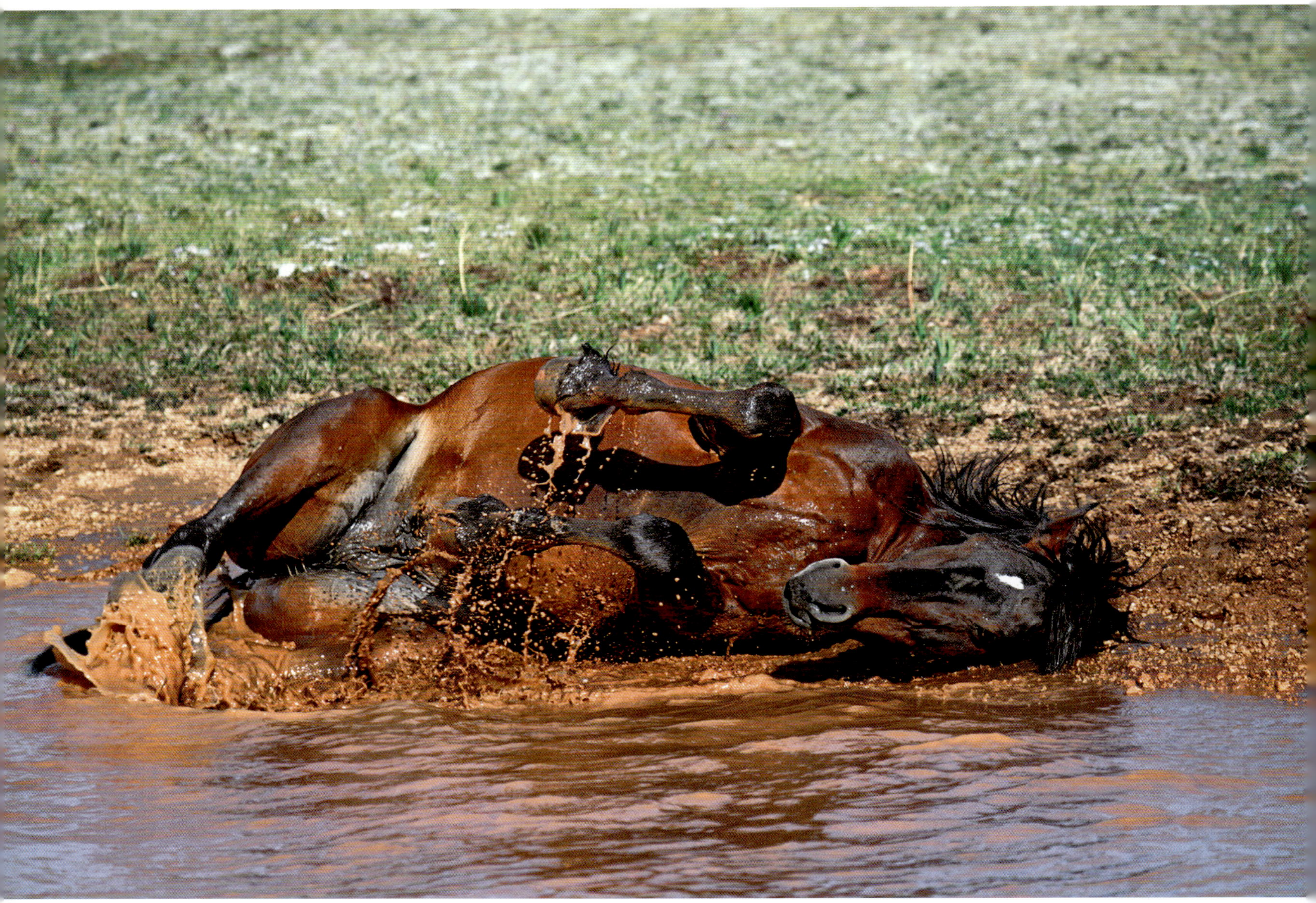

180 • Again, the daily wash of a female Mustang who is trying to take a bath on the edge of a pool.

181 • The same bay mare is rolling over to scratch herself and 'powder' her coat.

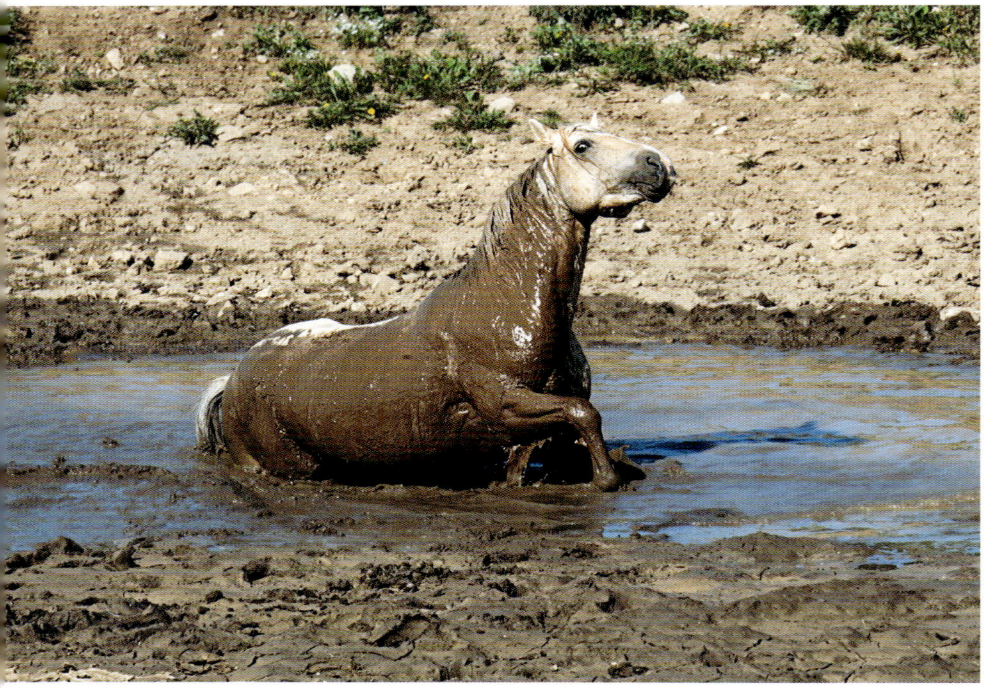

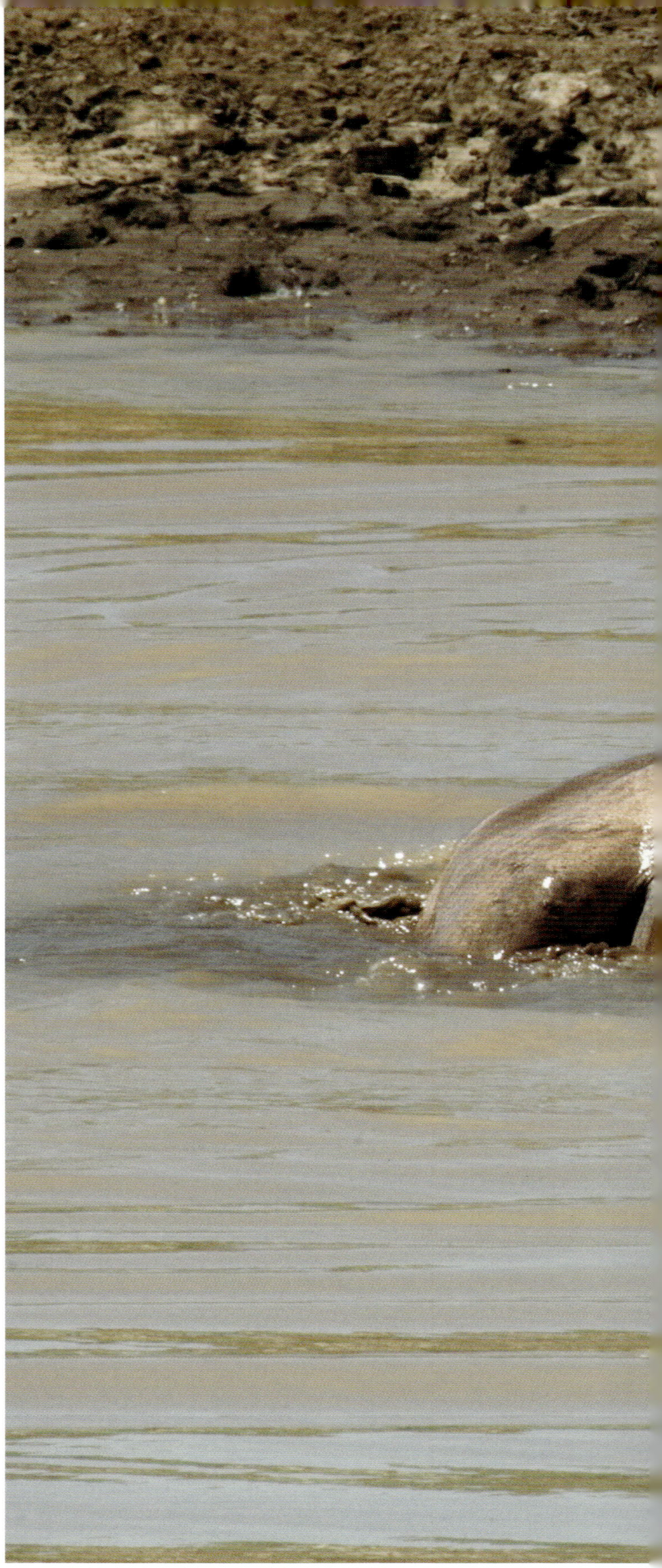

182 and 182-183 It is not just the females who love mud-bath beauty treatments, as we can see from this Palomino stallion pictured in the Pryor Mountains in the State of Nevada. • **184-185** Besides the desire to cool down and to protect his coat it seems that this young horse particularly enjoys digging in the mud.

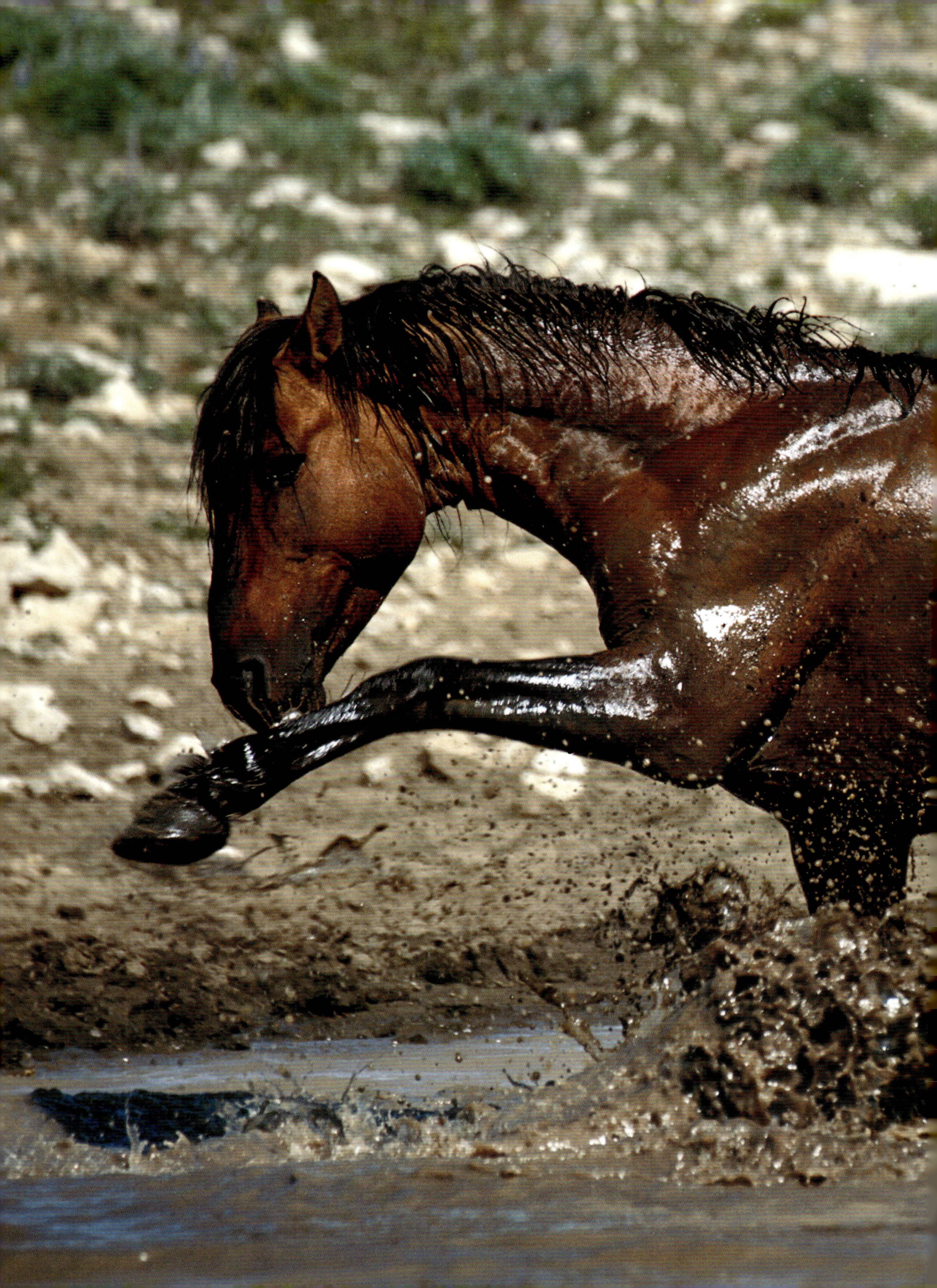

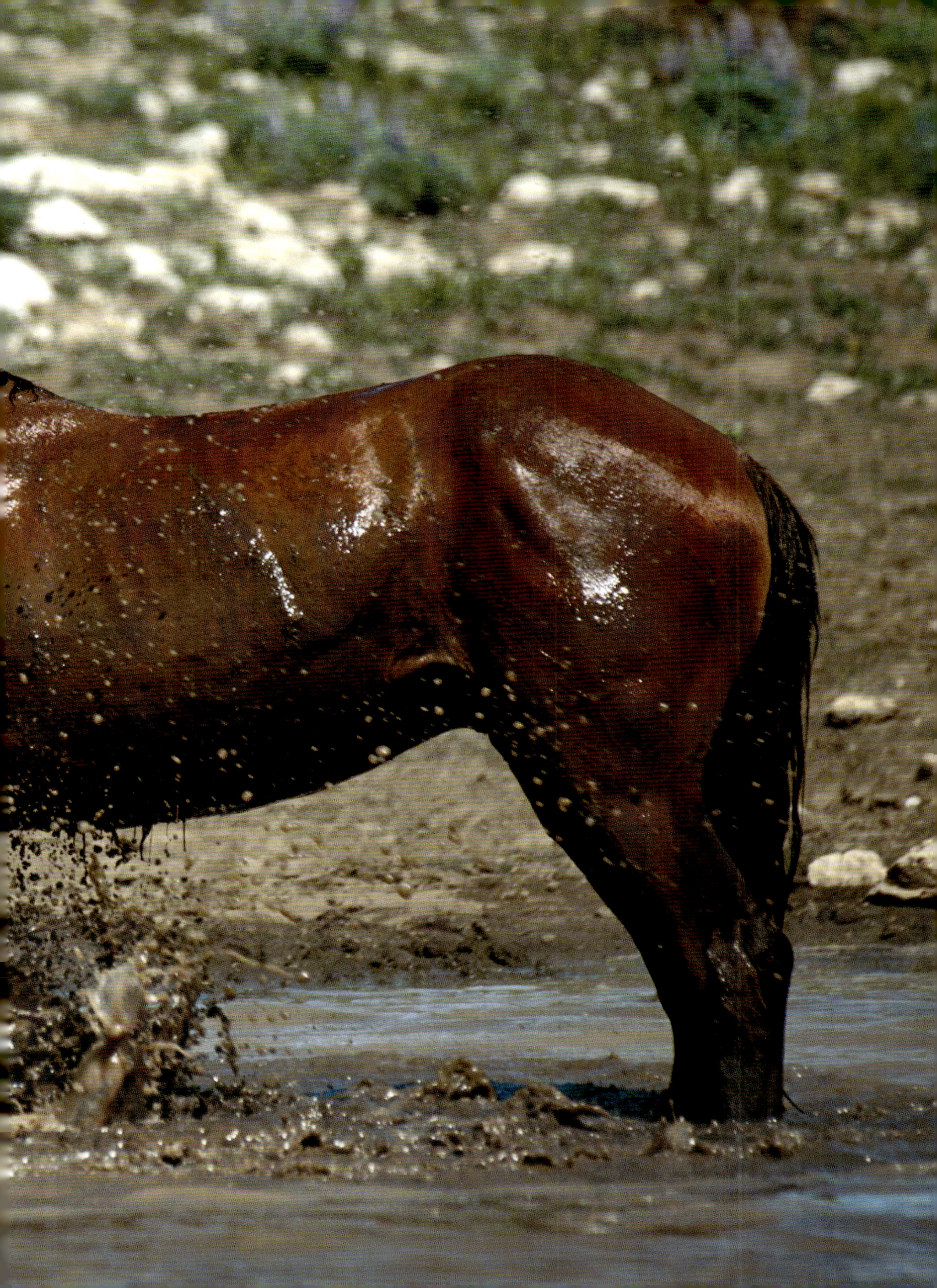

THE KING OF THE PAMPAS

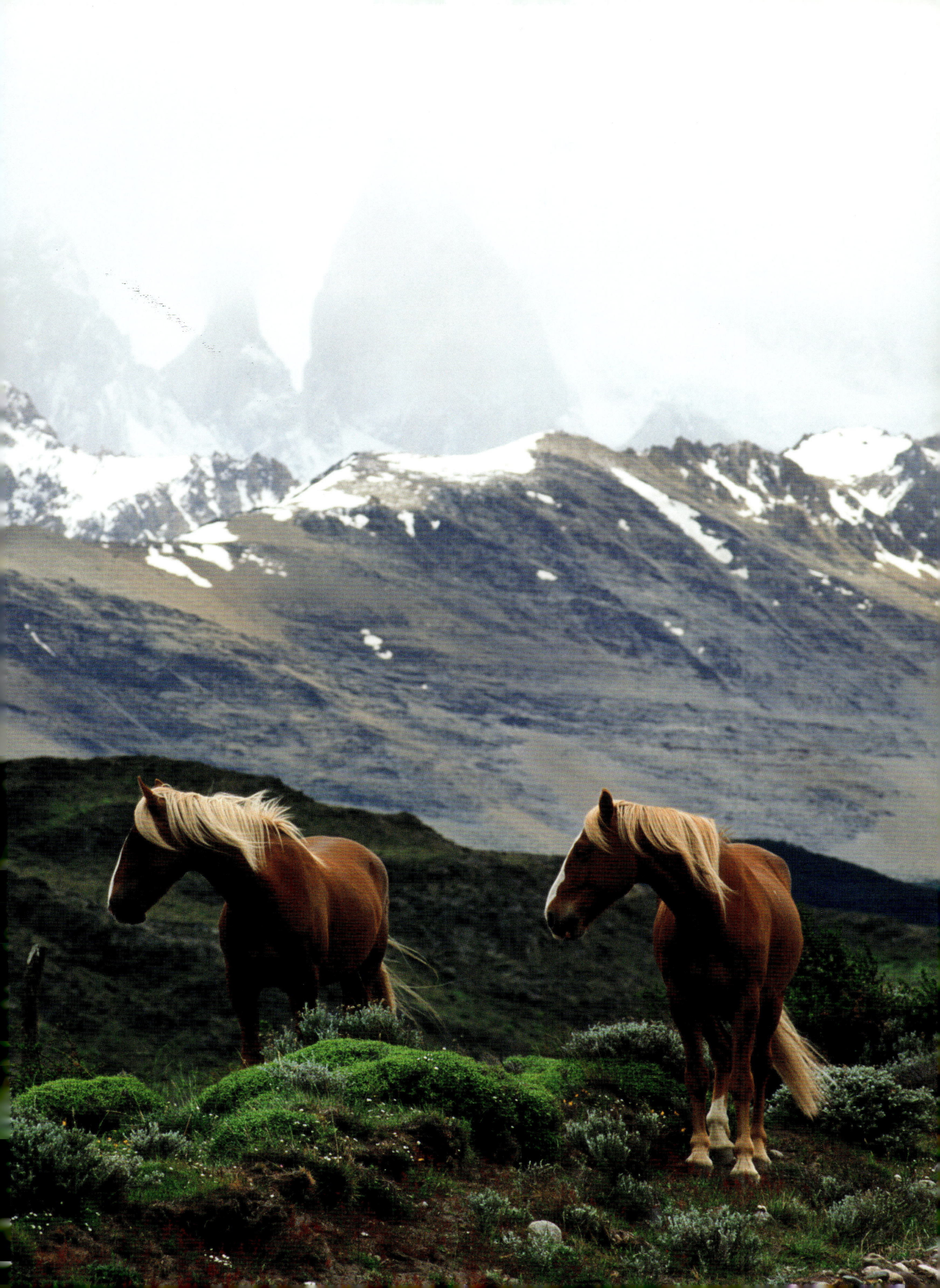

Is there anyone who hasn't heard of the gauchos? They were the famous cowboys of the Argentine pampas: hats with the front brim turned up, vest and baggy pantaloons, 'gaucho style' to be precise, galloping on strong and swift horses, decked out in 'homemade' saddlery of raw leather that was hand-weaved like the riders' belts.

They rode the famous Criollo horses ('Creoles' in Spanish), which descended from the horses of the Conquistadors of the sixteenth century, that is, from Andalusian horses that escaped and returned to the wild in the boundless spaces of South America. We could say that the Criollos are 'cousins' of the North American Mustang, sharing in the same origin, but with different experiences and evolution.

The horses imported by the Spanish into the southern part of the American continent were first, and foremost, improved in 1535 with a strong input of Arab and Berber blood – the work of Don Pedro De Mendoza, the founder of Buenos Aires. Later on when the city was destroyed, many of these horses scattered and they found the enormous planes of the Rio de la Plata to be the ideal habitat for reproducing and flourishing in the natural world, finally becoming wild again. The 'splendid isolation' in which they lived for three hundred years led to a morphological and aptitudinal homogeneity that made them an authentic breed in their own right.

Indeed, besides their recurring and easily identifiable traits (strong build, largely dun-colored coat) they acquired above all, and in this their Arab blood may have been crucial, their spartan nature and proverbial stamina.

The Criollo is generally a medium-sized horse (from 1.33 to 1.50 meters) with a wide but not heavy head, a muscular neck and broad chest, a short back, a rotund rump, short and shapely limbs and strong bones. Its feet are small and very hard. These characteristics make it agile and fast, surefooted on uneven ground, capable of sudden movements and bursts of speed. It is therefore an ideal horse for working with cattle and this is why they are frequently captured from the free roaming herds and tamed for the gauchos to ride in the 'fazendas' of the big landed estates. Excessive and ill-considered crossbreeding with other types of horse in the early 1900s led to a decline of the Criollo.

In order restore its original hardiness and stamina, a purebred stud-book was created in 1918 that re-established the original characteristics and set the standards. Every year, Argentine farmers organize an annual 405-mile, 15-day race, without any supplemental feed for the horses, which have to live off what they can forage during the race. Its purpose is to monitor respect for the breed's characteristics, in particular its hardiness and stamina.

If the principle of isolation from external influences that is encouraged in the Rio della Plata plane favors the creation of a breed with homogenous characteristics, the vast expanse of the South American continent and the varying environmental and climatic conditions of the various countries that compose it, have contributed (together with the influence of man) to diversify a number of the Criollo's characteristics in each country. However this has only happened to a degree as this horse has the same basic features wherever you go in South America.

Obviously the Argentine Criollo is the base-type, the best known and most widespread version of the breed. The even hardier Chilean Criollo is derived directly from its Argentine cousin.

In Colombia the Guajira Indians bred Criollos, from whom they take their name.

However, the type that most recalls its Andalusian origins is the Llanero – the Venezuelan Criollo. It has a more 'gracious' morphology than the Argentine horse, but is also less hardy. A few of them even have a slightly convex forehead, reflecting the relationship of the Criollos with Arab and Berber horses.

In Peru the Criollo is known as the Salteno. It is generally shorter and is in turn subdivided into three typologies. The Costeno is the standard-breed – it does not trot, the two-beat diagonal gait, but rather it moves with a lateral stride, making it an extremely smooth ride – and this is why it is known as the Peruvian Paso. Then there is the Andean Morchucho, which is the shortest of the three and has a convex forehead and finally, the stockier Chola, which is suitable for agriculture due its great stamina.

In Brazil the Crioulo of the Lower Rio Grande is very much like the Berber and is also used in equestrian sports. The other type of Brazilian horse, the Campolino, is similar to the Andalusian though a little less noble-looking. It comes from Cassiano Campolino (from which it takes its name). Finally, although the Mangalarga is descended from the original Criollo it has developed its own characteristics due to intensive crossbreeding with the Andalusian and the Portuguese Altèr-Real breeds. In fact this has occurred to such an extent that it is now considered to be separate breed.

The Criollos imported into Europe during the last thirty years (above all to Germany and Italy) have contributed to the spread of Western equestrianism, being excellent and far cheaper substitutes for Quarter Horses.

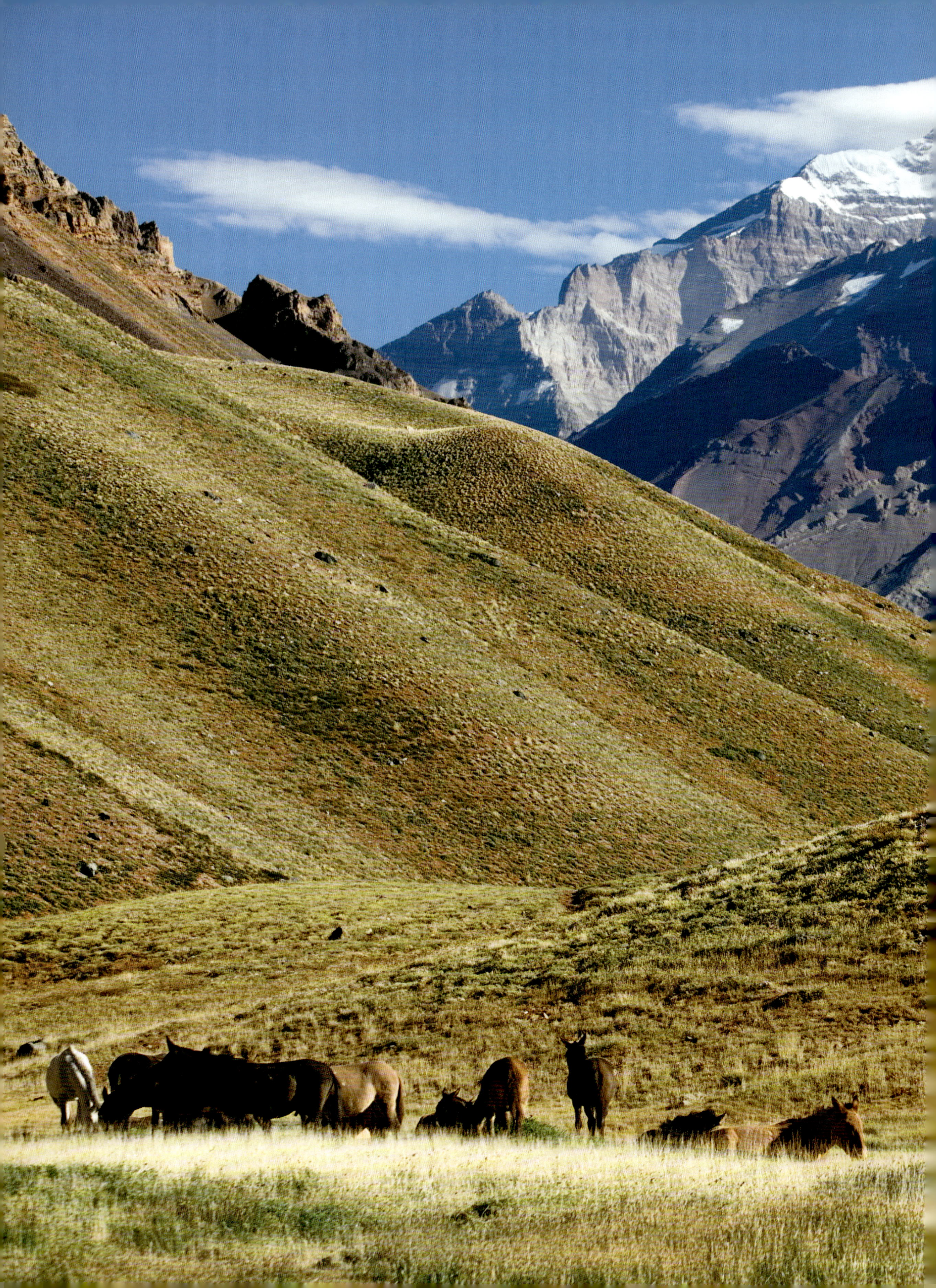

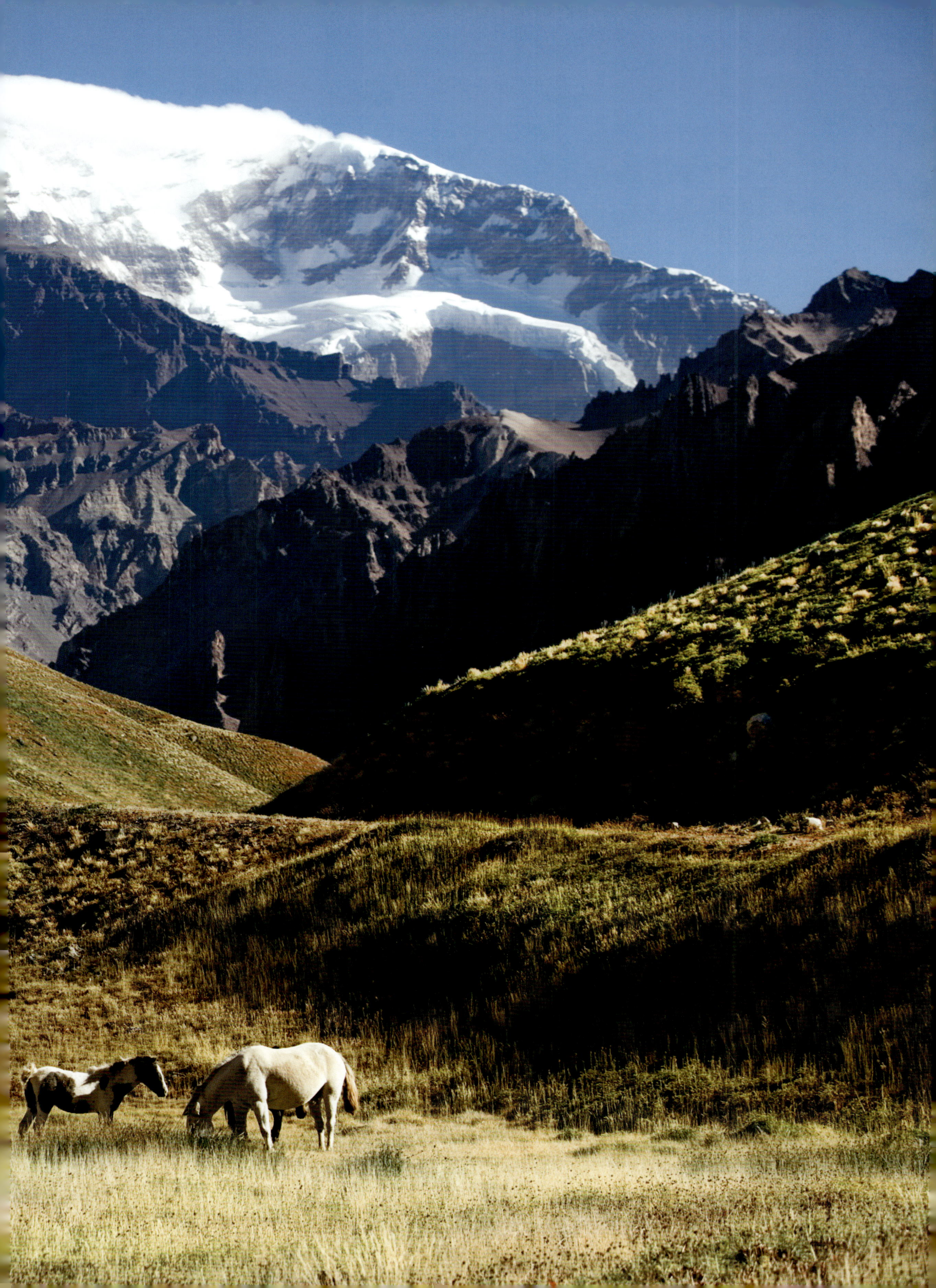

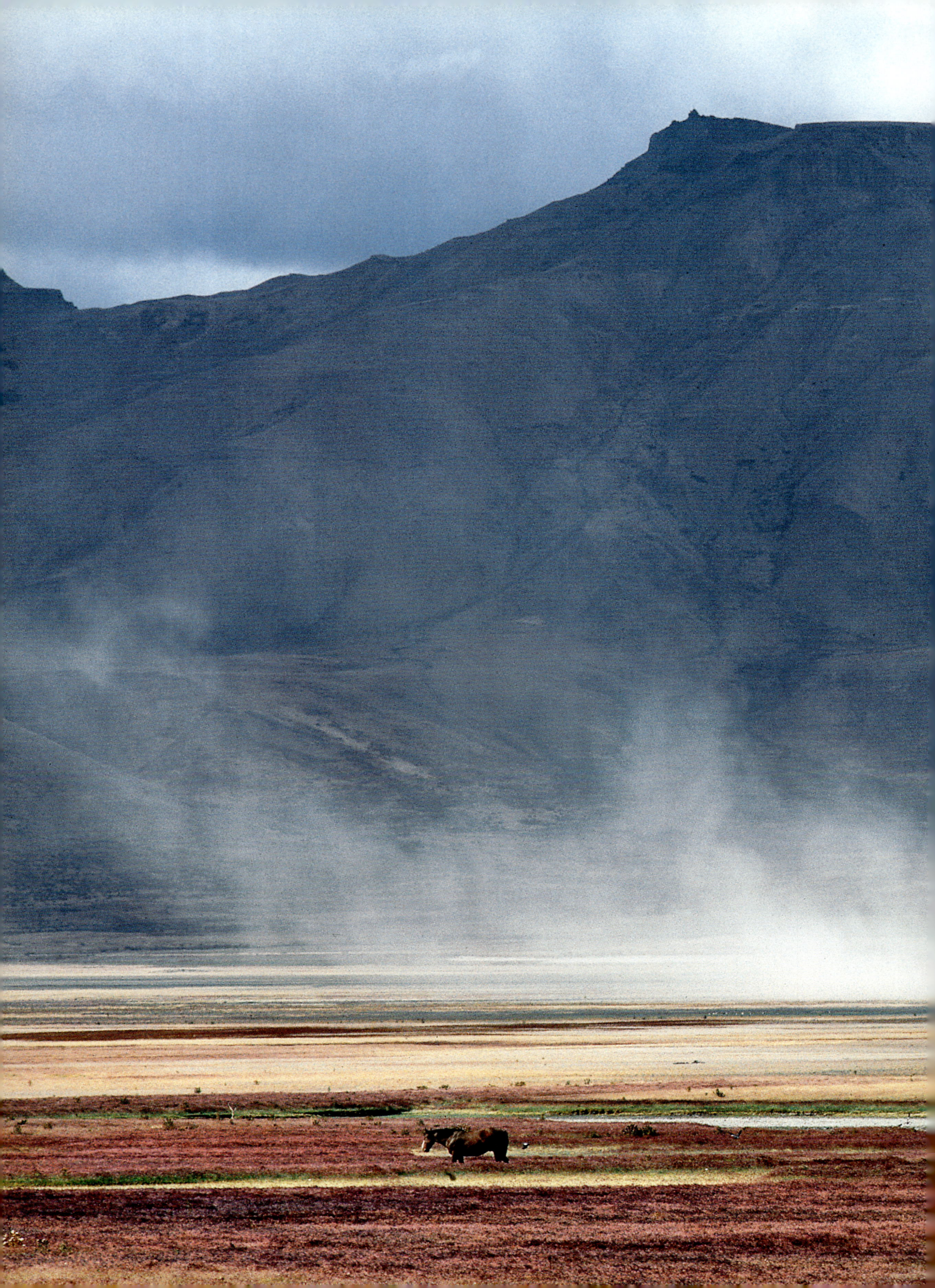

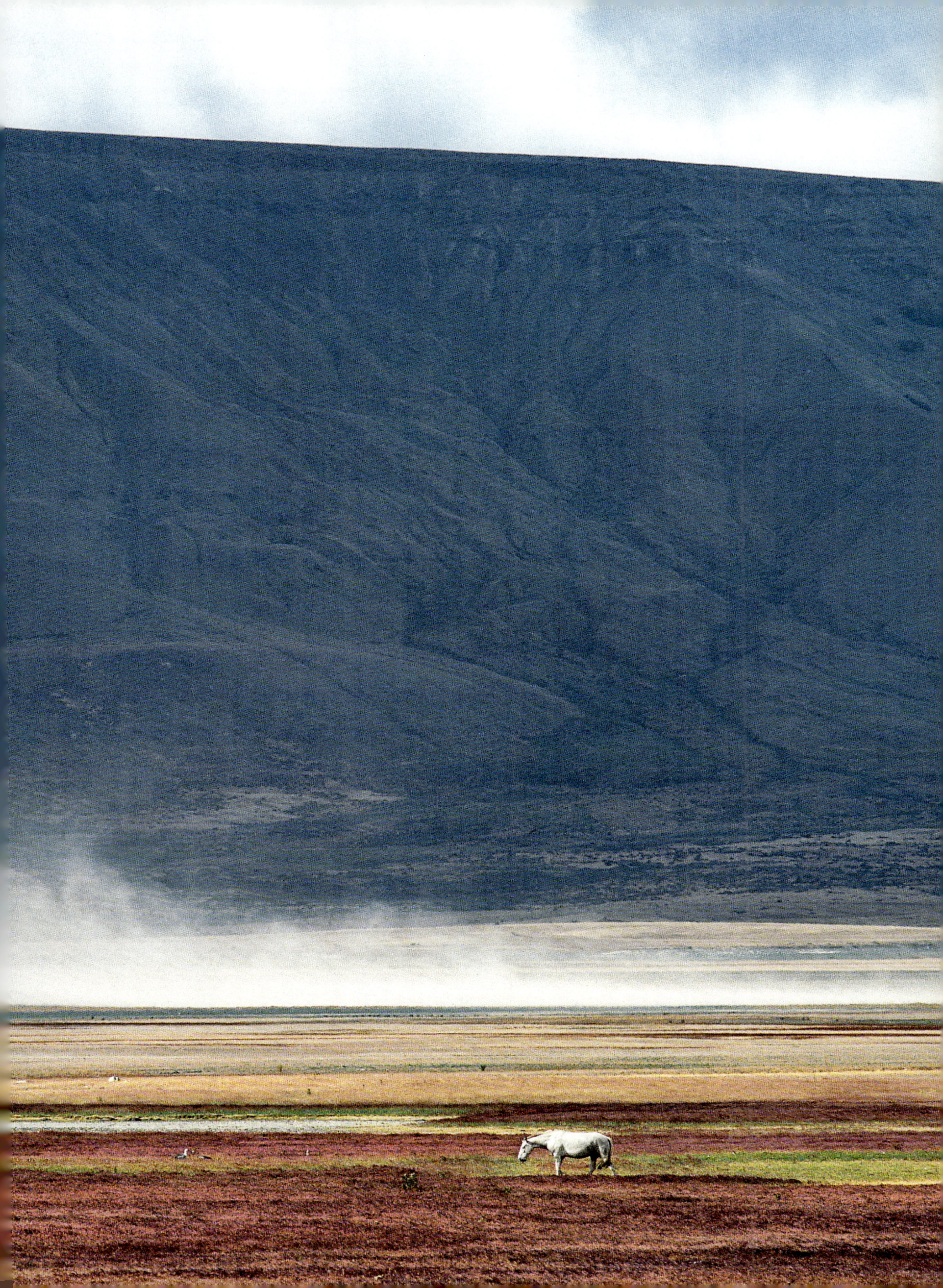

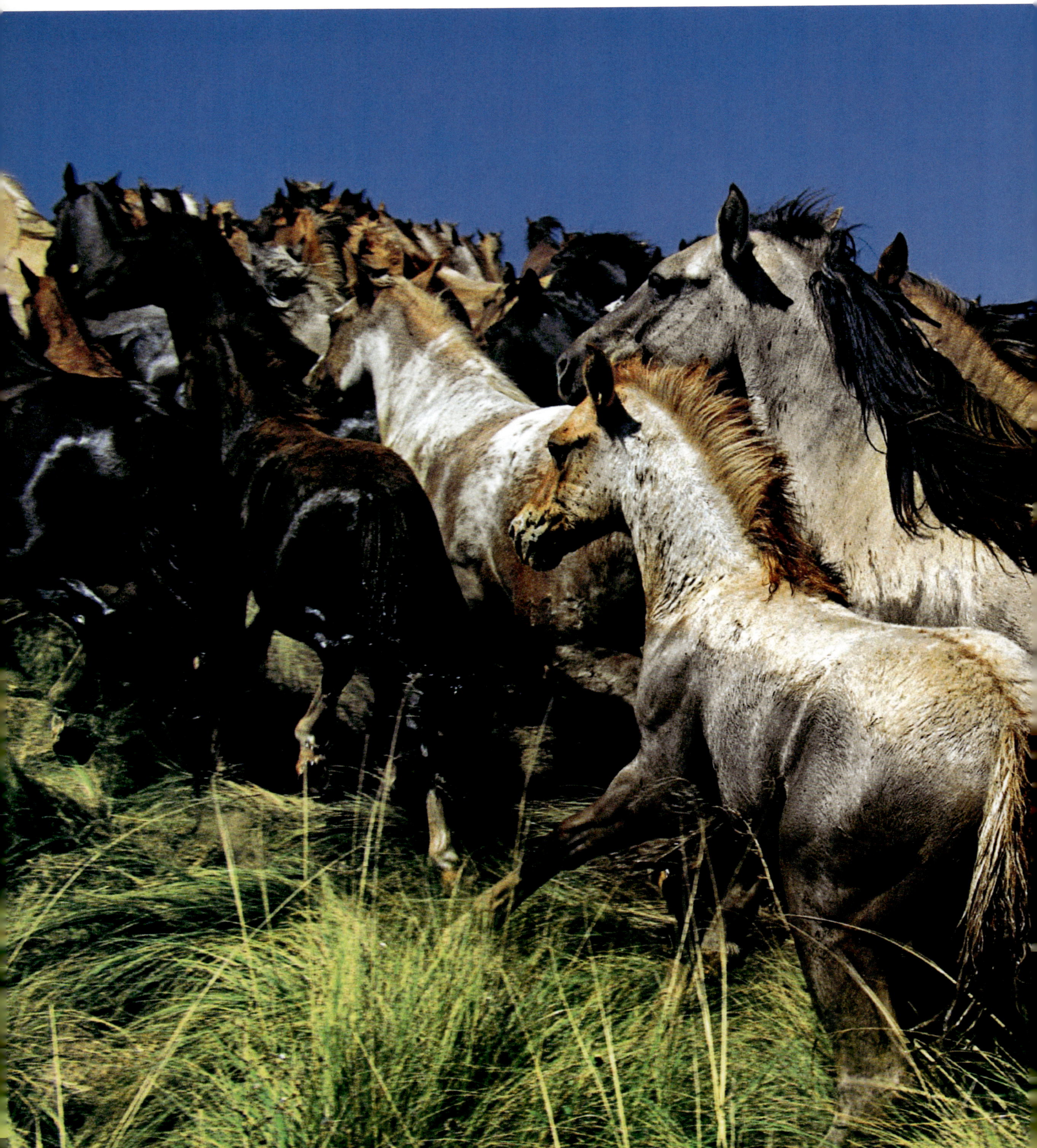

187 • This beautiful photograph shows two Criollos roaming free in the Torres National Park, Paine, Chile; a typical South American natural environment where the more 'rustic' variety of the breed lives and flourishes.

190-191 • A herd of horses grazing in a glade at the foot of Mount Aconcagua.

192-193 • This foreshortened view shows the typical habitat of the Argentine Criollo, the base-type of the famous breed that populates all of South America; in this case the plateau of Santa Cruz.

194-195 • The vast range of coats – roans, bays, overos, blacks, appaloosas, buckskins etc – turn a herd of Criollos on the move into a kaleidoscope of colors.

196-197 and 198-199 • We can see all the hardiness and strength of the Criollo in the pictures of these two wild stallions and the roan mare: in the powerful neck, in the angular, but never heavy, head and in the wonderful coat colors of these beasts, which rather closely resemble their Spanish ancestors.

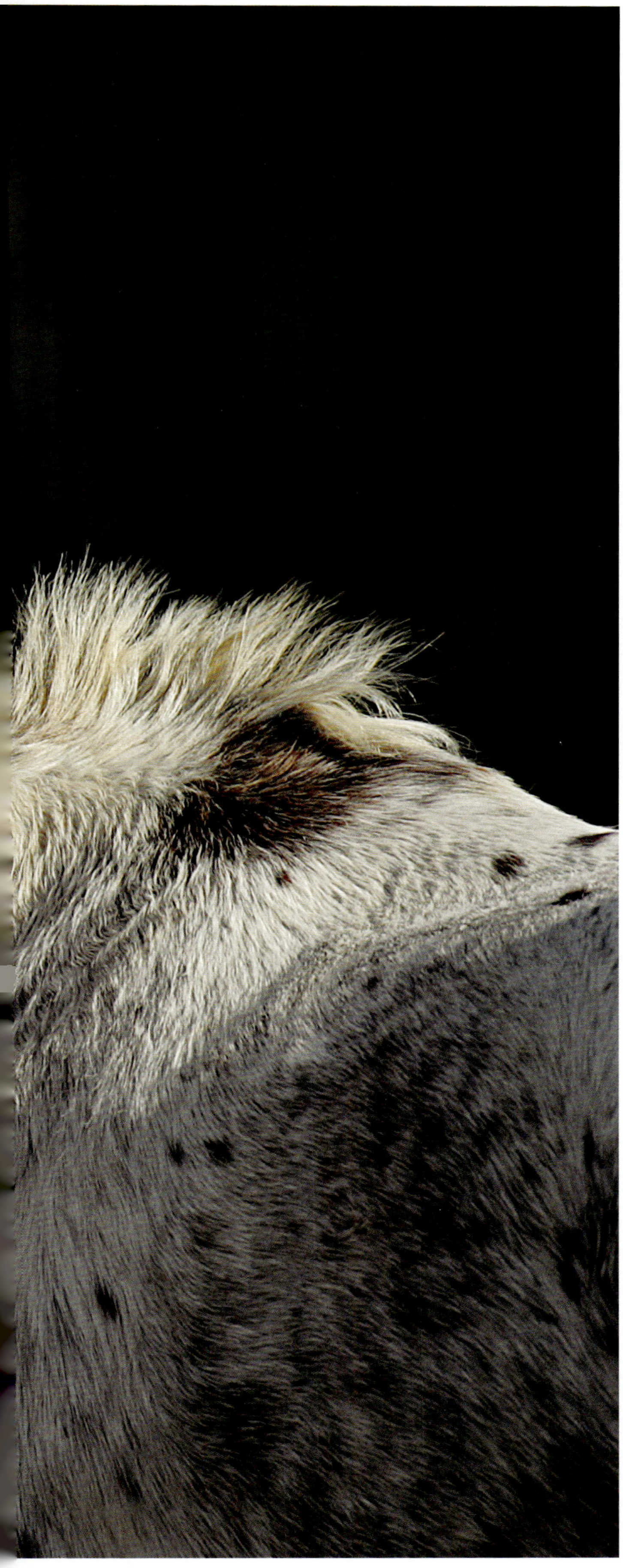

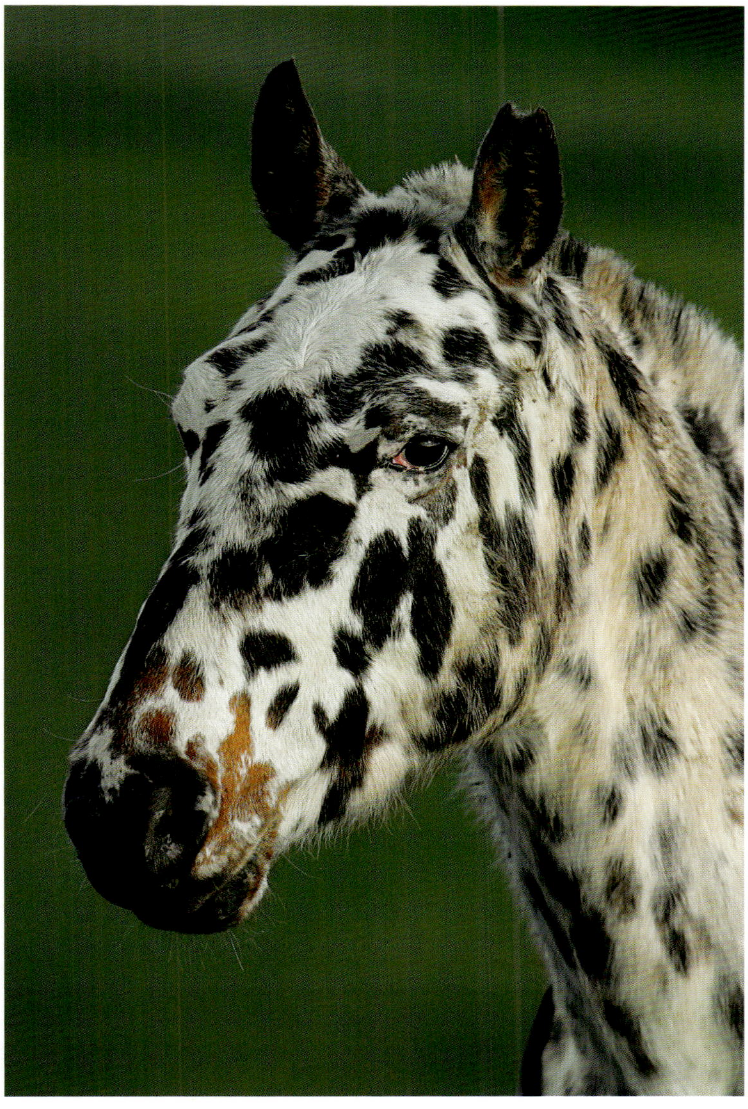

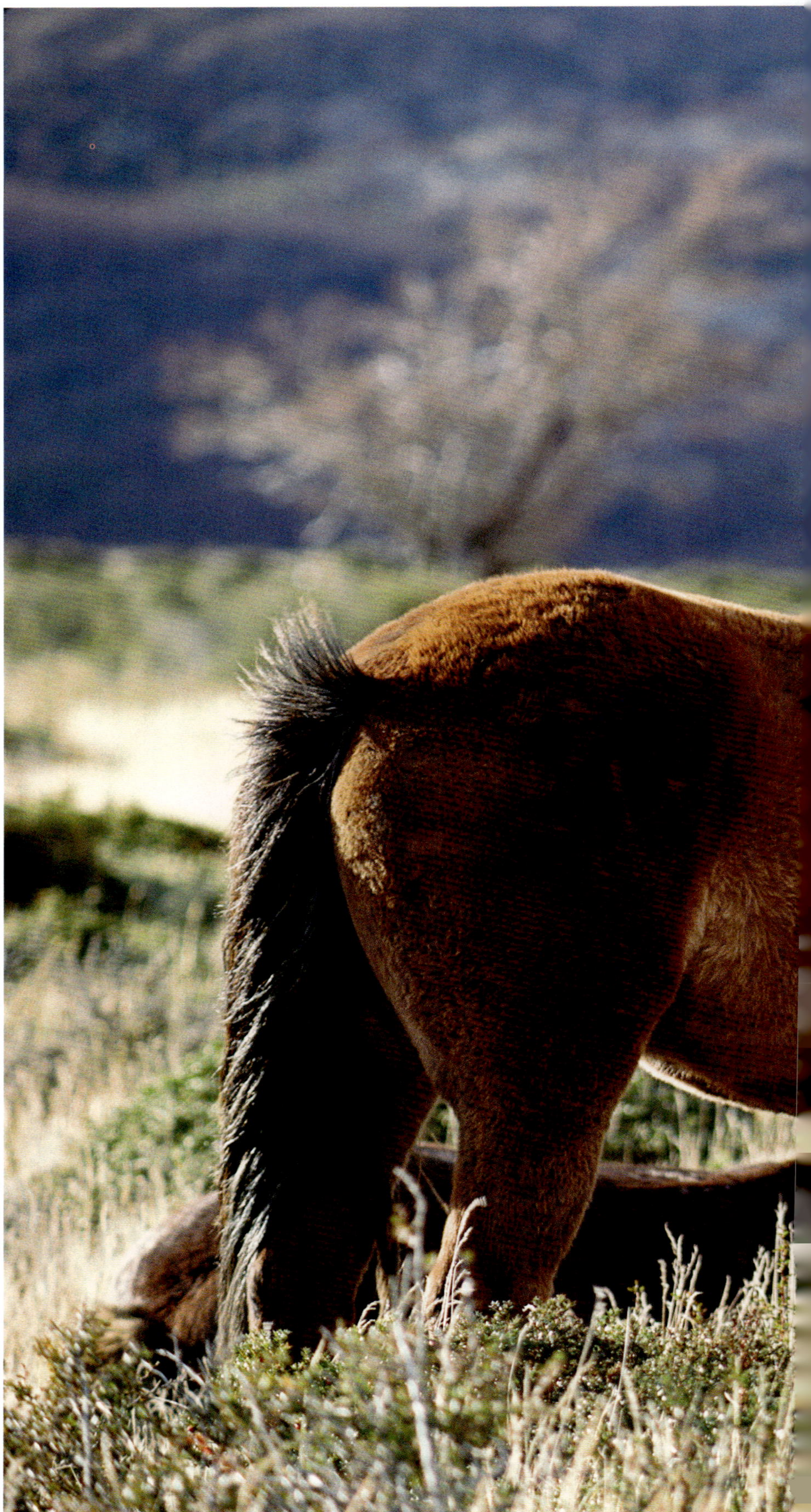

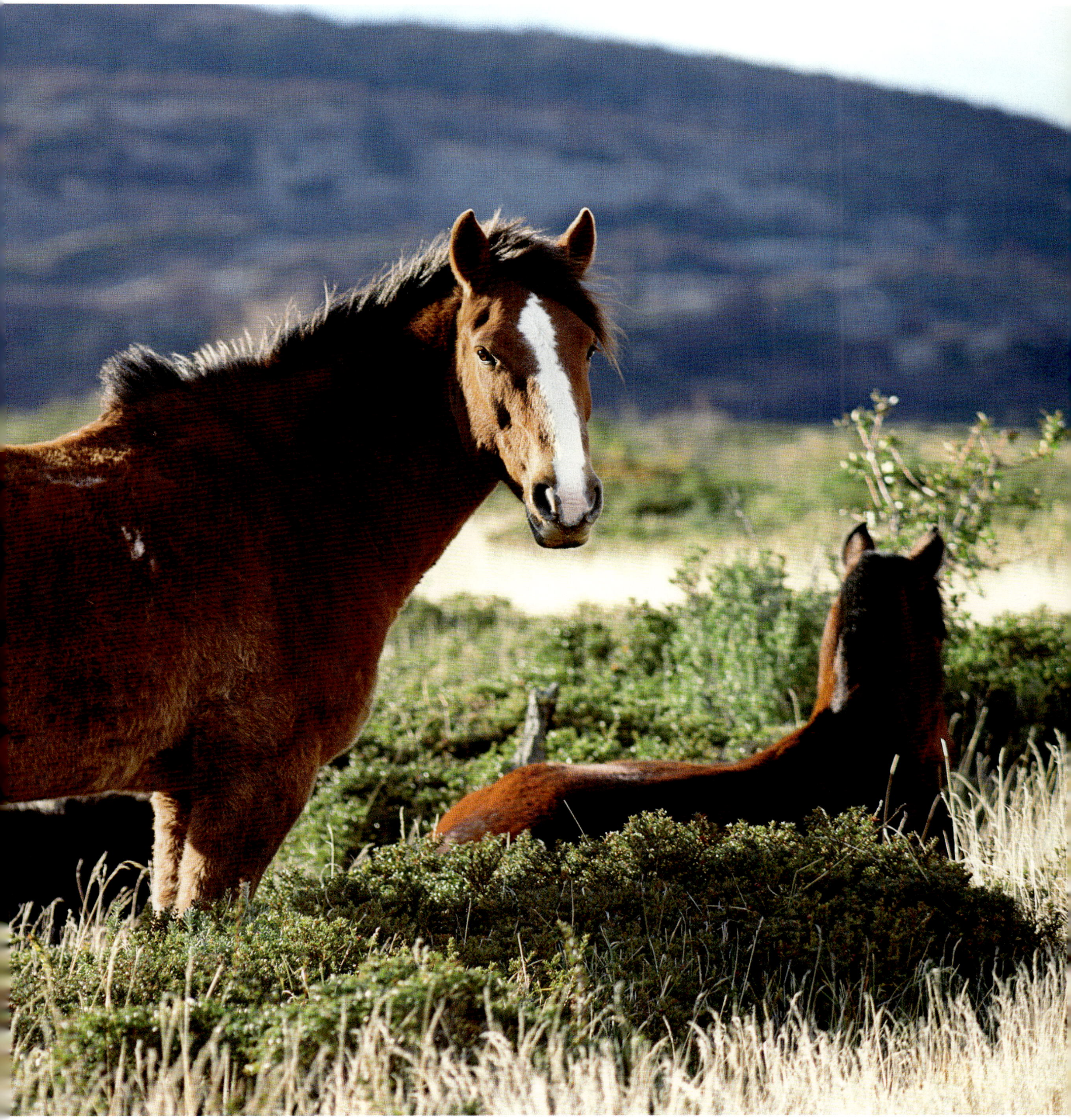

the king of the pampas

200 and 200-201 • The photographs show the limitless plains of the Torres National Park in Paine, Tierra del Fuego, in the extreme south of Chile, whose rainy and grassy pastures are ideal for horses.

202-203 and 203 • Thousands of kilometers separate the two apparently similar environments and their horses: Chile's Tierra del Fuego, left, where the Criollos are hardy and rustic, and the Lanin National Park in the Argentine province of Nequen, in which this mother and her foal are grazing.

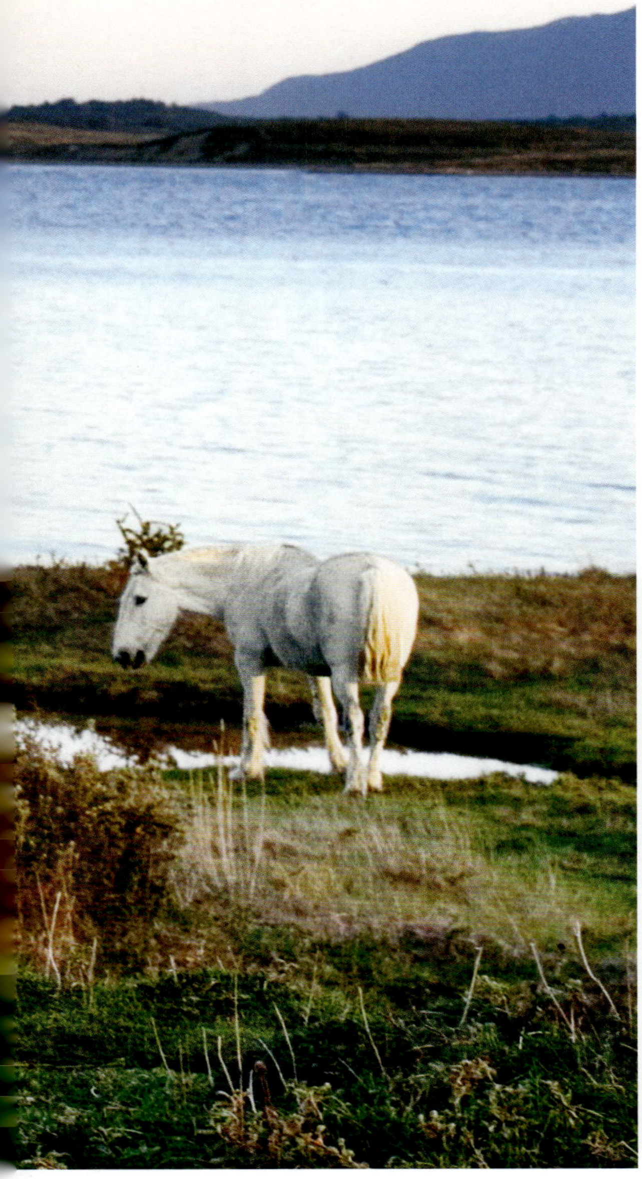

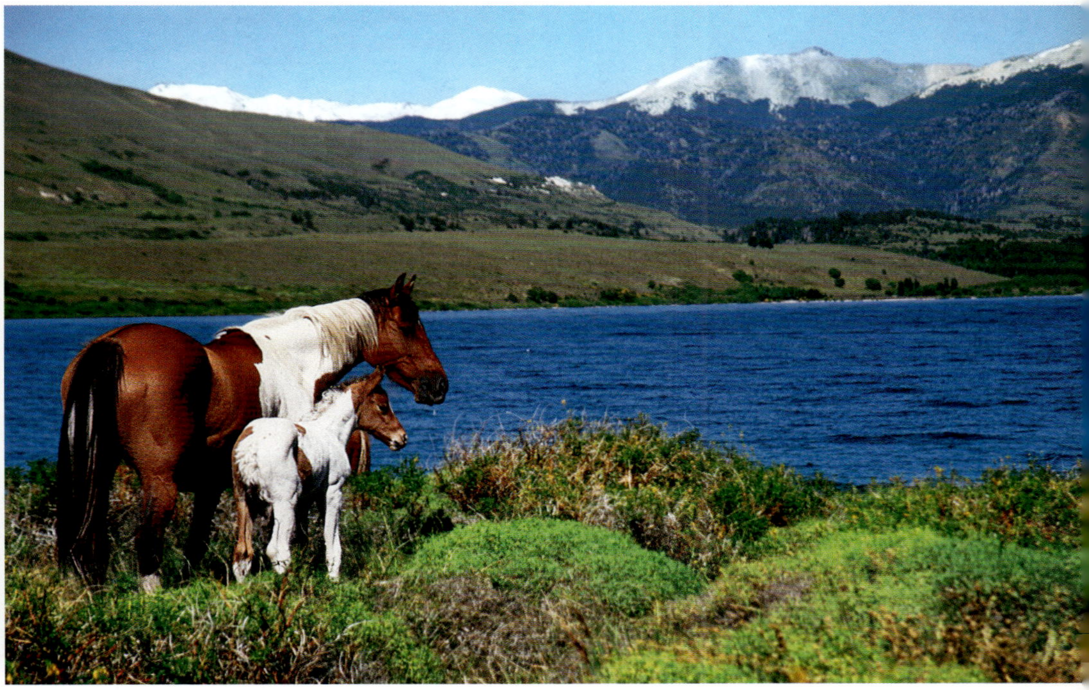

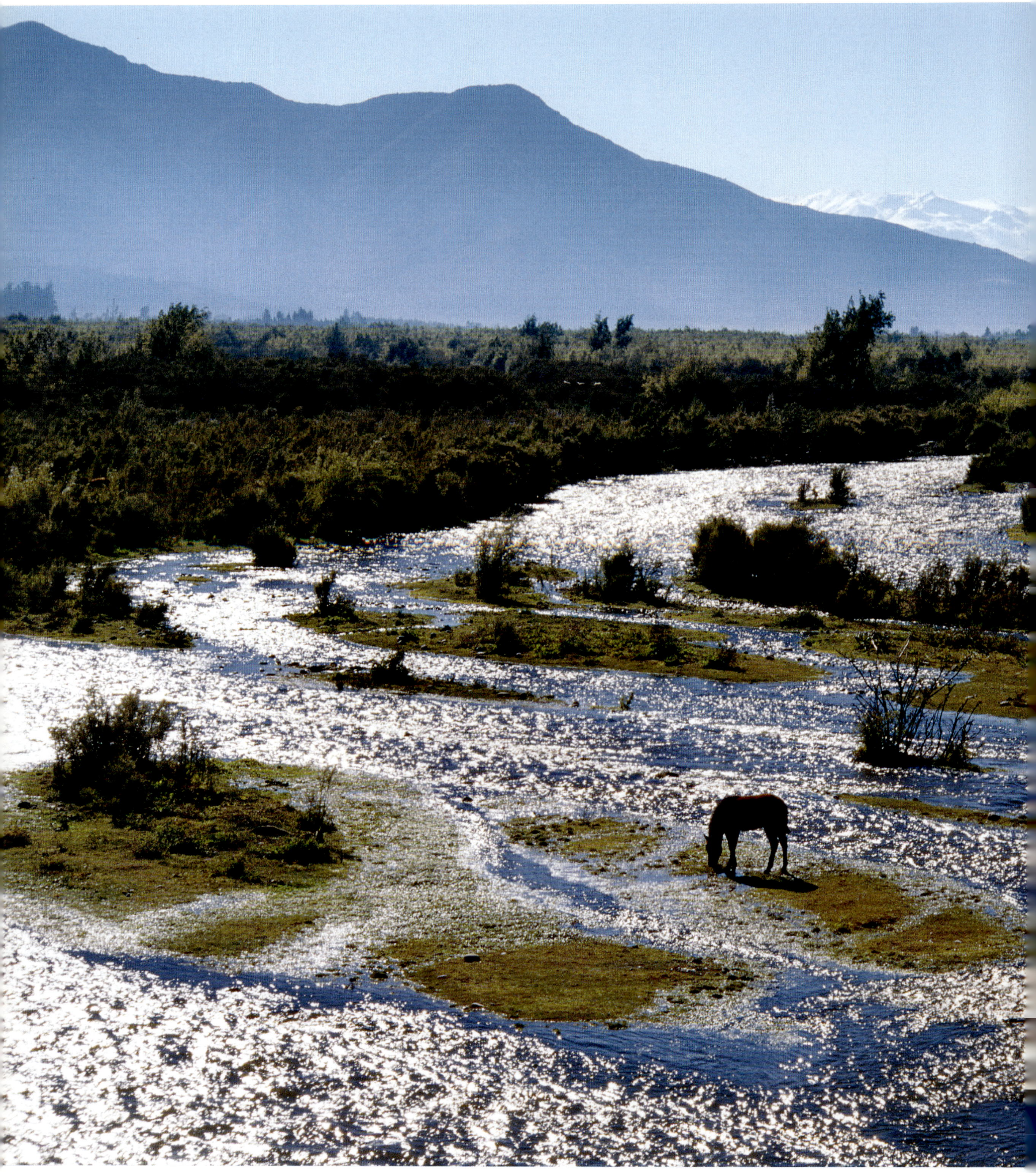

204-205 • A solitary Criollo grazes upon an island in the Aconcagua river, in Chile, with the Andes providing a very evocative background.

THE ELEGANT SON OF THE HIGH PLANES

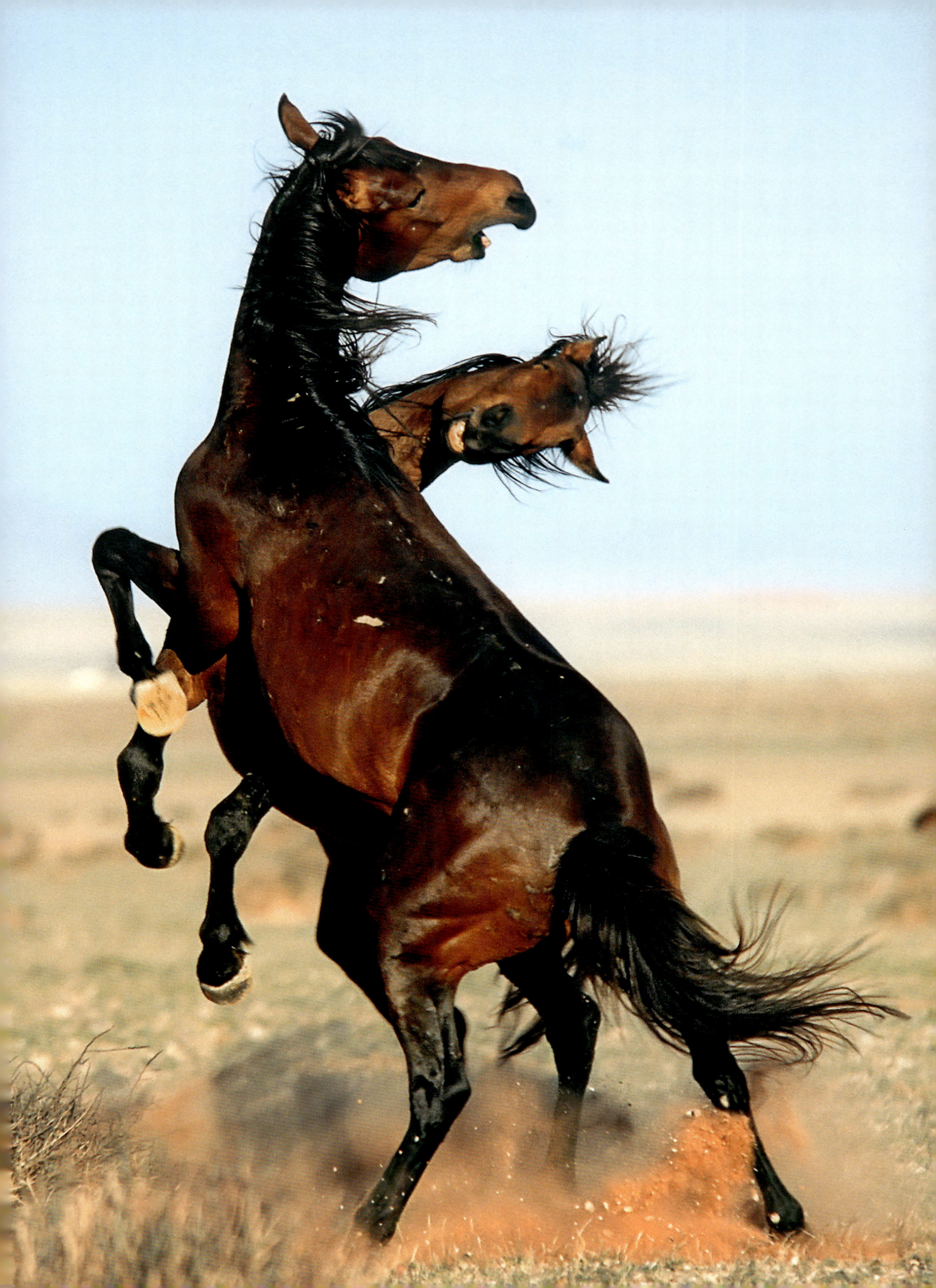

The case of the wild horses of Namibia is unique. If the vast open spaces of North America, South America or Australia gave escaped horses the scope to go looking for water, food and the other necessities for survival, in Namibia everything took place in a relatively confined area of 'just' 135 square miles and in such extreme environmental conditions that the horses adaptation constitutes a genuine feat of Nature.

Namibia's wild horses live in a desert area, with a torrid climate, practically without water and vegetation, separated from the less arid areas of the country by a long mountain range. It acts as a sort of wall that has stopped the horses from finding their own patch of vegetation on the plateau that vertically bisects the country.

Namibia, to the northwest of South Africa, faces the southern Atlantic Ocean and its coastal strip is a desert. In the middle a plateau runs north to south. Its southeastern border faces the terrible Kalahari Desert, in which the red ant represents one of the major animal life forms, with the exception of snakes.

'Prisoners' of the coastal desert, Namibia's horses have found within themselves and their genetic makeup, exceptional abilities to adapt and survive up to the present day. In recent times, with the growth of environmental awareness, academics and local governments have paid them greater attention.

There are various explanations as to why these horses ended up in such an inhospitable territory and perhaps, in the end, the answer is a mixture of all of them.

The first version says that they are descendents of horses that escaped during the First World War from German (Namibia was a German colony from the early 1900s) and South African troops (South Africa was part of the British Empire) during a number of clashes that led British troops to occupy the Luderiz-Ketmanshoo railway line, which is today the B 24 highway, one of the most panoramic and picturesque in Namibia.

A second legend talks of a German aristocrat, Baron Hans Heinrich von Wolf, who had at least three hundred horses in the stables of his castle at Duwisib, on the edge of the desert. The baron returned to Europe to take part in the Great War and when news came of his death, the castle and stables were abandoned and the horses escaped, returning to the wild.

A third legend says that Namibia's wild horses owe their origin to a shipwreck: a ship carrying thoroughbred racing horses from Europe to South Africa sunk at the mouth of the Orange River. The horses that managed to escape drowning landed and reached the Garub plane.

Whichever version is the truth, it is a fact that the horses established themselves on the Garub plane because there was water, a requisite for their survival.

The Garub's water was also used by men: it was transported by train from the small station at Aus, to the main water-deprived city of Luderiz, 75 miles further east. After an aqueduct was built at Luderiz, Aus station closed but water pumping in the Garub was continued by an Anglo-American diamond company, which in the meantime had been assigned mineral rights in the area. That water has thus continued to keep the wild horses alive.

In 1986 the diamond company gave the northern part of the area to the Namibian authorities and since then the managers of the Namib Naukluft Park have safeguarded the wild horses. Today alongside Aus's little station (it was never knocked down, just abandoned) naturalists have erected an observation post to see the wild horses close up, without disturbing them, as they drink at the Garub Waterhole.

After a tremendous drought in 1992 that killed 40 horses, the Ministry for Environment and Tourism acted to safeguard the 'pasture land' and to protect a base-group of horses: some were captured and sold to farmers and enthusiasts, while they fed the remaining 80 horses, mostly during rain-free periods – which means most of the year. The latest figures show that there are 150 wild horses in the Garub region.

The Ministry and environmentalists have not only had to fight the climate and adverse natural conditions, but they have also battled those who wanted to eliminate these horses (not by killing them but by relocation, a frequent practice in African natural parks), considered not native to the area and damaging to other wild animals, with which they fight over the small amount of water and food that nature provides. However, behavioral monitoring has clearly demonstrated that there is no competition between the horses and other herbivores and indeed they graze and drink together, just a few meters apart. Having thus been 'accepted' by nature, the skeptics now also have to accept them and the wild horses have become a definitive part of the history and fauna of Namibia.

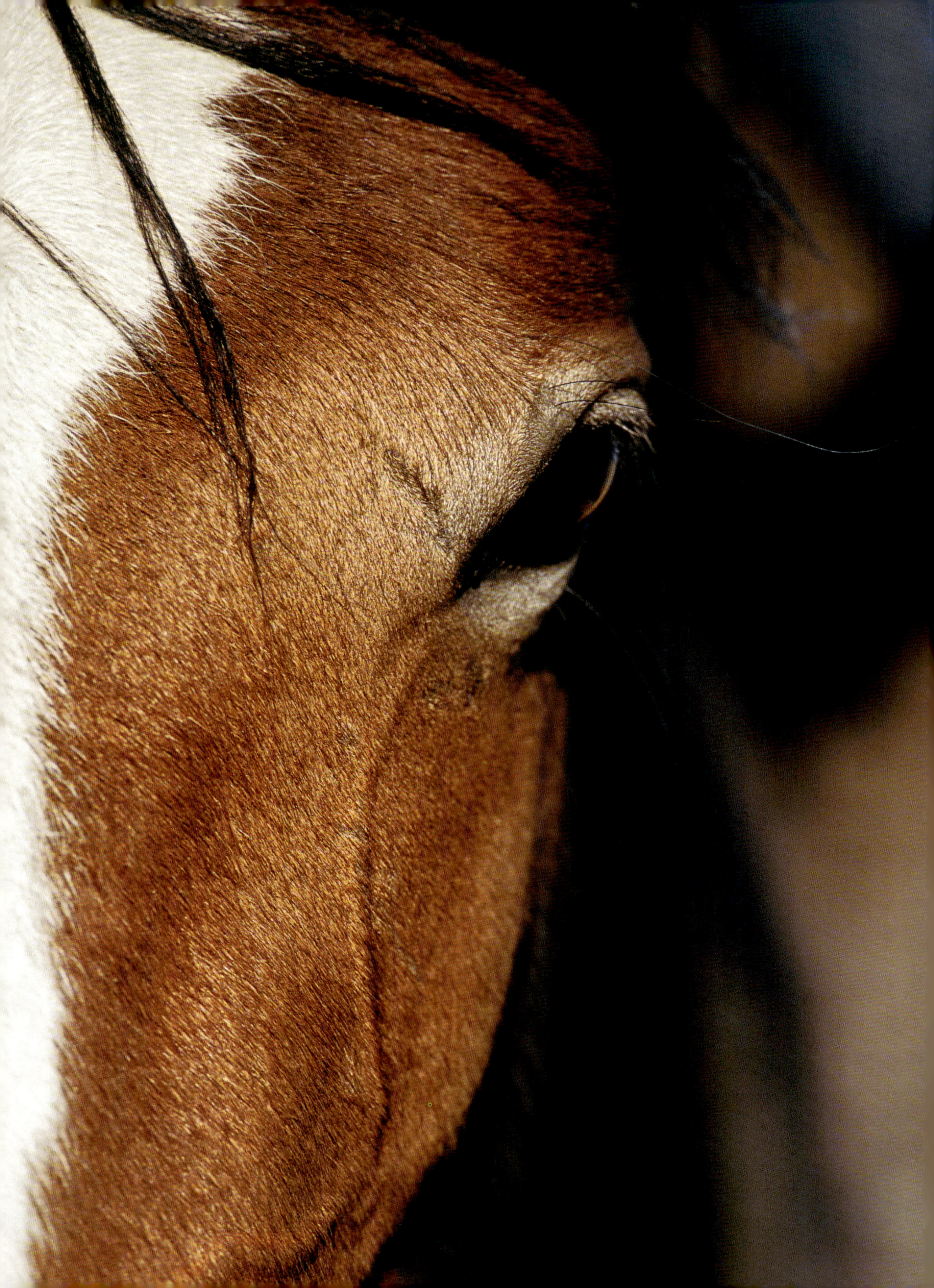

207 • Two horses photographed during a fight, a common occurrence between these untamed wild creatures.

210 • A striking foreground shot of a stallion. These horses roam wild in the Garub, a desert that extends along the coastline of western Namibia.

211 • Natural selection has provided a dark coat color for these horses living in a sun-drenched, scorching desert habitat.

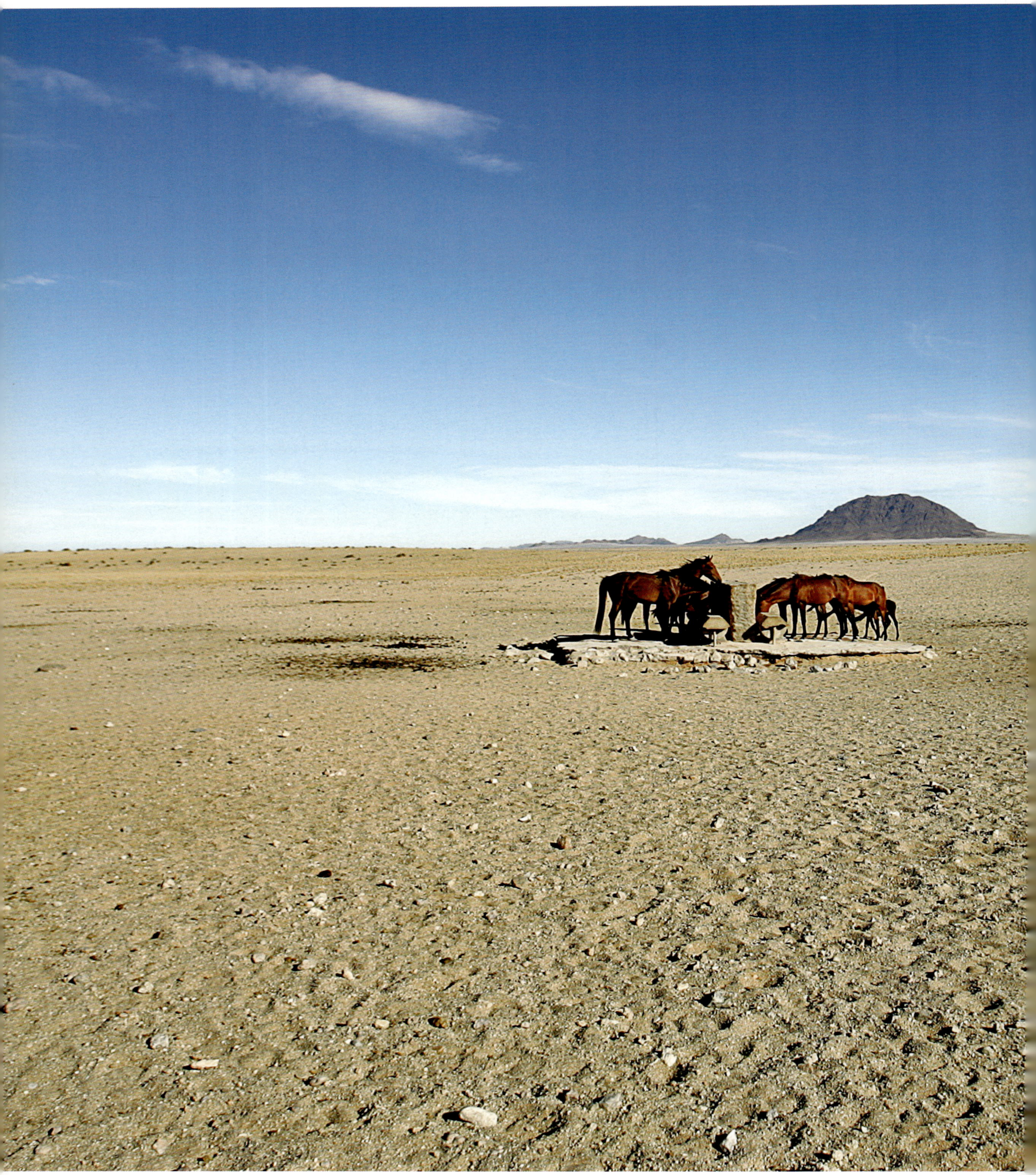

212-213 A small herd of wild horses drinks at one of the wells fed by a water pump that a diamond mining company has kept in working order. • 214-215 This wonderful picture shows that at the Garub Waterhole there is no 'competition' between horses and other wild animals for the water and food they all need.

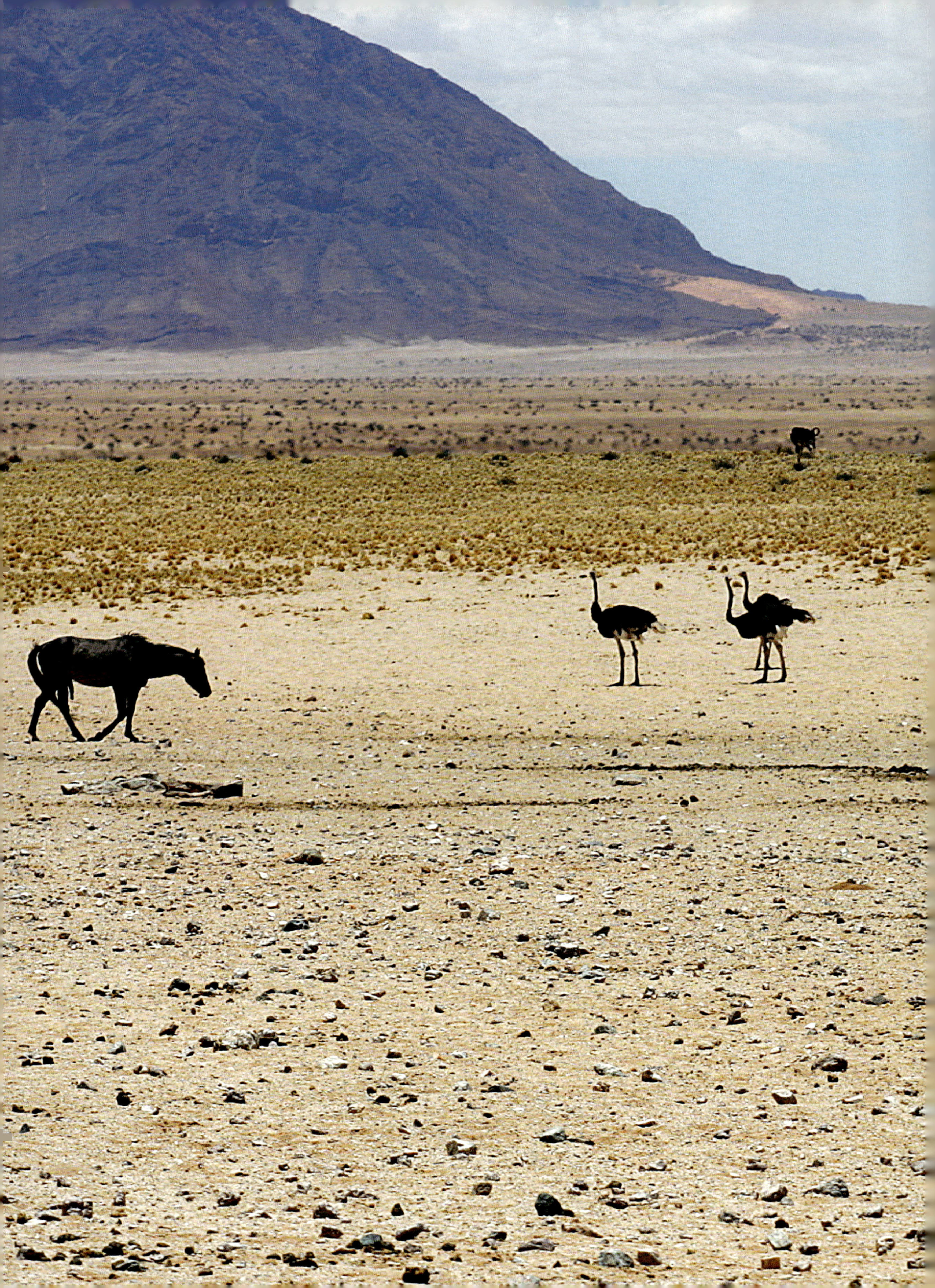

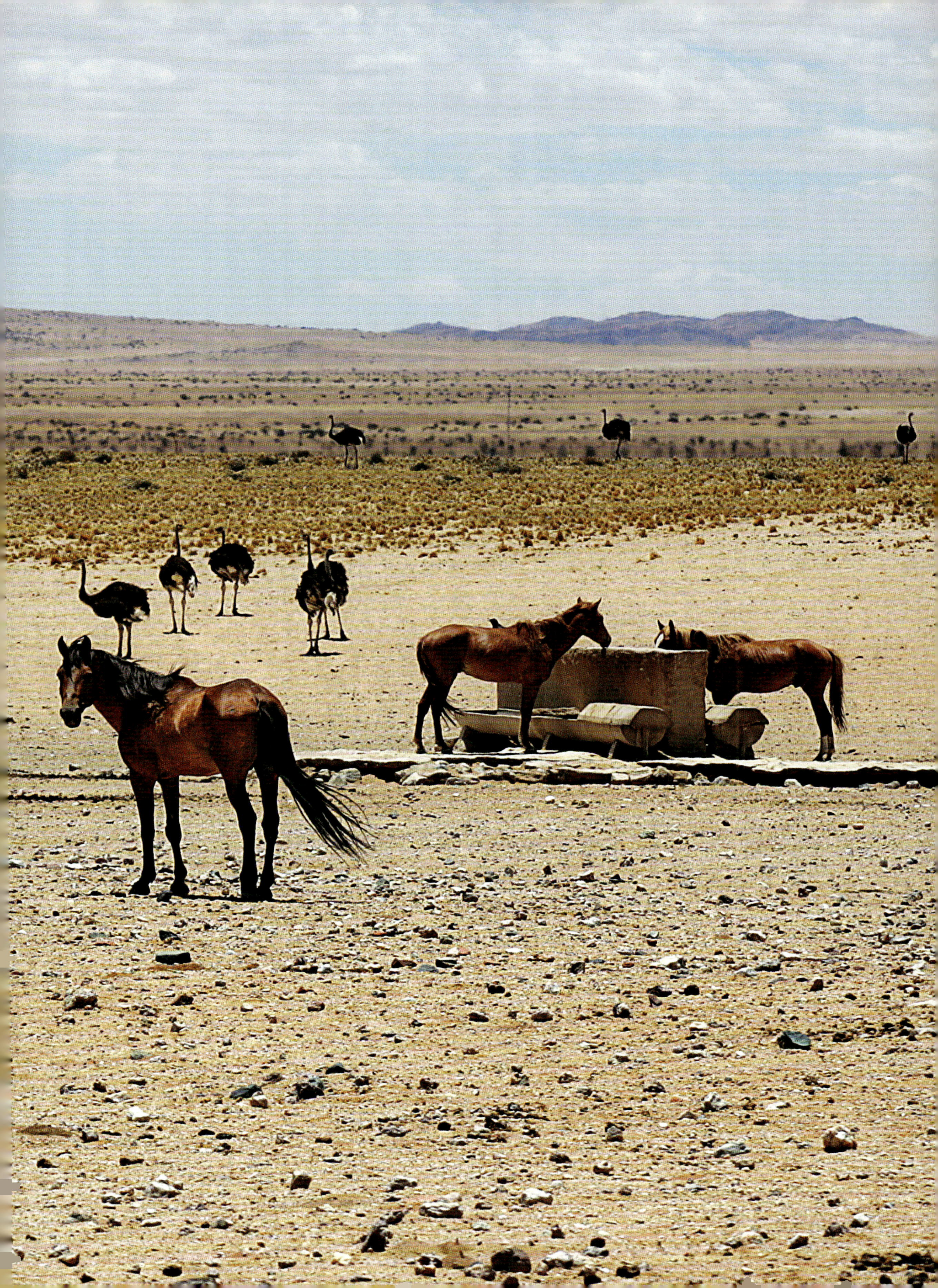

216 • Namibian horses behave just like their cousins the world over — they roll on the ground to scratch themselves and cover themselves with sand to protect their coats.

217 • A Namibian horse with an unusual blond-colored mane digs in the desert sand and finds a water source indispensable for quenching the thirst of the whole herd.

218-219 • This young horse eliminates irritating parasites and cleans its coat by rolling on the ground.

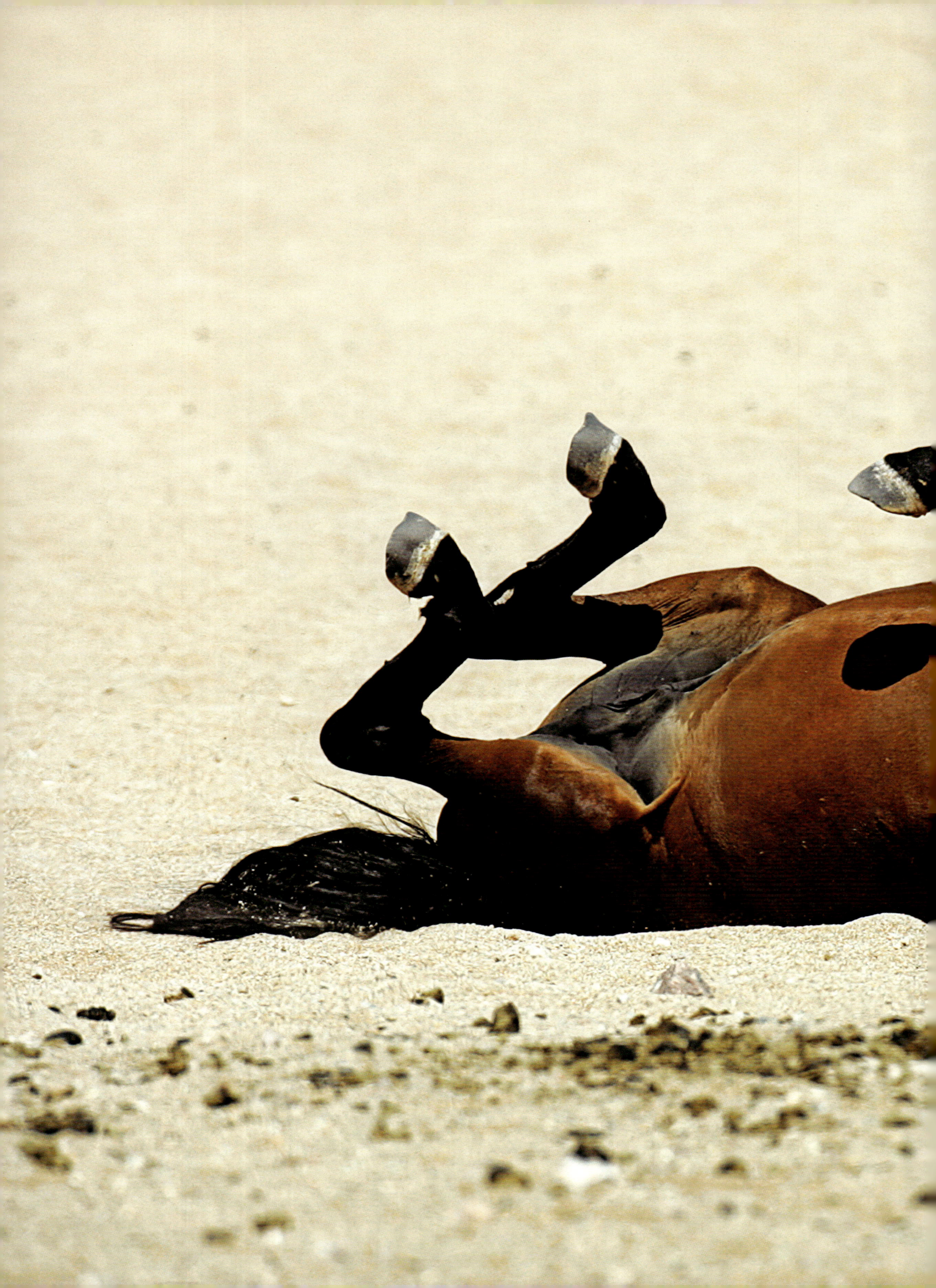

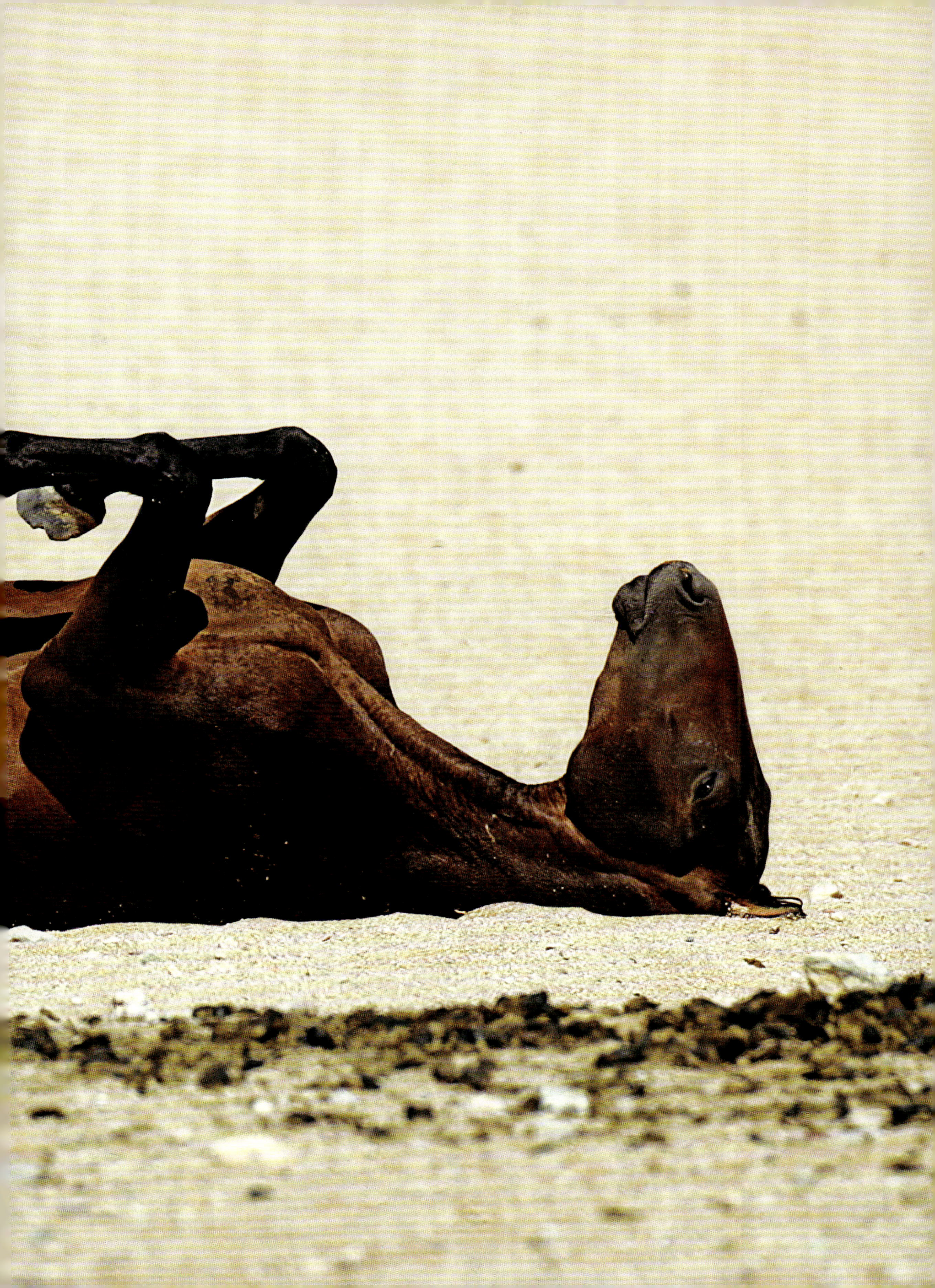

the elegant son of the high planes

220-221 • A young mare flees at a gallop across the desert dunes scattered among which the sporadic tufts of grass represent a very precious food source.

222-223 and 223 • Even in an environment as difficult and torrid as the Namibian desert, the younger horses of the herd find time to test themselves in play fights and skirmishes.

the elegant
son of the
high planes

224-225 • Sometimes the adults fight for real, like these two stallions caught on camera in the Aus zone.

the elegant son of the high planes

226-227 and 227 • Two exceptional photographs of wild stallions fighting during the mating season at Namibia's Garub Waterhole.

the elegant son of the high planes

227

228-229 The males of the herd fight over territory and for the right to approach the females in heat. • **230-231** The horses of the Garub are continually monitored by an agency that the Namibian government has created specifically to safeguard them. The latest figures record 150 of these horses.

the elegant son of the high planes

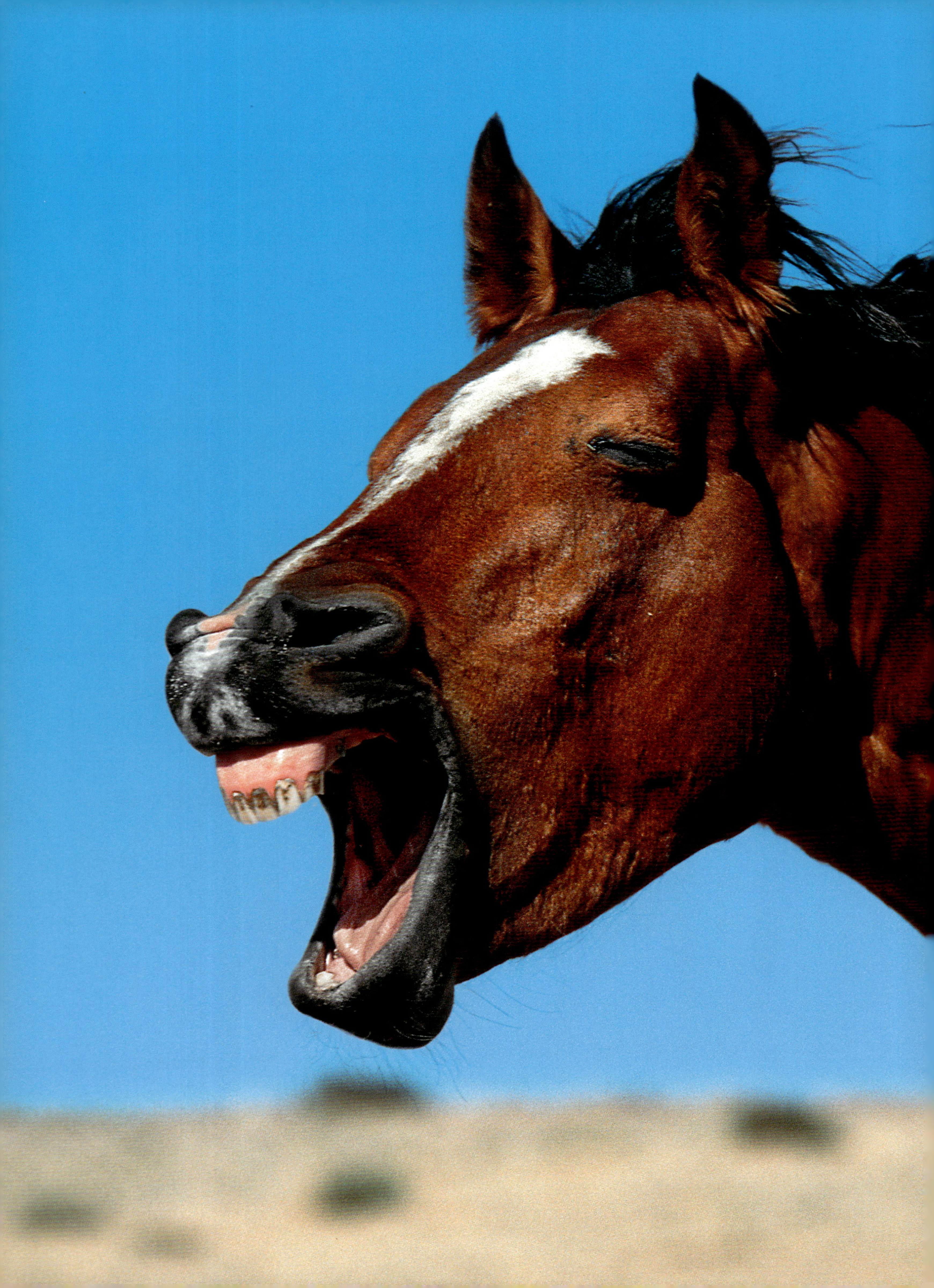

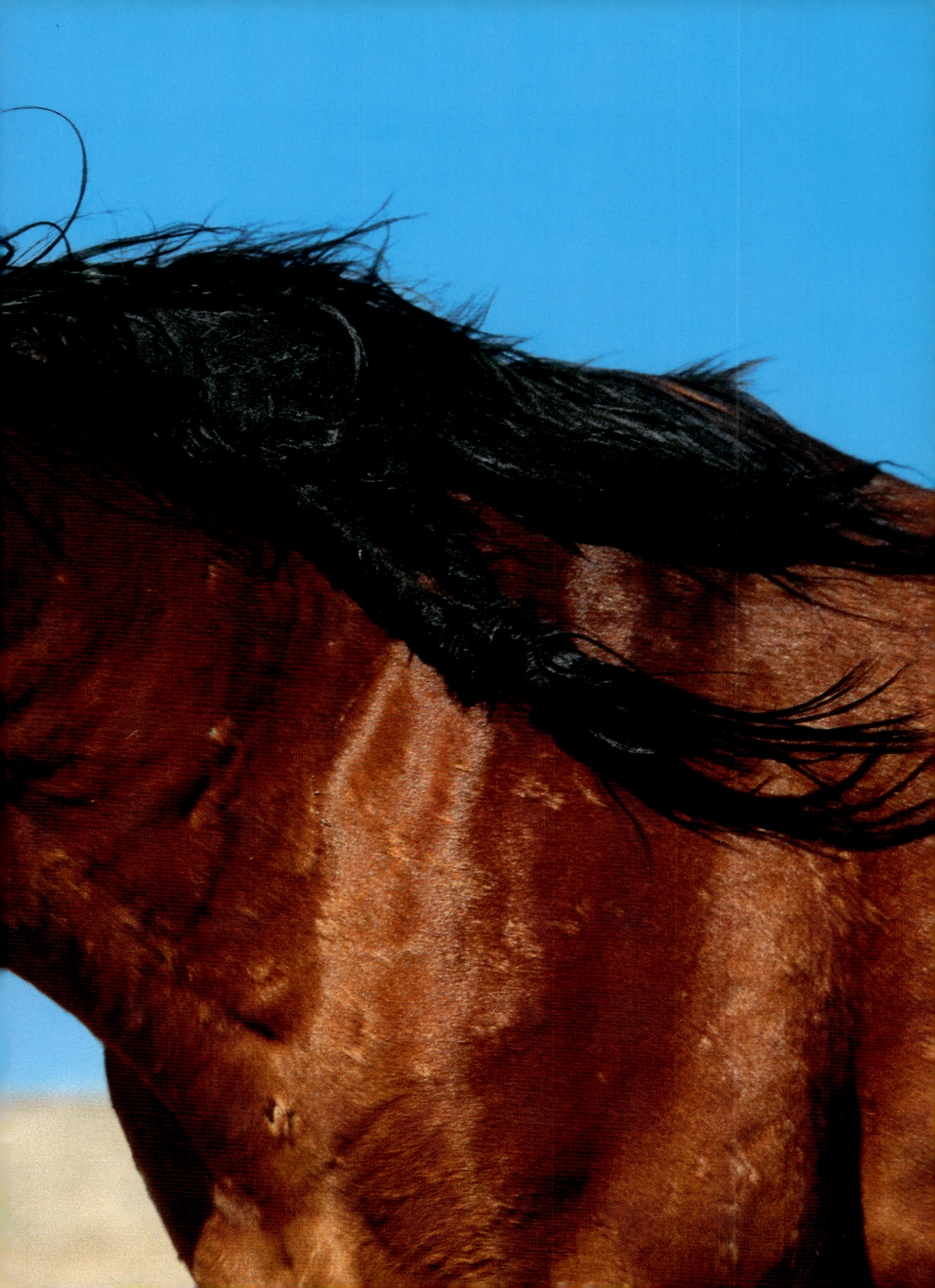

232-233 and 233 • Namibia's horses have had to find exceptional resources for adaptation from within their species' DNA in order to have survived the hostile desert environment up until today.

the elegant son of the high planes

234-235 and 235-237 • In these extraordinary photographs, the fiery sky of the African sunset tinges the Namibian desert a shade of red, highlighting the elegant profiles of these animals, before the night brings a bit of quiet to their daily struggle for survival.

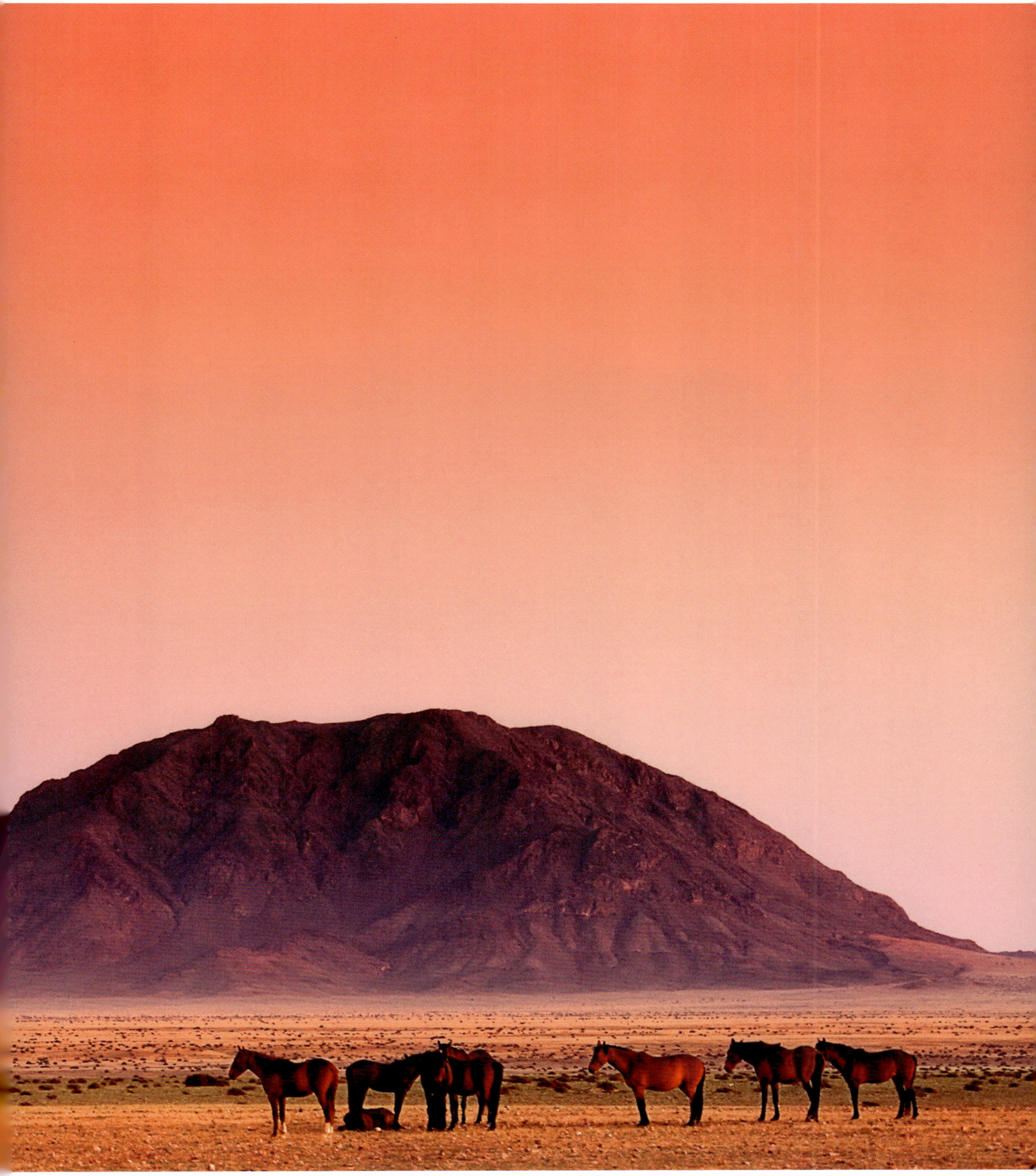

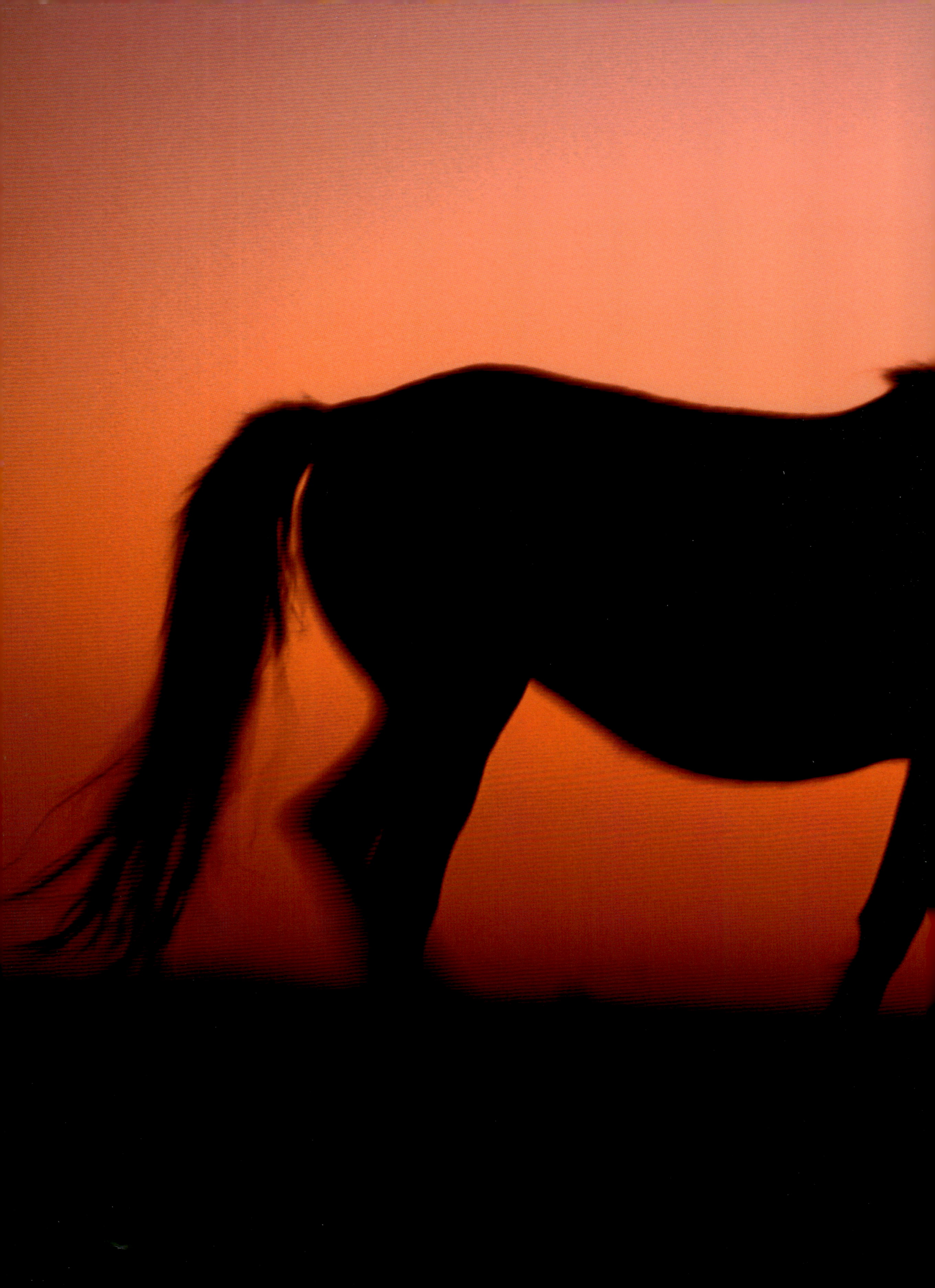

PHOTO CREDITS

page 5 Klein-Hubert/KimballStock
pages 7, 11 Ragnar Th Sigurdsson/Artic Images
pages 14-15 Tim Flach/Getty Images
pages 16, 17 Ragnar Th Sigurdsson/Artic Images
page 18 Junior Bildarchiv/Tips Images
pages 18-19 Arctic-Images/Corbis
pages 20, 21, 22-23, 24, 25, 26 Ragnar Th Sigurdsson/Artic Images
pages 26-27 Thomas Micek
pages 28, 29 Martina Gates
pages 30-31 Thomas Micek
pages 32-33 Junior Bildarchiv/Tips Images
page 33 Arco Digitale Images/Tips Images
pages 34-35, 36 Jeremy Woodhouse/Masterfile/Sie
page 38 Gabriele Boiselle/NHPA/Photoshot
page 39 Jupiterimages
pages 40, 40-41 Jeremy Woodhouse/Masterfile/Sie
pages 42, 43 John Daniels/ardea.com
pages 44-45 Gabriele Boiselle/NHPA/Photoshot
pages 46-47 Martina Gates
pages 48-49 Tim Flach/Getty Images
pages 50-51, 51 Thomas Micek
pages 52-53 SuperStock/Getty Images
page 53 Arctic-Images/Getty Images
page 55 David Tipling/Getty Images
pages 58-59 Jim Zuckerman/KimballStock
pages 60-61 Arco Digitale Images/Tips Images
pages 62-63 Jim Zuckerman
pages 64-65 Robert Tixador/TOP/Eyedea/Contrasto
page 65 Henry Ausloos/Eyedea/Contrasto
page 66 Junior Bildarchiv/Tips Images
page 67 Gérard Sioen/RAPHO/Eyedea/Contrasto

page 68 Sylavain Cordier/Jacana/Eyedea/Contrasto
pages 69, 70 Henry Ausloos/Jacana/Eyedea/Contrasto
page 71 Jean-Michel Roignamt/Hoa-qui/Eyedea/Contrasto
page 72 Klein-Hubert/KimballStock
page 73 Bob Langrish
pages 74-75 Jim Zuckerman/KimballStock
page 76 Junior Bildarchiv/Photolibrary Group
page 77 ArtWolfe
pages 78, 79 Henry Ausloos/Jacana/Eyedea/Contrasto
pages 80-81 Bob Langrish
pages 82, 82-83 Henry Ausloos/Jacana/Eyedea/Contrasto
page 84 top Gérard Sioen/RAPHO/Eyedea/Contrasto
pages 84 bottom, 84-85 Henry Ausloos/Jacana/Eyedea/Contrasto
page 86 Art Wolfe/Getty Images
pages 86-87 Eric Soder/NHPA/Photoshot
pages 88, 88-89, 90, 91, 92 top, 92 bottom, 92-93, 94 top, 94 bottom, 94-95 Henry Ausloos/Jacana/Eyedea/Contrasto
pages 96-97 M. Watson/ardea.com
page 98 L. Lenz/Blickwinkel
page 99 Henry Ausloos/Jacana/Eyedea/Contrasto
pages 100, 101 Morales/Agefotostock/Marka
pages 102-103 Sylavain Cordier/Jacana/Eyedea/Contrasto
pages 104-105, 106-107 Jim Zuckerman/KimballStock
page 109 Bob Langrish
pages 112-113 L. Lenz/Blickwinkel
pages 114-115 John Carnemolla/AUSCAPE

pages 116-117 A.N.T. Photo Library/NHPA/Photoshot
pages 118-119 Bob Langrish
pages 120-121 Wayne Lawler/AUSCAPE
pages 122-123 L. Lenz/Blickwinkel
page 125 Mark Terrell
pages 128-129 Yva Momatiuk & John Eastcott/Minden Pictures/National Geographic Stock
page 130 Ron Kimball/KimballStock
page 132-133 Yva Momatiuk & John Eastcott/Minden Pictures/National Geographic Stock
pages 134-135 Ron Stroud/Masterfile/Sie
page 136 Arco Digitale Images/Tips Images
page 137 Tom & Pat Leeson/ardea.com
pages 138-139 Bios/Tips Images
pages 140-141 Robert Franz/Photolibrary Group
page 142, 142-143 Bios/Tips Images
page 144 Eastcott Momatiuk/Getty Images
page 145 Yva Momatiuk & John Eastcott/Minden Pictures/National Geographic Stock
pages 146-147, 147 Bios/Tips Images
pages 148-149 Klein-Hubert/KimballStock
pages 150-151 Yva Momatiuk & John Eastcott/Minden Pictures/National Geographic Stock
pages 152 top, 152 bottom, 152-153 Carol Walker/Naturepl.com/Contrasto
page 154 Bios/Tips Images
page 155 Junior Bildarchiv/Photolibrary Group
pages 156-157 Bob Langrish
pages 158-159, 159, 160, 161 Bios/Tips Images
pages 162-163 John Giustina/Photolibrary Group
pages 164, 165 Bios/Tips Images
pages 166-167 Gay Bumgarner/Tips Images
pages 168, 169, 170, 170-171 Bios/Tips Images

page 172 Oxford Scientific/Photolibrary/Getty Images
pages 172-173 Jim Doberman/Getty Images
pages 174, 175 Bios/Tips Images
pages 176-177 Klein-Hubert/KimballStock
pages 178-179, 179, 180, 181 Bios/Tips Images
pages 182, 182-183 Carol Walker/Naturepl.com/Contrasto
pages 184-185 Bios/Tips Images
page 187 Chad Ehlers/Tips Images
pages 190-191 Patrick Bennett/www.DanitaDelimont.com
pages 192-193 Giulio Andreini/Agefotostock/Marka
pages 194-195 Gabriele Boiselle/NHPA/Photoshot
pages 196-197, 197 Bob Langrish
pages 198-199 Jason Edwards/Getty Images
page 200 Galen Rowell/Corbis
pages 200-201 Frank Lukasseck/Corbis
pages 202-203 Karl-Heinz Raach/laif/Contrasto
page 203 Arco Digitale Images/Tips Images
pages 204-205 R & K Muschenetz/Photolibrary Group
page 207 Manfred Delpho
page 210 Winfried Wisniewski/Jacana/Eyedea/Contrasto
pages 211, 212-213, 214-215 Bob Langrish
pages 216, 217 Thomas Dressler
pages 218-219 Bob Langrish
pages 220-221 L. Lenz/Blickwinkel
pages 222-223, 223 Bob Langrish
pages 224-225 Werner Bollmann/Agefotostock/Marka
pages 226-227 Manfred Delpho
page 227 Arco Digitale Images/Tips Images
pages 228-229, 230-231, 232-233, 233, 234-235, 236-237 Manfred Delpho

WHITE STAR PUBLISHERS

WS White Star Publishers® is a registered trademark
property of Edizioni White Star s.r.l.

© 2009 White Star s.r.l.
Via Candido Sassone, 24
13100 Vercelli, Italy
www.whitestar.it

TRANSLATION: Alan Goldwater
EDITING: Emma Greenwood

All rights reserved. No part of this publication may be reproduced,
stored in a retrieval system or transmitted in any form or by
any means, electronic, mechanical, photocopying, recording or
otherwise, without written permission from the publisher.

ISBN 978-88-544-0480-9
1 2 3 4 5 6   13 12 11 10 09

Printed in Italy